WORLD GOVERNMENT BY STEALTH

Also by Guy Arnold

THE END OF THE THIRD WORLD

World Government by Stealth

The Future of the United Nations

Guy Arnold

BKJ 5102 - 9/3

First published in Great Britain 1997 by
MACMILLAN PRESS LTD
Houndmills, Basingstoke, Hampshire RG21 6XS and London
Companies and representatives throughout the world

A catalogue record for this book is available from the British Library.

ISBN 0–333–65582–6

First published in the United States of America 1997 by
ST. MARTIN'S PRESS, INC.,
Scholarly and Reference Division,
175 Fifth Avenue, New York, N.Y. 10010

ISBN 0–312–17494–2

Library of Congress Cataloging-in-Publication Data
Arnold, Guy.
World government by stealth : the future of the United Nations /
Guy Arnold.
p.   cm.
Includes bibliographical references and index.
ISBN 0–312–17494–2 (cloth)
1. United Nations—Developing countries.   2. Security,
International.   I. Title.
JX1977.2.A1A76 1997
341.23'1—dc21   97–6554
                                                   CIP

This book is printed on paper suitable for recycling and made from fully managed and
sustained forest sources.

10   9   8   7   6   5   4   3   2   1
06   05   04   03   02   01   00   99   98   97

Printed in Great Britain by
The Ipswich Book Company Ltd
Ipswich, Suffolk

Contents

Preface

The end of the Cold War has changed all the parameters of international relations; it has also provided an opportunity for the major powers to inject new life into the United Nations. This, however, is only likely to happen if the permanent members of the Security Council, above all the United States, want to make the world body a competent instrument of peacekeeping, for only if it is able to discharge that function properly will the United Nations also be able to progress to the next logical stage of its development, to form the nucleus of an effective world government. During the course of the twenty-first century international relations will become more complex and dangerous as the world population increases and the scramble for resources accelerates, and the alternative to an effective United Nations will be a 'dog-eat-dog' world in which the strongest will triumph in the short term at the price of an appalling longer-term future of strife and antagonism.

Guy Arnold
October 1996

Abbreviations and Acronyms

ANC	African National Congress
ANS	Armee nationale Sihanoukist
ASEAN	Association of Southeast Asian Nations
CACM	Central American Common Market
CARICOM	Caribbean Community and Common Market
CIEC	Conference on International Economic Cooperation and Development
CIS	Commonwealth of Independent States
CIVS	International Verification and Follow-up Commission
CNA	Cambodian National Army
CPP	Cambodian People's Party
CSCE	Conference on Security and Cooperation in Europe
DFSS	Democratic Front for the Salvation of Somalia
ECOMOG	Economic Community (of West African States) Monitoring Group
ECOWAS	Economic Community of West African States
ESCAP	(UN) Economic and Social Commission for Asia and the Pacific
EU	European Union
FAO	Food and Agricultural Organization
FLN	National Liberation Front (Front de liberation nationale)
FMLN	Farabundo Marti National Liberation Front
Frelimo	Liberation Front of Mozambique (Frente de Libertacao de Mocambique)
Frodebu	Front for Democracy in Burundi
FUNCINPEC	United National Front for an Independent, Neutral, Peaceful and Cooperative Cambodia
IAEA	International Atomic Energy Agency
ICRC	International Committee of the Red Cross
IDA	International Development Association
ILO	International Labour Organization
IMF	International Monetary Fund
KPNLF	Khmer People's National Liberation Front
LDC	Least Developed Country
MFN	Most Favoured Nation

MINURSO	UN Mission for the Referendum in Western Sahara
MPLA	Popular Liberation Movement of Angola (Movimento Popular de Libertacao de Angola)
NATO	North Atlantic Treaty Organization
NIC	Newly Industrialized Country
NIEO	New International Economic Order
NGO	Non-Government Organization
OAS	Organization of American States
OAU	Organization of African Unity
OECD	Organization for Economic Cooperation and Development
ONUSAL	UN Observer Mission in El Salvador
OPEC	Organization of Petroleum Exporting Countries
PLO	Palestine Liberation Organization
PNGC	Provisional National Government of Cambodia
Polisario	Popular Front for the Liberation of Saguia al-Hamra and Rio de Oro
Renamo	National Resistance of Mozambique (Resistencia Nacional Mocambicana)
RPF	Rwandese Patriotic Front
SADC	Southern Africa Development Community (formerly SADCC)
SADCC	Southern Africa Development Coordinating Conference
SADR	Saharan Arab Democratic Republic
SIPRI	Stockholm International Peace Research Institute
SNA	Somalia National Alliance
SNC	Supreme National Council
SNM	Somali National Movement
SWAPO	South West African People's Organization
UDI	Unilateral Declaration of Independence
UNAMIR	UN Assistance Mission in Rwanda
UNAVEM (II)	UN Angola Verification Mission
UNDP	UN Development Programme
UNEF	UN Emergency Force
UNESCO	UN Educational, Scientific and Cultural Organization
UNHCR	UN High Commissioner for Refugees
UNICEF	UN Children's Fund
UNIKOM	UN Iraq–Kuwait Observer Mission
UNITA	National Union for the Total Independence of Angola (Uniao Nacional para a Independencia Total de Angola)
UNMIH	UN Mission in Haiti
UNOMIG	UN Observer Mission in Georgia

UNOMIL	UN Observer Mission in Liberia
UNOMOZ	UN Operation in Mozambique
UNOMSA	UN Observer Mission in South Africa
UNOSOM	UN Operation in Somalia
UNOMUR	UN Observer Mission Uganda–Rwanda
UNPROFOR	UN Protection Force in Former Yugoslavia
UNTAC	UN Transitional Authority in Cambodia
UNTAF	UN Task Force
UNTAG	UN Transition Assistance Group
USC	United Somali Congress
WEU	Western European Union
WFP	World Food Programme
WHO	World Health Organization

1   The First Half-century

At the beginning of the 1990s, after 40 years of Cold War stalemate, there was a sense that at last the United Nations could be employed fully both to keep the peace and otherwise to act as the core of a growing world government. This new optimism was given a major boost by the unprecedented circumstances surrounding the Gulf War in 1991 when the United States and the Soviet Union worked together instead of in opposition to one another and it seemed, briefly, that the original functions and purpose of the United Nations could be fully realized. The sense of euphoria released by the end of the Cold War was to prove as short-lived in relation to the United Nations as it was in relation to almost everything else including US President Bush's much trumpeted 'New World Order' which, alas, soon gave evidence of being very much an unregenerate old world order of squabbling big powers.

At the heart of UN problems lies the composition and powers of the Security Council whose five permanent members (the United States, Russia, Britain, France and China), the victors of World War II, have always seen the world body as an instrument to be manipulated for their own political ends rather than as an embryo world government to which they would be prepared to surrender real authority with appropriate power to sustain it. In 1945, when the membership of the newly formed United Nations stood at a manageable 51, the Security Council of 11 members (the five permanent members and six non-permanent members elected by the General Assembly) stood in a ratio of 1 to 4.6 between Council and General Assembly; by 1995, although the Security Council had been increased in size to 15 with four more non-permanent members, UN membership had grown to 185 (more than three and a half times the original numbers) so that the ratio between Security Council and General Assembly then stood at 1 to 12 making it even more unrepresentative of the whole than at the beginning.

The stultifying effects of the Cold War upon UN operations can be seen in the peacekeeping figures for these years: between 1945 and 1987 the Security Council authorized 13 peacekeeping operations; then from 1987 (when Moscow finally agreed to support peacekeeping exercises) to 1993 21 peacekeeping operations were authorized.[1] By the mid-1990s peacekeeping was costing US$3.5 billion a year. By contrast, the General Assembly budget for development aid stood at only one-third this figure, emphasizing the huge power difference between the Security Council whose real decisions still lie with the original five permanent members and the General Assembly of 185 nations. It is unsurprising, therefore, that much discontent within the United

Nations concerns the unrepresentative nature of the Security Council in relation to the total membership.

In the aftermath of World War II the UN Charter pledged to 'save succeeding generations from the scourge of war, which twice in our lifetime has brought untold sorrow to mankind'. The five permanent members then saw their role, in the words of US President Roosevelt, as 'global policemen' and Article 42 of the Charter gave the Security Council the right to wage war in the name of world peace. Given the appalling problems faced by the United Nations in Bosnia and elsewhere during the 1990s when, apart from political problems, it has never had adequate means to carry out its tasks, it is instructive that the United States then (1945) proposed a standing force be placed permanently at the disposal of the United Nations; this was to consist of 20 army divisions, 3800 aircraft and 200 ships including aircraft carriers, battleships, destroyers and submarines. The USSR made similar if more modest proposals. The Cold War ensured that such a force was never created.[2]

Thereafter, throughout the Cold War, the Security Council was frozen with all power in the hands of the permanent five and, moreover, such power largely stalemated by the ideological antagonisms that the Cold War represented with the two sides using their veto powers whenever they believed their interests to be threatened. Reform of the Security Council, which also means reform of the United Nations as a whole, can only be achieved by enlargement. Apart from any other considerations, the permanent five are no longer representative of the world power situation as they were in 1945. In terms of economic weight alone both Germany and Japan ought to be permanent members of the Security Council; India with its huge population and long-term potential ought to join China; while neither Africa nor Latin America are represented at all. There are various possibilities (see below, Chapter 14) including regional as opposed to country representation on the Security Council but reform is essential if the United Nations is to retain the support of the world it represents and on whose behalf it acts.

The difficulties attending enlargement are those of persuading major nations to be more democratic in relation to the powers they wield. The United States would find it relatively easy to agree an enlargement of the Security Council and an addition to its permanent members since it remains the most powerful country in the world, a position that would not be threatened by such a change; Britain and France, on the other hand, are powers in decline and any enlargement of the Security Council would be likely to lessen their influence at a time when both are anxiously aware of constant erosions of their economic strength and world impact. They favour the status quo. Just how countries in possession of an absolute veto are to be persuaded to agree changes that must lessen their authority remains to be seen. At the centre of all problems faced by the United Nations is the need to reconcile national interests, whether of major or minor powers, and the interests of world development and peace; too often, moreover, the permanent five see the resolution of world problems solely in terms of their own interests.

Symptomatic of the absurd levels to which the United Nations is obliged to descend in order to pacify the national interests of its members was the censorship applied to two books which had been commissioned to commemorate the world body's fiftieth anniversary: the names of all countries were removed from the books so that none should be deemed to have precedence over any other; and mention of the Dalai Lama was barred so as to placate China. One of these books, *A Vision of Hope*, was cut in 70 places while the second book, *The World in Our Hands,* which was written and designed by children from all over the world, was also heavily censored.[3] The determination not to upset the sensibilities of notoriously touchy (and often highly repressive) governments simply underlines the extent to which the United Nations is a prisoner of the very governments it is supposed to assist, but also discipline, in its world role.

The fiftieth anniversary of the United Nations which was celebrated in 1995 hardly coincided with a propitious time in the world body's history. Disasters in its peacekeeping operations in both Bosnia and Somalia were fresh in the public memory, bankruptcy stared it in the face (as a number of members led always by the United States consistently fell into arrears with their dues) while the United States which has never been an ardent supporter of the United Nations was showing increasing signs of antagonism that could spell the end of the world body's effective life. Major criticisms included charges of corruption and inefficiency while the Secretary-General, the Egyptian Boutros Boutros-Ghali, appeared to have made more enemies than friends, at least among the ranks of the leading Western powers whose attitudes towards the United Nations will prove decisive to its future. The United States Congress, in an act that emphasized US disillusionment, passed a new law to become effective on 1 October 1995, reducing the US contribution to the peacekeeping budget from 32 per cent to 25 per cent.

Although no one wishes to see the United Nations collapse, equally none of the major powers appears willing to change a system of institutionalized responsibility that is not accompanied by equivalent power. Perhaps too much had been demanded of the United Nations too quickly in the aftermath of the Cold War. As a comparison, for example, whereas during the three years 1980–3 there were 83 Security Council resolutions and 19 vetoes, in the first three years following the demise of the USSR there were 246 Security Council resolutions and only three vetoes while by 1994 a total of 17 peacekeeping operations were underway worldwide involving 70 000 troops.[4]

This was quite an achievement even when taking account of the glaring failures that had attended the UN operations in Bosnia, Somalia and Rwanda.

There are four areas in which it is generally agreed reforms are required. These are as follows: first, the need to expand the Security Council and make it more representative of the world which it serves; second, a reconstruction of the UN finances so that contributions reflect accurately the wealth of member states; third, the reduction of the Secretary-General's term of office to a single seven-year period so that he or she does not become involved in campaigning for renewal (this rule should also apply to the UN specialized agencies); and fourth, a radical rethink of the UN's most important role of peacekeeping so that operations, for example, can be subcontracted to regional powers.

The fiftieth anniversary celebrations were held in New York during October 1995 and were attended by 150 heads of government, but if the turnout was impressive so, too, were the doubts as to the United Nations' future. Agreement upon the need for reform was not matched by any comparable sense of what had to be done. Reform priorities are most likely to highlight the growing gap between the rich North (essentially the major Western powers) and the developing South. The wealthy Western nations would like to see a more streamlined, cheaper United Nations concentrating upon those areas where it can achieve results; the small, poor countries want, first and foremost, to obtain a bigger say in UN decision making which means a reorganization of the Security Council. As Zambia's President Frederick Chiluba put it: 'The Security Council can no longer be maintained like the sanctuary of the holy of holies, with only the original members acting as high priests deciding on issues for the rest of the world.'[5]

The United Nations is not a world government, a fact that the major powers do not wish to alter, and has no independent peacekeeping forces of its own while it is constantly obliged to seek funds for any operations it undertakes yet, despite these limitations, the world repeatedly turns to it to solve problems. This expectation that it both can and should solve problems is the key to its future. At present, as a result of this situation, it is blamed when things go wrong (as in Bosnia) while credit for successes is claimed by the major powers. In fact, though this is rarely acknowledged, the United Nations can only act effectively if its members both wish it to do so and provide it with the means to achieve the end.

The United Nations has only gone to war effectively twice: in the 1950–3 Korean War which was only possible because the USSR had temporarily absented itself from the Security Council and so was not present to cast its veto; and in the Gulf War of 1991 when in the immediate aftermath of the Cold War the USSR was prepared to support the US stand against Moscow's former ally Iraq. This immediate post-Cold War agreement helped raise expectations of UN capacity far too high before the debacles of Bosnia, Somalia and Rwanda inflicted grave damage upon its reputation.

During the 1980s, the United Nations had achieved a growing number of successes or partial successes as Cold War tensions slackened; these were in both Africa and Asia with interventions in Afghanistan, Cambodia and Namibia and more to come. The very successes of the United Nations encouraged a violence-weary world to call upon it too much and so it became embroiled in such quagmires as Yugoslavia and Somalia where there were no easy solutions while the major powers either had very clear ideas as to whose side they wished to support, as in Yugoslavia, or little or no wish to be involved at all, as in Somalia and Rwanda.

The failure of the United Nations to protect the Bosnian Muslim population was the result of disagreements between the leading Western powers as well as between the West and Russia rather than any incapacity as such on the part of the world body. Furthermore, the major powers refused to provide the necessary arms, money or authority to the United Nations to carry out the Security Council resolutions effectively. In the end (see below, Chapter 4) the individual Western powers and Russia, the European Union and NATO each became involved in disintegrating Yugoslavia with separate or at least differing policies and when chaos and disaster inevitably followed, the United Nations provided an easy scapegoat upon which to lay the blame. None of this means that the United Nations does not make mistakes in such situations but no international organization can be effective unless its principal members are in agreement and are prepared to provide the organization with real authority and a mandate that they subsequently uphold.

The fiftieth anniversary celebrations provided the occasion for a range of criticisms which between them reinforced the general sense of a United Nations in crisis. Many countries criticized the United States for failing to pay its arrears which then amounted to US$1.3 billion. US President Bill Clinton called for swift action to reform the United Nations, to rationalize its bureaucracy and streamline its operations while Britain's Prime Minister John Major called for an early expansion of the membership of the Security Council. When Cuba's President Fidel Castro attacked the privileged position of the five permanent members of the Security Council – 'The obsolete veto privilege and the ill-use of the Security Council by the powerful are exalting a new colonialism within the UN itself' – he expressed a view that had great appeal for many of the smaller members of the world body.

At least the world's leaders gave the United Nations a new lease of life, at any rate in theory, when they produced a document in which they vowed to 'give to the 21st century a UN equipped, financed and structured to serve effectively the peoples in whose name it was established'. Such statements of principle have long been part of the United Nations' story; what will matter in the years leading to the opening of the new century is the extent to which actions and involvements by the United Nations make its continued existence essential to world peace and security.

During the three-day commemorative meeting of the General Assembly, held on 22–24 October 1995, the largest ever gathering of world leaders, a total of 91 heads of state, eight vice-presidents, one crown prince, 37 prime ministers, 10 deputy prime ministers, 21 foreign ministers, nine chairmen of delegations and 23 observers – a total of 200 speakers – addressed the meeting. Their theme was reform.[6] Such attendance, at least, ought to augur well for the future of the United Nations.

THE UNITED NATIONS SINCE THE COLD WAR

During 1989, as the Cold War structures which had dominated international politics for the previous 40 years began to break up, the United Nations mediated an accord in Afghanistan which allowed Soviet troops to withdraw. This represented a major achievement for the world body and a significant change of policy for the USSR; if the United Nations could assist one of the two superpowers in this manner where else, at last, could it play an effective role? In Africa it was deeply involved in what turned out to be the last (successful) phase in its long effort to bring the UN Trusteeship Territory of Namibia to independence and as a result of this operation was becoming committed to a new involvement in war-torn Angola where both the United States and Cuba, which then had 50 000 troops in the country, were willing for the United Nations to take over and allow them to retreat. In war-torn Sudan the United Nations was carrying out its 'Operation Lifeline' to provide southerners affected by the ongoing civil war with essential food supplies. Each of these operations represented a plus for the world body although it was forced to withdraw its agencies from Somalia due to fierce and escalating fighting between the factions in that country's civil war. The new readiness on the part of the two superpowers – the USSR in Afghanistan and the United States in Angola/Namibia – to allow the United Nations to act effectively and bring about positive conclusions to long-lasting conflicts gave rise to the hope that a new era was about to open.

In 1990 the United Nations faced ongoing tasks in Cambodia, the Middle East, Cyprus and Nicaragua but what made the year memorable was the high level of cooperation that was achieved over the explosive issue of Iraq's invasion of Kuwait on 2 August. The Security Council invoked Chapter VII of the Charter which deals with 'acts of aggression', condemned Iraq and then demanded its immediate and unconditional withdrawal from Kuwait. US Pesident George Bush and Soviet President Mikhail Gorbachev spoke warmly of their new found ability to cooperate with one another. If the two superpowers which had spearheaded the Cold War confrontation over more than 40 years could now work closely together through the United Nations then anything was possible – or so it must have seemed to optimists and those who had argued constantly through the bleak years for greater trust in the world body.

The Cold War might have come to an end but there was growing evidence that the relaxation of tensions between the superpowers had, if anything, helped release restraints elsewhere so that the world was becoming a more violent if not more absolutely dangerous place in which to live. The Gulf War and its aftermath remained at the centre of attention and there US/Soviet cooperation continued: it was the first time since the Korean War that the United Nations approved the use of force. Elsewhere the United Nations was involved in civil war situations in Angola, Cambodia, El Salvador and the rapidly deteriorating situation in Yugoslavia; on economic and development matters it was responsible for drawing up a Code of Conduct for Transnational Corporations to control their relations with host countries and conducted a series of environment debates in preparation for the Rio Earth Summit scheduled for 1992. In general, the United Nations had never been busier.

UN commitments became even greater during 1992: in Western Sahara it postponed a referendum at the insistence of Morocco; in Angola, Mozambique and El Salvador it worked to bring an end to civil wars; in South Africa it became involved in the process of reconciliation, as apartheid was dismantled, and preparations for the first universal franchise elections; with regard to Libya (under pressures from the United States, Britain and France) it applied sanctions to force Colonel Gaddafi to hand over the Lockerbie bomb suspects; it tried to induce Israel to improve its treatment of the Palestinians and was also involved in strife-torn Lebanon. In November the Secretary-General forbade the sale of arms to Liberia in a move to end the civil war in that country. The United Nations was also involved in the fight to curb international drug-trafficking, in combating the spread of AIDS, in running the Rio Earth Summit on the environment, in preparing a draft treaty to ban the use of chemical weapons, in the humanitarian supply of food and drugs to various troubled regions of the world, in drawing up demographic projections (part of its ongoing and massive work updating international statistics), and international law. Indeed, there were few aspects of world affairs in which the United Nations was not involved and in a number of cases it was in the lead in seeking solutions. It had precise commitments – whether in peacekeeping or other activities – in at least 18 countries. The new Secretary-General, Boutros Boutros-Ghali, presented his report, *An Agenda for Peace*, in which he made a plea for regional organizations to become involved in peacekeeping operations as the United Nations had become overstretched and overburdened.

The United Nations was equally active during 1993. The Security Council in its deliberations concluded that social and economic development should be given equal importance with political and security concerns. As of 31 December 1993, there were UN Peacekeeping Operations in no less than 17 countries:[7] of these, two – UN Truce Supervision Organization in Palestine (UNTSO) and the UN Military Observer Group in India and Pakistan (UNMOGIP) had been ongoing since 1948 and 1949 respectively; the UN Peacekeeping Force in Cyprus (UNFICYP) had been ongoing since 1964; the UN Disengagement Observer Force in the Golan Heights (UNDOF) and the UN Interim Force in Lebanon (UNIFIL) had been ongoing since 1974 and 1978 respectively; while the remaining 12 operations had all been undertaken since 1990. These were as follows:

UN Angola Verification Mission (UNAVEM II) 1991
UN Mission for the Referendum in Western Sahara (MINURSO) 1991
UN Observer Mission in El Salvador (ONUSAL) 1991
UN Iraq–Kuwait Observer Mission (UNIKOM) 1991
UN Observer Mission in South Africa (UNOMSA) 1992
UN Operation in Mozambique (UNOMOZ) 1992
UN Protection Force in Former Yugoslavia (UNPROFOR) 1992
UN Observer Mission in Georgia (UNOMIG) 1993
UN Observer Mission in Liberia (UNOMIL) 1993
UN Operation in Somalia (UNOSOM II) 1993
UN Mission in Haiti (UNMIH) 1993
UN Assistance Mission in Rwanda (UNAMIR) 1993

Despite being overstretched the United Nations and its agencies constantly took on new responsibilities: partly because it could not refuse involvement, for example in a new refugee crisis; and partly because, despite growing criticisms, it suited the major powers that the United Nations should undertake tasks which they themselves were not anxious or prepared to tackle.

The pattern of growing and widespread involvements continued through 1994 and into 1995 when a deeply overburdened and heavily in debt United Nations celebrated its first 50 years. By that year, however, the post-Cold War euphoria had evaporated and overt criticisms of the United Nations appeared to be greater and far more persistent than any comparable understanding of its problems. These problems, moreover, were changing very rapidly in both scope and kind as the world moved towards an increasingly globalized economy that paid less and less attention to national boundaries. The movement of people, whether as refugees from civil wars or as economic migrants, threatens to become one of the most tenacious world issues as the century draws to its close. And that problem is closely intertwined with the question of attitudes as between the rich North and the developing South. The old established powers of the West still assume that the transformation of Third World countries into Western-style states is most likely to solve their development or other political problems. It is an assumption that is both arrogant and dangerous but as long as it persists (and there is no sign of any abatement of it) the relationship between North and South will continue strained. Moreover, since the great majority of the members of the General Assembly belong to the Third World this will mean continuing and escalating tensions in the United Nations.

In its report *Our Global Neighbourhood*, published in 1995, the Commission on Global Governance said, bleakly enough, 'The Gulf War, the enormities of ethnic cleansing in the Balkans, brutal violence in Somalia, and genocide in Rwanda' between them have done much to change the world mood for the worst.[8] Yet despite or because of these doubts, the Commission advances a powerful plea on behalf of the United Nations:

> It is our firm conclusion that the United Nations must continue to play a central role in global governance. With its universality, it is the only forum where the governments of the world come together on an equal footing and on a regular basis to try to resolve the world's most pressing problems. Every effort must be made to give it the credibility and resources it requires to fulfil its responsibilities.[9]

In an increasingly violent world the need for an effective United Nations has never been greater; whether the major powers in the troubled aftermath of the Cold War will provide the world body with the authority and the means to deal with the tasks that they so readily thrust upon it remains to be seen.

2   Peacekeeping

Maintaining world peace was always seen as a primary object of the United Nations; deciding when and how to intervene remains the crucial test for the Security Council. According to the UN Charter, member states must settle their disputes by peaceful means and in such a way that international peace, security and justice are not endangered or threatened. Member states are to refrain from the threat or use of force against other member states; the Security Council is the UN organ primarily responsible for maintaining peace and security and under Article 25 of the Charter member states agree to accept and carry out the Council's decisions. Peacekeeping operations are mounted to help control conflicts which arise between members to threaten international peace; such operations are meant to be impartial and can only be mounted with the consent of the warring governments concerned. The object of a peacekeeping operation is to create a ceasefire and then, after establishing a buffer zone between the warring parties, facilitate the search for a peaceful settlement of the dispute by diplomatic and mediatory channels.

Prior to the end of the Cold War peacekeeping operations were designed to monitor ceasefires, control buffer zones and prevent the resumption of hostilities. 'Peace-keeping forces are made up of contingents of troops provided by Member States and financed by the international community. The soldiers of the United Nations peace-keeping forces have light weapons, but can use them only in self-defence.'[1] A crucial aspect of UN peacekeeping has always been its perceived impartiality: 'An operation must not interfere in the internal affairs of the host country, and must not be used in any way to favour one party against another in internal conflicts.'[2] This perception of peacekeeping has been radically upset in the period since 1990. The Gulf War, events in Yugoslavia, Somalia and Rwanda as well as enormous extra demands upon the United Nations to monitor a variety of highly explosive and dangerous conflicts have produced a situation that was hardly envisaged when the United Nations Charter was drawn up.

A majority of world disputes are now, in fact, disputes within countries – civil wars – and intervention in such circumstances requires a different set of rules. What is slowly evolving is a new and fundamental principle that the United Nations can and should intervene in the internal affairs of individual states and that the peoples within a state have the right to protection if, for example, they are a minority, and that they can call upon the United Nations to assist them to safeguard these rights, if necessary against the actions of their own governments. During the 1990s there has been a steady erosion of the principle that there should be no international interference in the internal affairs of individual states.

In *Our Global Neighbourhood* (the report of the Commission on Global Governance) a number of principles of security for a new era are laid down and if these recommendations become enshrined in UN practice then we are about to enter an era in which it will be seen as the duty of the United Nations to intervene in the internal affairs of member states in particular circumstances. The report states: 'All people, no less than all states, have a right to a secure existence, and all states have an obligation to protect those rights.'[3]

Effectively this would give the United Nations the right and the duty to intervene – and not just for humanitarian purposes – when such conditions were not being met, as in the civil war disputes of the 1990s such as those in Rwanda, Burundi, Somalia, Yugoslavia and Chechnya and though, as we shall see, the interventions that have taken place to date have been far from successful, yet, very gradually, new precedents are being established.

As the United Nations undertakes ever more interventions which are increasingly varied in their scope so it is exposed to a wider range of political pressures as well as the physical dangers facing its peacekeeping forces. 'The UN is now commonly asked to reduce tensions between warring parties, encourage political reconciliation, and supply humanitarian assistance to affected civilian populations.'[4] One of the problems facing UN peacekeeping efforts is purely practical: demands for peacekeeping have become so numerous that the capacity of the organization to respond has been hampered by the unwillingness of the member states to provide needed resources. This problem may be met, at least in part in the post-Cold War era, by the use of regional organizations under Chapter VIII of the Charter which deals with regional security issues. This has already been done in relation to Cambodia (with help from ASEAN), in Central America (with help from the OAS and the Contadora group) and in the former Yugoslavia (with help from NATO, the EU and the WEU) though with varying degrees of success. For the United Nations to be effective, 'Military, political, humanitarian, and development work should be seen as complementary and mutually supportive.'[5]

What the United Nations lacks is a standing force that can be deployed at once in emergency situations. In 1948 the first Secretary-General, Trygve Lie, called for the creation of a UN 'guard force' which would be at the disposal of the Security Council but his suggestion was ignored at the time. The idea of a UN Volunteer Force of up to 10000 personnel has been resurrected by the Commission on Global Governance at a time when the United Nations was running 17 peacekeeping or peace enforcement operations worldwide involving more than 70000 troops at an annual cost of US$3.2

billion. The point of a standing UN force, in addition to ongoing or new peacekeeping operations, would be to enable the Security Council to deploy 'credible and effective peace enforcement units at an early stage in a crisis and at short notice'.[6]

The 1990s witnessed parallel and contradictory pressures being exerted upon the United Nations: on the one hand, the sudden sense of release which followed the end of the Cold War led to it being asked to undertake more and more operations as governments pledged themselves to use it to solve problems; on the other hand, it was subjected to increasingly vitriolic criticisms as the added burdens placed upon it revealed the shortcomings of the organization. Some of the criticisms – corruption and stifling bureaucracy – were deserved; but others resulted from the gap between what it was asked to do and the readiness of the major powers actually to provide it with the means to carry out the mandates it was given.

At the beginning of the decade, in the immediate aftermath of the Gulf War, world leaders began to turn again to the United Nations in the hope it would be able to perform its original purpose of resolving conflicts, as they recognized 'the destructiveness of seeking military solutions to the world's ills'.[7] On 31 January 1992, 15 heads of government met as their countries' Security Council representatives and pledged to strengthen UN peacekeeping capacities. In June 1992 the Secretary-General, Boutros Boutros-Ghali, responded to the Security Council's January pledge with his *Agenda for Peace* which recommended a permanent UN armed force to be supervised by the Security Council and an active Military Staff Committee. He also proposed an 'early warning' system to settle disputes before they escalated into confrontations and asked for authority to stop disputes in their initial stages. He suggested that additional peacekeeping funds should be provided out of national military budgets and taxes on arms sales and international air travel. These suggestions were imaginative and remain 'on the table' but, at least for the time being, they were overshadowed by events.

Another factor complicating efforts at rejuvenation of the United Nations was that of simple fatigue on the part of its most consistent supporters upon whom it had to rely for peacekeeping operations; thus in 1992, after 28 years' failure to persuade Greeks and Turks to resolve their differences in Cyprus, Austria, Canada, Denmark and Britain threatened to withdraw their peacekeeping forces.

During 1993 there was a dramatic rise in the demand for UN peacekeeping forces round the world and in some cases troops were authorized to enforce order for the first time. It was not clear, however, who would fund the increased peacekeeping operations whose estimated cost for the year was US$3.6 billion. In February 1993 a Ford Foundation panel picked up the proposal from the *Agenda for Peace* that peacekeeping should be charged to national military budgets and that the United Nations should be authorized to charge interest on arrears of dues. The need for peacekeeping forces grew during 1994 with the Secretary-General asking member states to make troops available to cover the many commitments which the Security Council had undertaken. In April it was announced that 15 states had pledged at least 54000 troops and specialists for future operations and on 12 July the German courts ruled that German nationals might legally take part in UN operations, a change of the German constitution (which had prevented German military personnel serving outside Germany) that would make available substantial new sources of highly trained manpower.

On 14 March 1994 the Secretary-General issued a report, 'Improving the Capacity of the United Nations for Peace-Keeping', which contained concrete proposals for standby arrangements as well as civilian policy, training, the principle of UN command, the strengthening of the Secretariat and the recruitment of civilian personnel. The Secretary-General also advanced proposals covering the financing of peacekeeping operations. By September 1994, 22 member states had made written offers amounting to a total of 31000 troops to be available on a standby basis for peacekeeping operations but, as the violence escalated in the Rwanda refugee camps and the Secretary-General asked for some of these forces to be made available, he discovered a marked unwillingness of major contributing countries to commit their personnel.[8] In March 1995, at Vienna, the Secretary-General suggested that the United Nations should 'contract out' peacekeeping operations; he cited France in Rwanda and the United States in Haiti. The suggestion held great possibilities – good and bad – for the future.

By late 1994 the disastrously complex civil war or wars in disintegrating Yugoslavia made any staightforward appraisal of peacekeeping impossible. Speaking in London, the Secretary-General, Boutros-Ghali, said: 'The problem is the member states are not ready to do peace enforcement ... The 36 members who are participating in the operation have done so on the basis of a peace-keeping operation. They have not the necessary equipment to do peace enforcement. So how can we do peace enforcement? NATO air strikes will not solve the problem and our troops will be in danger.' Responding to US pressures at that time to lift the arms embargo on Bosnia, Mr Boutros-Ghali said: 'It's very simple. The message I receive from Great Britain, from France, Spain, Canada and Russia [is] that if the embargo is lifted they will withdraw their troops. So if I want to keep troops on the ground for humanitarian reasons, for political reasons, for protecting the Muslims, I have to take this into account.' He also referred to the fact that it was easier to obtain troops for one problem (Yugoslavia) than another (Rwanda) and he made the point which goes to the heart of half the problems faced by the United Nations: 'Everyone is equal but some persons are more equal. This is a political body and the member states have national interests so they will obtain a resolution in their favour and not pay attention to others.'[9]

By May 1995, as the Bosnian ceasefire began to fall apart, UN impotence was becoming more marked and the Secretary-General said that UNPROFOR would have to reconsider its role. For the first time in the war, the UN forces fought the Serbs for control of territory that was supposed to be under UN control; France demanded that the UN mandate should be clearer and tougher or it would withdraw its troops (they then had 4000 on the ground, mainly based in Sarajevo). At the same time the United States increased its denunciation of the Bosnian Serbs, describing them as international outlaws for seizing and killing UN peacekeepers. An apparent stalemate had been reached with the Serbs holding UN hostages and shelling safe areas. Some UN sources in Sarajevo believed that the international community had lost its stomach for the fight and that realization highlighted yet another problem: peacekeeping in one part of the world, no matter how important, may have little appeal to a power whose troops and logistics are essential to the operation if it is not seen to be in its national interest. Once too many body bags began to return home from Somalia, for example, the United States decided to end its operation there and withdraw its troops.

Backing for the United Nations is often given for the wrong reasons and that does not help to make its operations effective. In the crisis-ridden month of May 1995 the US Republican presidential candidate Pat Buchanan said, 'If you use air strikes you have to ask yourself: "Are you ready to escalate to total war?" I don't think the US is.' Furthermore, despite its involvement, the United States was determined not to commit troops to Bosnia although it had promised to provide them to assist a NATO withdrawal. In fact, at the time, fear of being drawn into a Balkan Vietnam was uppermost in American calculations and since Washington did not wish to see US leadership and the West humiliated it continued to support the UN mission.[10]

Attacks upon the United Nations' peacekeeping record are easy enough to mount but rarely take account of the conflicting political forces with which it has to contend. The British charity Save the Children called for major changes and a new UN approach to crisis intervention.

No structure or mechanism capable of tackling the world's forgotten emergencies has been created. Safe havens, military interventions and peace-keeping have all failed because they have been damagingly short-term. Changes should include drastic reform of UN structures and mandates to meet the challenges of a new era. We need sensitive and appropriate international diplomacy carried out by the right people for the job and free from UN bureaucracy and member states' self-interest.[11]

Stating the problem, however, is no substitute for finding a solution. Just how does the United Nations free itself of 'member states' self-interest'?

While Save the Children was laying down criteria of UN behaviour the French commander of UN forces in Sarajevo, Major-General Hervé Gobilliard was telling his troops to avoid confronting either Serbs or government forces so as to reduce the risk to French peacekeepers. 'I do not want to accept any more casualties', he said. 'Under no circumstances will we engage either warring party [in ways] which might put the life of one of our soldiers in jeopardy.'[12] If that is the attitude of the peacekeepers it is not to be expected that those who have embarked upon a war will be persuaded to keep the peace.

At the end of three years at a cost of many billions of dollars it was still not clear in mid-1995 whether the United Nations' operation in Bosnia was to feed civilians and protect safe areas or to stop the fighting, and, though much of the blame for this had to be laid at the door of UN bureaucracy, incompetence and poor leadership could be assigned to the major powers which had signally failed to come up with any consistent policy but presented instead a series of perspectives – American, West European, Russian, EU or NATO – that constantly teetered between new initiatives to solve the problem and face-saving gestures to show that the world cared about the tragedy which continued to unfold relentlessly in front of the world's media.

As the former British permanent representative to the United Nations, Sir Anthony Parsons, argues in his book *From Cold War to Hot Peace*,[13] the whole nature of peacekeeping changed during the 1990s; it is no longer a question of dealing with interstate wars but civil wars of which there are about 30 being waged worldwide at the time of writing. Furthermore, another new factor of immense importance is the communications revolution which allows people to see horrific pictures of what is happening on their television screens leading them to demand that their governments do something. Unfortunately, what governments do in response to such public pressures is often the wrong thing. Politicians consistently shy away from tough action; instead they opt for policies which are designed to demonstrate that they are doing 'something' rather than opting for tougher and more costly policies which will achieve results. (More costly policies of effective action in the first place often turn out to be the cheapest in the long run.) The various failures of the 1990s have shown clearly that there is little point embarking upon a policy unless the political will exists to follow it through to a conclusion. This was not done in either Somalia or Rwanda and it remains an open question as to whether it will eventually be done in Bosnia.

By mid-1995 there were bitter resentments among the peacekeepers in Bosnia: senior UN representatives claimed that Washington, backed by Germany, had pushed the UN into acting as an intervention force in Bosnia, something Washington had always wanted although it would not deploy its own toops to such an end. Huge pressures had been mounted by top members of the US administration, including President Clinton, upon the Secretary-General to mount air strikes against the Serbs and this had been done before the UN observers had been withdrawn. The United Nations first sent troops to Bosnia in 1992 to act as peacekeepers and deliver humanitarian aid; subsequently, a series of Security Council resolutions led the troops on the ground to undertake enforcement duties as all sides in the conflict refused diplomatic solutions. While Germany supported the Croats and the United States supported the Muslims, the other European powers were more ambivalent and opposed lifting the arms embargo on Bosnia although the Russians supported the Serbs. This was far closer to the big power politics that had characterized diplomacy in the Balkans prior to World War I than to the kind of support the United Nations had a right to expect. Furthermore, Western governments did not wish to send troops to Yugoslavia to fight in a war which the logic of the situation increasingly seemed to demand; instead, they treated the UN force as a substitute for more comprehensive action as they tried to ease their consciences by maintaining a presence and then did not provide the United Nations with sufficient personnel, materiel or authority to do an effective job.

Postponement of effective action has been the hallmark of Western behaviour towards the Balkan problem. Britain and France which had troops on the ground became increasingly disenchanted with the United States which did not; Germany remained ambiguous in its attitudes with an eye clearly on its own historic sphere of influence in the region; Russia, when it did become engaged, supported its historic ally Serbia. At the same time no one wished the United Nations to withdraw: it was and remains too convenient a scapegoat for failures on the ground.

The British Foreign Scretary, Malcolm Rifkind, who succeeded Douglas Hurd in 1995, followed an American demand for reform of the United Nations and said: 'Recent experience has shown the UN is in some ways ill-fitted for its tasks, underpowered in some areas, like peace-keeping and preventive diplomacy; but still bloated in other parts of the system.' The British Foreign Secretary was taking part in the 1995 50 years celebrations when it was more or less *de rigueur* for foreign ministers to level criticisms and suggest what reforms their own countries would like to see being adopted. He told the General Assembly:

Bosnia and Somalia have shown the limits of peace-keeping. They offer a clear lesson. The UN is not yet suited to fight wars. Peace enforcement is perhaps better left to coalitions of the willing acting under UN authority. We must not send in the UN to keep a peace which does not exist, then blame it for failure.[14]

That, exactly, was what had happened.

The changing nature of war in the post-Cold War era must affect the way the United Nations operates. If peacekeeping is to have any meaning the world community will have to be prepared to intervene more often and more effectively in civil wars: not just to keep the peace after a ceasefire has been achieved, which really means supporting whatever new status quo has been arrived at, but intervening before or at the start of a civil war to prevent it taking place or escalating. According to the Stockholm International Peace Research Institute (SIPRI) all 30 of the wars being fought in 1995 were civil wars and they were being fought in what SIPRI describes as 'weak' or 'failed states'. Most civil wars are relatively contained: that is, they are confined within a particular state and do not affect neighbours or a wider world except in so far as other states or their nationals become more wary of dealing with such a state while the conflict lasts. Such wars, nonetheless, can be just as devastating and horrific in terms of human suffering as wars between states. The question now facing the United Nations and the world community is whether to abandon the approach which has been accepted as the norm up to the present time – that there should be no intervention in the internal affairs of a member state – and be prepared, instead, to intervene in civil wars. Can a civil war only be regarded as an internal affair or should the suffering and bloodshed be seen as a world concern? The answer, at least in the light of experience during the 1990s, is a highly qualified 'yes'. Since the United Nations Charter was not designed to deal with civil wars there exists no consensus on when or if other states ought to intervene. But if such intervention is to become the norm – and that is a real possibility – then the main military powers will have to consider just how much of their military potential is to be assigned, more or less on a permanent basis, to interventions under the umbrella of the United Nations. And following that decision comes the even more fraught one: do they intervene as peacekeepers or as peace enforcers? And further, how is a civil war defined? The terrible slaughter in Rwanda during 1994 in which perhaps one million people were killed was both a civil war and a war of genocide and there were powerful arguments for intervention by the world community which, however, stood aside. But what of the long-lasting war in Peru between the radical Maoist Shining Path movement and the government: was that a civil war or was it no more than an insurrection which the government by 1996 appeared to have got under control (an estimated 28 000 people had been killed by that year). Some civil wars, such as those in East Timor or the South Philippines, continue for years and are largely – and deliberately – ignored by the world community.

Major armed conflict has been defined as that in which 1000 people or more are killed in a year. In 1995 the United Nations played a role in nearly every conflict situation worldwide although this may well prove impossible in the future. The new emphasis, perhaps, should be on conflict prevention rather than peacekeeping after a war has taken place but conflict prevention will require as great a readiness to intervene as peacekeeping does and, in many cases, would only be permitted if the United Nations had at its command sufficient forces to allow it to intervene whether or not the government of the potential conflict state wished it to do so. If conflict prevention is to become a major aspect of United Nations activities then the United Nations Charter needs to be amended accordingly.

A good deal of speculation about the changing nature of war has followed the end of the Cold War and, according to one qualified observer,[15] the clear distinction between war and peace has now become blurred and while the major powers, including Russia and France which have long relied upon conscript armies, are now moving back to smaller highly professional armies, there is a growing sense that the international community should be prepared to intervene in civil wars in order to enforce international standards of behaviour. The nuclear stalemate and the assumption that war would be total has now been replaced by a growing belief that much smaller but highly dangerous civil wars should be contained and then controlled. As the UN Secretary-General Boutros-Ghali wrote in 1992: 'The centuries old doctrine of absolute and exclusive sovereignty no longer stands, and was never so absolute as it was conceived to be in theory.'[16] As his predecessor, Perez de Cuellar, also wrote in 1991: 'We are witnessing what is probably an irresistible shift in public attitudes towards the belief that the defence of the oppressed in the name of morality should prevail over frontiers and legal documents.'[17] He was referring to the decision to intervene in Iraq to assist the Iraqi Kurds. Crucial to this new approach must be the readiness of the major powers, which possess the military means and the finances to intervene effectively, and their readiness (or not) will, in its turn, be dependent upon public attitudes as these are affected by modern communications. Wars today cannot be ignored but what does seem to be emerging is a distinct element of choice: the major powers, through the United Nations, intervened in the Gulf in 1991 and intervened in Yugoslavia because their interests were involved; in Somalia and Rwanda, after initial forays, they disengaged because those civil wars did not threaten their interests. And in the case of Chechnya the world community left the Russians a free hand.

3 The Gulf War of 1991 and its Aftermath

The Iraqi invasion of Kuwait on 2 August 1990 led to an unexpectedly high level of cooperation between the United States and the USSR which had not been seen throughout the years of the Cold War. The UN Secretary-General, Perez de Cuellar, invoked Chapter VII of the UN Charter which deals with aggression and demanded Iraq's immediate and unconditional withdrawal from Kuwait. On 6 August he ordered a comprehensive trade and financial boycott of Iraq and on 9 August the Security Council invalidated Iraq's annexation of Kuwait. On 18 August the Security Council demanded that Iraq should release foreign citizens held as potential hostages.

Further pressures against Iraq were mounted during September: food supplies entering the country were to be screened, Iraq's violation of diplomatic premises was condemned and the Security Council again demanded the release of all foreign personnel while air traffic to Iraq was embargoed and member states were authorized to seize Iraqi ships violating UN sanctions. On 29 October the Secretary-General held Iraq responsible for all damage resulting from the invasion of Kuwait and requested nations to prepare financial claims against Iraq. On 29 November the Security Council authorized states to use 'all necessary means' including force against Iraq if it failed to comply with these UN resolutions by 15 January 1991.

Perez de Cuellar visited Iraq at the end of August but announced on 2 September that President Saddam Hussein would not agree to comply with the UN resolutions. In the meantime Iraq prepared for war. Already, on 3 July 1990 (prior to the invasion of Kuwait), Iraq had agreed to end ten years of hostilities with Iran so as to secure its eastern frontier; then, on 15 August, Iraq gave up all the gains it had made during the fighting in the Gulf War with Iran (1980–8) while diplomatic relations were resumed with Teheran in September.

It became clear at this point that the United States was determined, if necessary, to use force to make Iraq relinquish Kuwait and it is worth asking upon what principle Washington acted? The United States and its Western allies (especially Britain which was equally forthright in demanding action against Baghdad) could hardly claim to be acting on the principle that it was automatically right to enforce a UN resolution as such since blatantly, over the years, they had ignored many UN resolutions in relation to Israel, South Africa and other parts of the world where their interests dictated inaction.

Nor could they argue that they were taking action to prevent annexation *on principle* since they had remained quiescent in the case of China's annexation of Tibet in the 1950s, over Israel's annexation of the Golan Heights in 1967, Turkey's annexation of the northern third of Cyprus in 1974 or Indonesia's annexation of East Timor in 1975. Apologists for earlier Western inaction over the issue of annexation were quick to point out that the Cold War made intervention far more dangerous and difficult in those previous cases but this raises the question as to whether, even had there been no Cold War, the West would have intervened? In fact, there was only one principle of overriding importance which led the West to intervene in the Gulf and that was oil. Had there been no oil in Kuwait there might have been outraged denunciation of a bullying regime but there would not have been a war. It was the fear in Washington, London and Paris that Saddam Hussein, a highly volatile and unpredictable leader, would end up controlling the largest oil resource in the world outside Saudi Arabia that dictated Western intervention. A recognition of that fact is essential if we are also to understand the later dilemmas faced by the United Nations when it tried but failed to secure major Western support for other interventions elsewhere in the world. In direct proportion, as national interests are involved in a crisis so are the major powers prepared to take part in UN peacekeeping or other acts of intervention.

Even so, there was almost universal condemnation of the Iraqi invasion of Kuwait although the Arab world was thrown into disarray for, though its conservative members – Saudi Arabia and the small Gulf states – knew that their safety depended upon ousting Iraq from Kuwait, they also knew that this could only be done with Western – American – assistance and this would mean the return of a neo-colonialist military presence to the Arab world. Moscow's willingness to cooperate with the United States to force Iraq to obey UN sanctions (despite the fact that the USSR was Iraq's ally and its main source of military equipment) ensured that massive US intervention could be swiftly mounted. A rapid build-up of forces to oppose Iraq now took place and as early as 9 August the United States had begun to despatch 40 000 troops and 100 F-15 and F-16 fighter bombers to the Gulf. Britain joined the United States at this stage in sending troops to the Gulf and both powers actively sought UN backing for the use of their forces against Iraq.

During the remainder of 1990 the American-led Alliance built up its strength in the Gulf to more than 500 000 men, of whom over 400 000 were US personnel. They formed the core of the Alliance in terms of both numbers and sophisticated weaponry. British forces numbered 30 000, French forces 10 000 while a further 100 000 troops were deployed by Saudi Arabia, Egypt and Syria with small contingents from other states. It was the first time since the Korean War of 1950–3 that a UN-backed alliance had been prepared to wage war according to UN Security Council resolutions but with the significant difference that the two communist giants – the USSR and China – had decided to support the United Nations so that there was no threat of a Cold War split over the crisis.

On 13 January the Secretary-General, Perez de Cuellar, met with President Saddam Hussein in Baghdad in a last attempt to persuade him to withdraw from Kuwait but he refused. On 16 January following the expiry of the UN deadline the 28-nation coalition began massive air strikes against Iraq which were to continue for more than a month. The land campaign was only launched on 23 February 1991, and was to last a mere five days; the Iraqi forces were driven from Kuwait though not before they had fired most of the oil wells; then, on 28 February Iraq agreed to comply with the Security Council's requirements and on 2 March the Security Council agreed a ceasefire. Iraq had to abandon all its claims to Kuwait. On 9 March the UN Commission on Human Rights began to investigate abuses committed by Iraq both in Iraq itself and in Kuwait and a UN team in Iraq described the effects of the aerial bombardment as 'near apocalyptic'. On 3 April the Security Council formally ended the Gulf War although maintaining an arms embargo on Iraq. Food sanctions were to be lifted and an observer force was to be established in the buffer zone between Iraq and Kuwait.

The war part of the UN exercise had been relatively straightforward; endless complications were now to follow and persist through the 1990s. Almost at once, after the ceasefire, the Iraqi regime mounted military campaigns against the Kurds in the north of the country and the Shi'ite Muslims and the Marsh Arabs in the south leading the UN Secretary-General to condemn a level of repression that was causing waves of refugees to cross into Turkey, Iran and Saudi Arabia and, for the first time, the Security Council described action by a government against its own people as a threat to international peace while the UNHCR called Iraqi actions close to genocide.

The Kurds of northern Iraq make up 19 per cent of the total Iraqi population and have long been seen as an irritant by governments in Baghdad. By the beginning of 1990 the Iraqi Kurds were worse off than at any time in the preceding quarter of a century. When the Gulf War between Iran and Iraq came to an end in 1988, the government of Saddam Hussein prepared to crush Kurdish resistance; Turkey, which had a substantial and disaffected Kurdish minority of its own, showed little sympathy for the Iraqi Kurds, some of whom had crossed into Turkey as refugees and was ready to cooperate with Iraq. Iran, on the other border of northern Iraq and again with a Kurdish minority of its own, also showed little inclination to support the Iraqi Kurds who, in consequence, were isolated. In April 1989, therefore, the Baghdad government had embarked on a massive programme to relocate the Kurds away from their mountain homelands and this had been in progress at the time Iraq invaded Kuwait. In March 1991, in the immediate aftermath of the war between Iraq and the American-led United Nations coalition, the Kurds launched a widespread rebellion against Saddam Hussein.

It was this rebellion and Saddam Hussein's brutal reaction to it which led the United Nations to adopt a new principle of intervention with the widest possible implications for the future. The Security Council accepted a principle which overrides sovereignty; it was based upon a French proposal that there was a 'duty of humanitarian intervention'. This new principle was then applied to the Kurds of northern Iraq after attacks upon them (in which chemical weapons were used) by Saddam Hussein's forces in the wake of the Gulf War. On 8 April the proposal to create 'safe havens', an idea put forward by Britain's Prime Minister, John Major, was adopted by the United Nations and applied to the Kurds of northern Iraq, many of whom were then in camps under UN auspices. These were to be policed by Western troops including 10000 US, 4500 British, 1000 Dutch and 1500 French. At the same time, the United Nations, which was already administering the main Kurdish refugee camp at Zakho, now stationed 500 security guards there to observe and monitor the safety of UN civilians working in the camp. In their safe havens in northern Iraq the Kurds began to build schools and villages; allied air force planes stationed in eastern Turkey overfly the region to ensure that it is not attacked by Iraqi planes although how long such a situation will be allowed to continue is very much an open question.[1]

Meanwhile, on 24 April 1991, a 1400-strong UN Iraq–Kuwait Observer Mission (UNIKOM) headed by the Austrian, Major-General Gunther Greindl, took control of the buffer zone from US troops. In May Iraq accepted a rigorous UN system of inspections of its military and scientific installations and the UN inspectors had almost unlimited freedom to investigate Iraq's weapons programmes. During the course of the month a UN team announced its discovery of 26 lb (12 kg) of highly enriched uranium. In November 1991 the Secretary-General approved a plan to destroy all plant and equipment associated with nuclear, chemical or biological weapons programmes. None of this was plain sailing and from June 1991 onwards the UN inspection teams complained of constant Iraqi attempts to conceal or remove uranium-enrichment equipment. On 25–28 September the Iraq authorities detained 44 UN inspectors who had seized documents related to the country's nuclear programme and they were only released when the United Nations provided an inventory of the documents that had either been taken or copied. During October the UN teams discovered much evidence to point to the fact that Iraq had constantly violated its pledges never to acquire nuclear weapons and that it was approaching the capability of building hydrogen bombs. The

IAEA requested government intelligence agencies to report suspected cheating by other countries in an effort to discover who had been assisting Iraq and prepared to inspect 'suspicious installations'. On 21 October 1991, Iraq gave up its pretence that it had only developed peaceful nuclear capacity and admitted trying to build nuclear bombs. On 11 December the IAEA released a list of companies (mainly German) that had supplied Iraq with products to forward its nuclear programme. The Iraqi authorities defied, delayed or deceived the UN investigators whenever they could. Although Iraq desperately needed funds (which it could only obtain by selling some of its oil) to purchase food and medicines, it rejected a UN authorization to sell US$1.6 billion worth of oil because of the conditions attached to the sale. On 2 November Iraq forbade international relief organizations to distribute food, insisting that it must control supplies of food itself.

The battle between the United Nations and Iraq continued throughout 1992 with the Iraq authorities constantly hampering UN efforts to investigate its nuclear weapons programme. Even so, after a total of 14 inspections the UN teams reported that Iraq could no longer sustain nuclear activity. The search for scud missiles, however, was inconclusive and it was not established whether all of them had been discovered. UN sanctions were maintained through the year, in part because Iraq had refused to reveal the names of companies which had supplied it with nuclear technology. In a different area entirely, the Security Council tried to prevent harassment of the Shi'ites and the Marsh Arabs and banned all Iraqi flights south of parallel 32 north of latitude; on 27 December, when an Iraqi plane did fly south of this line it was shot down by a US fighter. In response to Iraq's attempt, beginning on 30 June, to stop all international aid programmes the Security Council voted on 2 October to take control of US$800 million of Iraqi frozen assets from which to finance relief and Baghdad then reversed its policy.

Iraq spent 1993 denying UN personnel access to its nuclear facilities. The United Nations, however, demonstrated several times during the year that it was prepared to use limited military force to ensure compliance with its demands. On 13 January allied forces carried out air strikes on Iraqi command posts and radar installations to force Baghdad to drop its ban on UN flights over the country. Iraq then attempted to impose other restrictions. Further Iraqi violations of the exclusion zones led the US forces to launch a Tomahawk cruise missile attack on a Baghdad industrial site on 17 January. On 27 June US forces launched a missile attack on the Iraqi Intelligence Service HQ because of the alleged Iraqi attempt to assassinate former President George Bush while he was on a visit to Kuwait. In September the UN teams increased their hunt for weapons sites 'declared and undeclared' while intelligence sources suggested that Iraq still had 200 Scud missiles hidden about the country. Iraq permitted the UN inspectors to activate monitoring cameras on two missile sites. During mid-November (16–20), in protest at the UN demarcation of the Iraq–Kuwait border, Iraqi forces mounted an incursion into Kuwait; subsequently, Baghdad accepted the UN international monitoring requirements. Iraq conducted a constant war of nerves against the United Nations during 1993 and at the end of the year it was still far from clear whether Baghdad still possessed the weapons and capability to pose a threat to its neighbours although the Secretary-General described this possibility as 'diminishing'. In his annual report to the General Assembly the Secretary-General said that Iraq had yet to fulfil its commitment to provide 'the full, final and complete disclosure of all aspects of its programmes that is needed to assess adequately its capabilities and facilities'.[2] Inside Iraq, meanwhile, great suffering continued to afflict the civilian population, especially in the north and south of the country.

In a move to pressure the United Nations into lifting the sanctions imposed in August 1990, Iraq moved 80000 troops to the Kuwait border at the beginning of October 1994; the United States promptly responded by moving troops up to the border while the Security Council condemned the Iraqi threat and demanded an immediate withdrawal and followed this on 15 October with Resolution 949 which imposed fresh restrictions upon Iraq's deployment of troops within its own borders. On 13 October the head of the UN Special Commission on Iraqi Compliance, Rolf Ekeus, reported that the United Nations had created an effective arms-inspection system although Iraq was threatening the inspectors and not providing 'straight and factual answers'. The United Nations now came under pressure from two major powers – Russia and France – to set a timetable for lifting sanctions since they wished to resume trade with Iraq but the Security Council refused to do so and the United States showed that Hussein had spent US$500 million on building palaces for his family while the people lacked food and medicines. In early November 1994 Iraq finally met the Security Council requirement and formally recognized Kuwait. There was strategy in Hussein's delaying tactics for he hoped that in the long run the West's interest in his huge oil resources and its desire to resume lucrative trading would override its willingness to prolong indefinitely the UN embargo and other punitive measures. Evidence of gross human rights abuses led the special rapporteur of the UN Human Rights Commission on Iraq to criticize Saddam Hussein's government as 'a barbaric regime' and call for the UN to deploy human rights monitors in the country.[3]

In a mood of defiance to mark the fourth anniversry of the start of the war in 1991 President Hussein said that United Nations sanctions against Iraq were the last weapon against his country but that nothing could vanquish his people: 'Those in the anti-Iraq camp have been facing increasing resistance that has weakened their influence. The number of enemies is decreasing and these enemies have become desperate or near desperate.'[4] Orchestrated demonstrations followed his speech and state-run newspapers attacked the United States which was blamed for the deaths of Iraqi soldiers in the war and for sanctions which, the newspapers claimed, had killed tens of thousands of people by cutting off vital supplies. In April 1995 the Security Council heard evidence to show that Iraq was developing biological weapons and though the Council authorized states to permit the import of up to US$1 billion of Iraqi oil every 90 days to allow Iraq to meet its humanitarian needs (of food and medicines) the Baghdad government rejected the offer as it had similar earlier offers on the grounds that it amounted to 'a dangerous violation of Iraq's sovereignty and national unity'.[5] The International Atomic Energy Agency (IAEA) investigated allegations that Iraq was still attempting to develop a nuclear weapons programme in defiance of the UN ban.

An argument in the Security Council between the United States and Britain on the one hand and France and Russia on the other over the proposed sale of oil by Iraq illustrated both the complexity of the UN embargo and the ability of Iraq to play off members of the Security Council against one another. The United States and Britain wanted to authorize Iraq to sell US$2 billion worth of oil over six months and, from each US$1 billion, US$650 million would be available to Iraq to purchase food, US$300 million would go in war reparations to Kuwait while US$50 million would meet UN costs. France and Russia, on the other hand, argued that there was no point adopting such a resolution unless it was accepted by Iraq as otherwise it would simply enable the United States and Britain to blame Iraq for the hardships inside the country.

The Security Council extended trade sanctions against Iraq several times during 1995. In October Rolf Ekeus, head of the Special Commission to eliminate Iraq's ballistic, chemical and nuclear weapons progammes, again reported that Iraq was withholding details. In August Lieutenant-General Hussein Kamel Hassan, the former Iraqi weapons chief, defected to Jordan to reveal that Iraq had a major biological and nuclear programme underway. As a result the Security Council refused to accede to President Hussein's demands that sanctions should be ended and insisted, instead, that he first comply with all the demands of the UN weapons monitors.

In January 1996, in an apparent climb down, Iraq announced that it would no longer cut off criminals' ears (a response to the UN Human Rights Commission complaints of Iraqi practices) and told the United Nations it was ready to discuss the offer made the previous year to allow it to sell US$2 billion of oil for food and medicine. The moves were seen as an effort to relieve some of the suffering of the population. In addition, the Iraqi Deputy Prime Minister, Tariq Aziz, wrote to the UN Secretary-General, Boutros-Ghali, to say: 'we would be prepared to enter a dialogue with you provided that no conditions were placed upon us'.[6] By February Iraq was closer to negotiating again with the United Nations over the sale of oil as it became clear the Security Council was not prepared to budge over sanctions although Saddam Hussein has shown himself to be a master of brinkmanship and prevarication. It was not until May 1996 that an agreement was reached and Iraq had won part of the argument since the proceeds from the sale of oil were to be spent exclusively on the purchase of food; the deal represented the return of Iraq to the world oil market after five years. The United Nations, however, retained the last word on how the money should be spent and how the food and medicine would be distributed inside Iraq. While Iraq's negotiator, Abdul Amir al-Anbari, described the deal as 'perfect', the US Ambassador to the United Nations, Madeleine Albright, insisted that the deal was 'a humanitarian exception, it is not a lifting of the sanctions. The sanctions regime remains fully in place.'[7]

During May and June 1996 a UN team worked to destroy the massive al-Hakam complex near Baghdad which, despite Iraq's earlier claim that it was an animal feed plant, turned out to be the country's main biological weapons plant used for producing anthrax and botulinum. Tensions then mounted as weapons inspectors were denied access to other installations and by mid-July Iraq was blocking the UN weapons team from inspecting sites. There was every sign that these UN–Iraq confrontations would continue indefinitely with Baghdad only making minimal concessions in response to increased threats of new UN sanctions or other actions.

The story of Iraq and the United Nations is instructive at two levels. First, if the major Western powers and, above all, the United States are determined, for reasons of their own interest, to take action then the United Nations will be given the full authority and means to act. Second, given the nature of UN mandates, a country as powerful as Iraq can find endless ways to thwart or slow down the legitimate demands for access of UN inspection teams and Iraq (in this instance) will do this to the limit to which it believes it can push the world body in the hope of weakening the resolve of the United Nations to carry out its tasks.

4 The Break-up of Yugoslavia

The break-up of the Yugoslav Federation began in June 1991 when the Yugoslav federal army was sent to impose central (Serbian) authority in Slovenia. The consequent fighting spread to Croatia in July. In the months and years that followed the world was to be treated to a spectacle of barbaric brutality as the term 'ethnic cleansing' became part of the international language; it was also to witness an object lesson in how not to deal with such a problem as the major powers – the United States, Britain, France, Germany and Russia – each pursued different and sometimes opposed policies or no policy at all while, in turn, the European Union, the CSCE (Conference on Security and Cooperation in Europe) and NATO were called upon to take the lead in finding a solution and the United Nations, often without adequate authority or the means to carry out its task which, in any case, was to be constantly redefined, nonetheless remained uneasily in the centre throughout. At the core of the problem was the reluctance of the major powers to commit troops to the ground on a scale commensurate with bringing an end to the fighting and the argument, that has yet to be resolved, is whether or when the business of the United Nations is to keep the peace (once this has been established) or to enforce peace between warring factions. It rapidly became plain that UN peacekeeping was not likely to succeed as ceasefire agreements were broken almost as soon as they were made yet no one with authority or power wished to move on to the next logical step: peace enforcement. Yugoslavia was not regarded as of sufficient importance to the major actors in the drama while the cost of peace enforcement was seen to be too high. If the major powers, led by the United States and under the auspices of the United Nations, had at once concentrated overwhelming force in the region (as they had done earlier that year in the Gulf) and made plain that force would be used to stop the fighting it is at least possible that a solution without the huge bloodshed and ethnic cleansing which were to follow could have been imposed. Such determined action, however, presupposes a level of common interest among the principal players that simply did not exist; the result has been close to disaster for both Europe and the United Nations.

Germany, which had historic ties with Croatia, recognized it as an independent state on 23 December 1991, thereby forcing its more reluctant EU partners to follow suit and on 15 January 1992 it was also recognized by the other 11 EU members followed by the United States on 15 April. It was admitted to the United Nations on 22 May. The recognition of Croatia signalled the break-up of Yugoslavia. In a referendum of 29 February and

1 March 1992 while 63 per cent of the population of Bosnia-Herzegovina voted for independence the majority of the Serbs boycotted the vote. Nonetheless, the EU recognized the new state on 6 April and the United States on 7 April even though Bosnia's Serb minority controlled the country's heavy weaponry and was supported by the federal army which was, in effect, a Serbian army. As Bosnia-Herzegovina was soon to discover, recognition did not also bring with it international protection from attack. Slovenia had similarly been recognized as an independent state by the EU on 15 January with Croatia.

Following the admittance of Bosnia-Herzegovina, Croatia and Slovenia to the United Nations as independent states the rump of Yugoslavia (Serbia-Montenegro) was disallowed by the Security Council in September 1992 from continuing to fill the former UN seat of the Federal Republic of Yugoslavia and was told to reapply for UN membership which was subsequently withheld. This was the first time that a sitting member of the United Nations had had its seat removed. The southernmost republic of Yugoslavia, Macedonia, also demanded its independence as Macedonia and while gaining recognition from Bulgaria, Russia and Turkey during 1992 was not to be admitted to the United Nations until April 1993 or to be recognized by EU members until the end of that year because of opposition from Greece. The stage had now been set, largely due to the unthinking speed with which Germany, and then the other EU members and subsequently the United Nations had recognized these states and so signalled the break-up of Yugoslavia without first guaranteeing the Serb minorities in either Croatia or Bosnia-Herzegovina. The wars that followed were due to Serbia's determination to create a Greater Serbia which would incorporate the 600000 Serb minority from Croatia (out of a population of 4.5 million) and the 32 per cent Serb population of Bosnia (which also then contained a 17 per cent Croat minority). The early Western mediators, Cyrus Vance of the United States and Lord Carrington of Britain, aimed to bring about a ceasefire and create a UN peacekeeping force (UNPROFOR) to police it. As they and their successors were to discover, this was a near impossible task.

The original mandate of UNPROFOR was to negotiate a passage for, or to safeguard UNHCR convoys to Sarajevo and other besieged cities and towns, courtesy of the Serbs who sometimes let these convoys through and sometimes did not. Right from the beginning this policy of ensuring that food got through to besieged Bosnians while they were being killed raised doubts as to the sincerity of the major powers or the point of the United Nations operation. As the *Washington Post* asked in August 1992, 'how to enforce international law and human rights without occupying the country with infantry on the ground, as no government is prepared to do'. There was no answer to that question and in the succeeding years even the United States, which was most reluctant of all to become involved in a Balkan war with troops on the ground, nonetheless came to accept that no solution was likely to succeed without troops on the ground. As the British *Independent* asked at this time, 'If the Shia Muslims and Marsh Arabs of southern Iraq deserve protection, what about the Slav Muslims of Bosnia?' The real problem facing the recipients of aid convoys was that they were being relentlessly fired upon day and night by the Serbs and the help they most needed was action to bring the firing to an end; as a doctor in Gorazde plaintively put the problem: 'We will all die with full bellies.'[1] Gradually, UNPROFOR's activities were extended and by the end of 1992 its peacekeepers had been deployed in the south on the Macedonian borders. In February 1993 the Security Council 'decided to establish an International Tribunal to prosecute persons responsible for serious violations of international humanitarian law committed in the territory of former Yugoslavia since 1991'.[2] What was totally unclear was just how such persons were to be brought to justice. Although by the end of 1993, UNPROFOR had over 27000 personnel comprising military, police and civilian personnel on the ground which included 12 infantry battalions in Croatia, nine in Bosnia-Herzegovina and 1000 observers in Macedonia at a cost of US$1.2 billion a year,[3] they were neither sufficient in numbers nor mandated to stop the fighting. So what were they supposed to do? The questions relating to international involvement multiplied while the killing continued to escalate.

In September 1991 the UN Secretry-General agreed to embargo the sale of arms and military equipment to Yugoslavia; he was also requested to help end the civil war in that country. But, as the United Nations and the other major mediators soon discovered, attempts to prevent the escalation of the civil war foundered on the unwillingness of the warring parties to accept either United Nations or European mediation. Nonetheless, on 21 February 1992, the Security Council authorized a UN Protection Force (UNPROFOR) of up to 14000 troops to take up positions in Croatia to protect the Serb minorities there; these were now under extreme pressure from the newly independent Croatian state. On 14 September 1992, additional NATO forces were assigned to serve as peacekeepers in Bosnia-Herzegovina. By November UNPROFOR had suffered 300 casualties including 20 dead. Meanwhile, on 30 May of that year, the Security Council had imposed sanctions on the rump of Yugoslavia (Serbia and Montenegro) and on 16 November it instituted a blockade to prevent supplies entering the country. During June the United Nations had opened the airport at Sarajevo (the capital of Bosnia) in order to begin an airlift of food and medical supplies to the 400000 Bosnians who by then were trapped in the city by the Serb armed forces. On 13 August the

Security Council authorized UN members to do whatever was necessary (including the use of force) to deliver humanitarian aid to the Bosnians. On 19 November French troops exchanged fire with Serbian forces while moving food and medical supplies to Bosanka Krupa which was the first Bosnian town outside Sarajevo to receive aid. The Security Council, which had banned Serbian flights over Bosnia on 9 October, requested the Secretary-General to consider creating secure zones for citizens of Bosnia-Herzegovina. On 11 December 1992, the Security Council authorized the deployment of UN forces to the borders of Macedonia to forestall any outbreak of fighting between Christians and Muslims.

The determination of the Serbs to carry out ethnic cleansing had become a major issue by the middle of 1992 and on 29 June and again on 13 August the Security Council unanimously condemned Serbia for ethnic cleansing and insisted upon Red Cross access to prison camps and detention centres. The Security Council also condemned human rights abuses in Bosnia-Herzegovina. On 6 October 1992, the Security Council established a war crimes commission for Yugoslavia while Serbia-Montenegro was barred from participating in the activities of the UN General Assembly.

Already in 1993 it was estimated that the Serbs had killed 200 000 Muslims and expelled a further 2 million from Serb towns and villages in the name of ethnic cleansing and their forces had largely destroyed Vukovar and Sarajevo by blockade and shelling. Moreover, recurrent attacks upon UN personnel constantly hampered relief work and repeatedly forced the United Nations to suspend its operations. Despite this, UNPROFOR continued with its work and twice had its mandate renewed during 1993 (on 20 June and 4 October).

Much of 1994 was spent in establishing when and how the increasing NATO forces committed to the former Yugoslavia might retaliate against Serb provocations. After the Bosnian Muslim forces had broken the siege of Bihac, which was a UN-designated safe area, in October, NATO obtained Security Council approval for its planes to bomb the runway at Udbina from which Serb planes were launching bombing attacks. By the end of November the Serb offensive against Bihac had been intensified and their forces had seized 450 UN personnel as hostages to prevent further air strikes. Earlier that year, in March, when the Security Council had sought a further 10 000 troops for its peacekeeping operation the initiative had been blocked by the United States which feared Congress would not agree to pay the US share of the extra costs and only 3500 fresh troops were deployed. Washington refused to supply troops unless the contending parties first agreed to a truce, an attitude which possibly reflected its Somali debacle. The British UN

Commander, Lieutenant-General Sir Michael Rose, showed reluctance to retaliate despite the Serb provocations, arguing that peacekeeping required 'patience, persistence, and pressure' if the United Nations was not to find itself in a shooting war.[4] In October, NATO formally requested the right to retaliate without warning against four targets at once in 'robust and effective fashion'. UNPROFOR, however, warned that the Bosnian Serbs, in control of 70 per cent of Bosnia, could lawfully ask it to leave the country. In August a new factor, for which the United Nations had been working, came into play when the Serbian President, Slobodan Milosevic, cut off supplies to the Bosnian Serbs; in return the Security Council suspended sanctions against Yugoslavia for 100 days and, instead, imposed sanctions on the Bosnian Serbs for rejecting the peace endorsed that July by the 'Contact Group' of Britain, France, Germany, Russia and the United States.[5] The situation changed yet again in October–November when the United States asked the Security Council to lift the embargo on arms to the Bosnian Muslim government by May 1995; Washington followed this by unilaterally ceasing to enforce the embargo and though the other members of the Contact Group, with troops on the ground, threatened to withdraw them because of the US action (fearing further retaliation against their troops by the Serbs) they did not do so and, instead, the General Assembly voted on 3 November to end the embargo by 97–0 with 61 abstentions.

If 1994 had been a complex year 1995 was to prove no better and, among other turns of fortune, witnessed the effective handover of authority in Bosnia from the United Nations to NATO. Although there was growing disillusion over the UN failure to maintain peace in the former Yugoslavia, US President Clinton did say that the fault lay in asking the 'Blue Helmets' to 'undertake missions they cannot be expected to handle ... to work miracles while [member states] were denying them the military and political support required and the modern command-and-control systems they need'.[6] During the year the Security Council reduced the number of UN troops in Croatia from 13 000 to 2500 and restructured its units in Serbia and Macedonia. In May the UN forces failed to stop the Bosnian Serbs seizing 300 peacemakers to be used as human shields against further NATO air strikes near Pale; nor were they able to defend Srebenica and Zepa as safe areas since they had neither the means nor the mandate to do so. On 11 July 1995, the Bosnian Serbs stormed Srebenica where, allegedly, they massacred 6000 Muslims. This led the chief UN investigator in Yugoslavia, Tadeusz Mzowicki, to resign on July 27 in protest at the UN failure to prevent the atrocity; he accused the United Nations of hypocrisy in claiming to defend Bosnia while abandoning it. The UN Secretary-General, Boutros-Ghali, was compelled to admit that the United Nations had failed in Bosnia and would have to disengage; gradually, between 31 May and October, it transferred its authority on the ground in Bosnia to NATO although Russia argued that this was illegally to bypass the Security Council.

On 25 July, at The Hague, the International War Crimes Tribunal for the Former Yugoslavia indicted Radovan Karadzic, the Bosnian Serb leader, and Ratko Mladic, the Serb military commander, as war criminals. Other indictments were then laid and those named were to be arrested and tried for their crimes anywhere in the world.

Towards the end of the year, on 1 November, the United States finally exerted sufficient pressure to bring the various leaders to peace talks at Dayton, Ohio, leading to the signing of a treaty in Paris on 14 December. During the course of these talks (12 November) the secessionist Serbs in Croatia agreed to give up eastern Slavonia to Croatia in the course of two years and it was agreed that the Security Council would establish a 'transitional administration' and deploy an international force to maintain peace and security. On 20 December the United Nations officially transferred its peacekeeping authority to a NATO force. By the end of the year the UNHCR warned that some 3 million refugees had to be returned to their homes.

Although, following the Dayton peace effort, it could be argued that a sort of resolution to the previous four years of internecine strife had been achieved, the achievement was precarious in the extreme. For most of the year neither the Bosnian government nor the Serbs showed any faith in the peace process. Endless talks to find common ground discovered none. The four-month ceasefire which ended at the beginning of May 1995 and allowed the West's main leaders to argue that diplomacy should be given a chance was in fact a farce, constantly ignored by the two main combatants. Shortly before his one-year term as UNPROFOR commander was up (at the end of 1994) General Sir Michael Rose said that the war would not end unless Bosnia returned to being the 'multicultural civilized state' that it had been historically. He was expressing a hope that could no longer be seriously entertained. And when, in May 1995, the United Nations refused to sanction air strikes against Bosnian artillery for fear of escalating the situation in Croatia, this was simply one more example of 'a mission with an impossible mandate in a conflict the world would rather avoid addressing'.[7] That, indeed, was the key to the endless failures and prevarications that had characterized everyone's involvement in Yugoslavia: none of the powers, either individually or collectively, wished to be there or to commit themselves beyond a minimal point that, by reason of its minimalism, could be effective. It was all very well for the British Foreign Secretary, Douglas Hurd, to tell the House of Commons: 'We have an interest in stopping a war spreading across the map of Europe, particularly a war which would range the US and Russia on different sides', but to express the interest was not to take the necessary action. As a UN official pointed out: 'The guidance has to come from the Security Council, which is basically the Contact Group, and because of a lack of ideas among those countries and consent, they cannot agree on a policy here but we [the UN] take all the crap.'[8] That would seem a fair summary of the situation in mid-1995. The fact that, in May, the five-power Contact Group, the European Union and NATO were each discussing what to do in Bosnia simply emphasized the inappropriate manner in which the main powers, who possessed the capacity to bring about a peace, were ready, instead, constantly to shift the responsibility round between different organizations.

A 16-nation conference in London during July 1995 merely served to demonstrate how hopelessly divided were the major participants in the Yugoslav imbroglio. Following a meeting of the defence chiefs of Britain, France and the United States in the wake of the fall of Srebenica and Zepa and the discussion of various options, it became clear that while the United States and France wanted to take 'tough' action to punish the Serbs the British and Russians did not and while these unproductive talks came to an inconclusive 'wait and see' conclusion 55000 Bosnian civilians remained trapped in Gorazde at the mercy of the Bosnian Serb General, Ratko Mladic. In the end the 'decisive' action proposed consisted of limited bombing but only if Gorazde was attacked. Unsurprisingly, in such a climate of indecision, the Serbs continued with their aggression. Nelson Mandela was surely correct when he declared that 'defence for basic human freedoms is what has held the community of nations together',[9] but if the Yugoslav question has demonstrated anything, it is how easily and how quickly such basic human freedoms are relegated to the background against the claims of self-interest advanced by indifferently committed powers. In mid-1995 the United Nations was effectively trapped between its mandate which was to deliver aid and protect the six designated 'safe areas' and the lack of any international will to help the peacekeepers enforce the mandate.

Part of the problem during a peacekeeping endeavour of this kind is the need constantly to reconcile the requirements on the ground with the individual agendas of the principal participants. Thus, in April and May 1995, France talked seriously of withdrawing its forces from Bosnia following the deaths of two of its soldiers in Sarajevo and it was not easy to disentangle motives. With 4800 troops in Bosnia, the French then had the largest national contingent in the former Yugoslavia and their presence there was seen as a potential political risk by the French Prime Minister, Edouard Balladur, that might affect his presidential ambitions. At the same time the French Foreign Minister, Alain Juppe (who was shortly to become prime minister), served notice that France would not keep its troops in Bosnia without political

progress towards a settlement. The new French government of Jacques
Chirac clearly used its troops as a bargaining counter in an attempt to bring
order to the chaotic peacekeeping process, an initiative that Britain backed.
But though both France and Britain, at this stage, seemed united in their
determination to keep their forces in Yugoslavia both were angry at the level
of casualties their troops were suffering. Britain had said it would withdraw
its forces if, to use the Foreign Secretary Douglas Hurd's formula, 'the risks
to our troops might outweigh the good which they can do'.[10] The difficulty,
as France and Britain saw things at this time, was that the other members of
the Contact Group – the United States, Russia and Germany – were pursuing
different policies. By mid-May there was a growing crisis of confidence in
London and Paris about the handling of the UN operation by its special envoy,
Yasushi Akashi, who had failed to stop the Serbs bombarding Sarajevo or
prevent the Croats recapturing western Slavonia from the Serbs. As an
official in London said: 'The perception that the UN is never going to
authorise NATO action is causing concern among troop contributors like
ourselves.'[11] The nub of the problem remained the degree of force that the
peacekeepers should use both to keep the peace and to protect themselves,
and the willingness of the United Nations to allow an escalation of military
activity commensurate with these two objectives.

There is an element of self-defeat in any peacekeeping force which
constantly talks of withdrawing, as was the case through 1995 with the
principal EU powers involved in Bosnia, just as there is something slightly
farcical about major military powers, such as Britain and France, threatening
to withdraw if their forces suffer casualties while carrying out their
peacekeeping duties, as both periodically did threaten. The more that such
talk is forthcoming from the peacekeepers the greater the temptation for the
combatants to continue with their fighting. First, why should they obey
peacekeepers who give every appearance of doubt both as to their role and
as to their readiness to withstand casualties? Second, if the peacekeepers are
seen as likely to withdraw under provocation then the war is equally likely
to begin again once they go even assuming it has been temporarily halted.
Once peacekeepers are on the ground they ought never to speak of
withdrawing for that is simply to play into the hands of belligerents who
probably did not want a peacekeeping operation in the first place. That
lesson was clearly not being learnt by the EU contingents in the former
Yugoslavia.

The EU, which brashly asserted at the beginning of the Yugoslav crisis
that this was the obvious issue where Europe could demonstrate its capacity
to produce a single foreign policy – 'This is the hour of Europe, not of
America', M. Jacques Poos, the Foreign Minister of Luxemburg had

announced – tried again in 1995 at the June meeting of the Internationl Conference on the Former Yugoslavia at Geneva which had been attempting to broker a settlement since 1992. The new EU mediator, Carl Bildt of Sweden, faced a difficult task. In 1994 the conference had lost much of its credibility when the United States, Russia, Britain, France and Germany took the diplomatic initiative to form the Contact Group to negotiate an end to the conflicts and by 1995 NATO was also becoming more directly involved and active. President Chirac of France indicated he would like Mr Bildt to speak for the Contact Group as a whole but neither the United States nor Russia accepted an idea which they saw as diminishing their own roles. In any case, the United States had fallen out with Carl Bildt's predecessor, Lord Owen of Britain, whom they regarded as a virtual apologist for the Serbian cause. A month later, following the London conference on Bosnia, one newspaper commented that the European Union's 'common foreign and security policy' was bleeding copiously but no one could be bothered to do anything about it.[12] Russia's Foreign Minister, Andrei Kozyrev, regretted the inability of the international community to reach a political settlement but suggested that this was because there were too many irons in the diplomatic fire. No major player, when it came to the point, was ever ready to hand over responsibility to any other player nor yet to withdraw. During the Cold War Europe found it relatively easy to act as one, under the US military umbrella, in face of real or supposed Soviet threats. In the post-Cold War era and in the face of conflicting interests in the Balkans that facade of unity, despite lip-service to a single European policy in the Maastricht Treaty, was soon shown to be a charade.

Almost no issue produced unity. Thus, while the UN tribunal on war crimes in the former Yugoslavia named the Bosnian Serb Leader, Radovan Karadzic, and his army commander, General Ratko Mladic, as suspects in an investigation into genocide, torture and ethnic cleansing, UN officials asked for a postponement of any such charges as likely to have a negative effect upon negotiations to extend the Bosnian truce. This was to introduce another astonishing principle into the Yugoslav story: that deals should be struck with named suspects before they are brought to justice. The chief UN prosecutor, Justice Richard Goldstone, wanted the tribunal to ask the Bosnian government to turn over suspects and evidence to the UN international prosecutor (himself). The evidence of atrocities and ethnic cleansing was overwhelming and included the fact that while, before the war, 355 000 Muslims lived in the Banja Luka area, by 1995 only 30 000 remained while an estimated 200 000 had either died or disappeared. The first person to face the international war crimes tribunal, Dusan Tadic, was accused of a sadistic terror campaign against both Muslims and Croats during 1992. The chances that bigger figures responsible for the initiation of such policies would be brought to justice seemed far more remote.

In mid-1995 the United Nations had 9600 personnel in its headquarters in Croatia and Serbia, 13500 in the four UN protected areas in Croatia and 19600 in Bosnia; these forces were on sufficient a scale to make the UN presence felt yet they were insufficient to peacekeep effectively. They were able, at least in part, to fulfil their humanitarian missions in the enclaves of Zepa, Srebenica and Gorazde (until the two former enclaves were overrun by the Serbs) but largely because much of the aid went to the Serbs. The London *Observer* made the point succinctly enough: 'As the Americans pull one way, the Russians another and the Europeans mouth platitudes, the UN forces are left in the middle, too weak to enforce the peace but too much of a presence to allow the conflict to go unheeded.'[13] At this time no Western government, and least of all that of the United States, was prepared to lose thousands of men in a Balkan war while direct NATO intervention, it was argued, would antagonize the Russians. A new formula was needed: either to give the United Nations real teeth; or to replace it with NATO (or some other force) as was to happen during the remaining months of 1995. Even so, it was only when Washington brought its weight to bear that a possible solution emerged with the Dayton agreement.

As arguments raged about the UN role in Bosnia, it was repeatedly asserted that its forces were protecting civilians in Sarajevo and the other enclaves. In the end the argument was proved wrong by what happened (the massacre in Srebenica, for example) but the assertions – that the United Nations had to be supported because it was protecting civilians – need to be examined in the light of what so-called humanitarian aid, which formed so large a part of the total operation, actually achieved. A number of questions need to be faced in the future in relation to this and other UN operations (such as Somalia or Rwanda) as they were not faced at the time. In broad terms, the question that needs to be addressed is as follows: does it make sense to concentrate resources upon delivering humanitarian aid to besieged civilians if those civilians are to be left in a state of siege and in imminent danger of being destroyed anyway? Would it not make far greater sense to bring an end to the sieges and military threats to their lives? That, surely, would be the most appropriate humanitarian aid and to pretend otherwise is to use the plight of the civilians to be aided as an excuse for not taking action to end the conflict. The number of refugees registered by the United Nations by August 1995 came to 2.3 million inside the former Yugoslavia, of which 1.37 million were in Bosnia, and that was before the expulsion of 40000 Muslims from the fallen enclaves of Srebenica and Zepa or the exodus of 100 000 Serbs from Krajina. In addition, a further 320 000 Bosnian refugees were in Germany.

It was clear by the end of May, when the Bosnian Serbs held UN observers as hostages and defied NATO to use more air strikes, that either the major Western powers escalate their involvement in Bosnia or allow the Serbs an effective victory. The Serbs were calculating that the West would not risk its relationship with Russia whose President, Boris Yeltsin, was demanding an end to NATO air strikes. In the event, NATO did increase its air strikes although uncertainty as to NATO's role led Britain and France unilaterally to form their own Rapid Reaction Force while the US Congress made President Clinton abandon his offer of US troops for a NATO force to help peacekeepers escape from tight corners. In August, after further months of dithering, NATO bombers struck Serbian ammunition dumps round Sarajevo (in support of UN Resolution 836 of June 1993 which authorized the UN to use force to deter attacks upon the safe areas). The bombers took out Serbian radar and missile sights and air defence systems and were supported by the guns of the Rapid Reaction Force. This action made possible the US initiaive which produced the ceasefire that came into effect on 12 October and was the prelude to the talks which began on 31 October. NATO then faced the problem of squaring the Russians as a lead role for NATO at last appeared to have emerged as the most likely way forward.

Although, by the summer of 1995, it could be argued that Bosnia had proved a disaster for the United Nations, this was hardly the fault of the world body. By that time the overall command was in the hands of a French general who took his orders from Paris, the Bosnian part was under a British general, the peace negotiations were in the hands of a European Union appointee (Carl Bildt) and the air cover was under NATO.[14] The UN operation, by then, had been reduced to potential conflict between the United States and Russia and major differences between the United States and its European allies. The lessons of this disaster for the United Nations had yet to be digested. The problem, to which we have to return again and again, is to determine how to intervene in a civil war. The tragedy of Yugoslavia made plain that peacekeeping was not a viable option; peace enforcement might have worked had the political will existed from the beginning to intervene on a scale commensurate with the size of the conflict.

One problem which persisted throughout the Yugoslav crisis was that of US reluctance to support the United Nations fully. As the Senate majority leader, Bob Dole, and the House Speaker, Newt Gingrich, had written to President Clinton: 'In our view, if you choose to support a UN Security Council resolution authorizing the expansion of UNPROFOR to accommodate the [force], the costs should be borne through voluntary contributions. We oppose funding through UN assessments.'[15] As Britain's Foreign Secretary, Douglas Hurd, said in response: 'Large sections of American opinion have been pressing for greater muscle. Well – here's the greater muscle. It has to be paid for.' There was understandable European resentment at American pressure for action when the European powers had troops on the ground while the Americans did not. The British and French, with the creation of their Rapid Reaction Force, thought to provide the United Nations with greater muscle on the ground so as to back calls for negotiations. What they had not done was to coordinate their policy with Washington and they were then to be horrified when they found the United States was not prepared to pay its share of the costs of the operation.

It was not until September 1995 under a new US negotiator, Richard Holbrooke, that Washington began to exert pressure to convene a rolling peace conference. By the end of September sufficient progress to this end had been achieved so that NATO ambassadors were able to agree the outlines of a plan to send thousands of alliance and non-alliance troops (including Russians) to police an eventual Bosnian ceasefire. President Clinton then thought he could convince the American people and Congress to consent to a US peacekeeping force of about 25 000 troops, after a peace had been concluded. 'I don't see how, as the leader of NATO and basically the leader of the West, we can walk away from it', he said.[16]

The Dayton Peace Accord, brokered by the United States under UN auspices and signed in Paris on 14 December, embodied the principle that European borders should not be altered by armed aggression. In order to assert this principle Dayton established a multi-ethnic state in Bosnia to comprise Sarajevo as the seat of a Bosnian federal government that would include the three nationalities – the Bosnian Muslims, Croats and Serbs. This federal government would stand above the Bosnian Serb Republic occupying the north and east of the country and the Muslim-Croat Federation in its south and west. The settlement was in the form of a direct rebuttal of the ethnic cleansing that had been carried out so ruthlessly in the previous four years; whether the three ethnic groups now incorporated in the newly legitimized multi-ethnic state of Bosnia would be able to work peaceably together in trust remained to be seen. The immediate task, ironically, was to reassure the Serbs in Bosnia that they would be safe under an arrangement that they had fought so hard to destroy. A new structure for peace enforcement was established in London just prior to the Paris signing of the accord. This abolished the old International Conference on Former Yugoslavia and created a Peace Implementation Council (which ended United Nations authority in the Balkans). The Peace Implementation Council was to be made up of the Group of Seven (Britain, Canada, France, Germany, Italy, Japan and the United States), Russia, the European Union and the Organization of Islamic Conference, with Carl Bildt, the former Swedish Prime Minister, as its High Representative.

Reconstruction in Bosnia was to be assisted by the World Bank and the International Monetary Fund; a Human Rights Task Force would operate throughout Bosnia which would hold elections within six to nine months. NATO troops including Americans would be stationed in the country until the end of the year. So much for the settlement in theory. Early in 1996, however, there were growing signs that multi-ethnicity would not work and that separate and suspicious communities were developing in place of the intended pluralism. Trust had not replaced bigotry and fear. By March 1996, for example, the Muslim-Croat Federation took control of Grbavica, the last of five Serb-held Sarajevo suburbs designated for transfer under the Dayton accord and while Serbs destroyed everything they could before leaving, marauding Muslim gangs were ignored by the authorities. What the new Bosnia discovered in 1996 was that mixed communities – the intention of Dayton – were a thing of the past. Already in March a Pentagon report warned that Bosnia was in danger of collapsing into civil war again once the NATO peacekeepers withdraw at the end of 1996. A continuing source of contention was the presence in Bosnia of the former Serb leader, Radovan Karadzic, who had been charged with war crimes but who, while debarred from participation in the elections scheduled for September 1996, wielded overriding influence in the Bosnian Serb Party. Few of the auguries were good.

Even with the NATO peacekeeping force in place the future for Bosnia in mid-1996 looked doubtful; when international troops are withdrawn the chances of renewed fighting seem high. The removal of Radovan Karadzic from power (if not influence) in Bosnia was due to the pressure of Slobodan Milosevic who is seen by many as the real architect of the Yugoslav war. But though he lost the military initiative and failed to create a Greater Serbia, he remained in total command of a truncated Yugoslavia, with its economy in ruins, and managed to emerge from Dayton with the image of an international peacemaker. The removal from power of Karadzic suited Milosevic who saw him as a potentially dangerous rival; his efforts in that direction had little to do with any sense of justice. And despite calls for such leaders as Karadzic to be brought to international justice for their war crimes all the signs point to their escaping as a matter of pragmatic political convenience. As Jonathan Eyal suggests, the Dayton accord 'offers the promise of *potentially* punishing *some* criminals at some unspecified future time'.[17] It may, perhaps, be claimed that the Dayton accord was the best resolution of the Yugoslav war that could be managed in the circumstances of 1995 and taking into account the extent to which the major players were prepared to make troop or other commitments. It leaves open the question: what does the international community propose to do if and when the accord breaks down as, unfortunately, there were more signs of it doing in August 1996 than anything else?

5   The United Nations in Africa (1)

Four African countries – Burundi and Rwanda, whose fortunes are closely linked, and Somalia and Liberia – have suffered the effects of brutal civil wars and massacres during the 1990s and through both involvement and default the United Nations has been shown up as less than effective in any of them. In Burundi, by mid-1996, there was ample and growing evidence that a genocidal explosion on a par with that which had taken place in Rwanda during 1994 was about to occur; here was a classic example of a country where a powerful case could be made for intervention in order to prevent a disaster that was clearly about to unfold. In Rwanda appalling genocide occurred during 1994 while the United Nations and the major powers remained onlookers and found it impossible to make any decisions about intervention. In Somalia US-led intervention exacerbated rather than diminished the existing problems so that the United Nations was forced to withdraw entirely. In Liberia, perhaps wisely, the United Nations kept to the sidelines and left peacekeeping operations to regional African states led by Nigeria and ECOWAS.

BURUNDI

Fundamental suspicions and ethnic rivalries between the Bantu-speaking Hutu and the Nilotic Tutsi peoples have existed for centuries. Burundi was incorporated into German East Africa in 1906; in 1923 it became part of the Belgian mandate of Ruanda-Urundi and tribal differences were emphasized as the Belgian administration entrenched power in the hands of the ruling Tutsi minority. Burundi became independent in 1962 as a kingdom under the Tutsi ruler Mwami Mwambutsa IV; growing Hutu unrest exploded in 1965 and though it was brutally suppressed the king was forced to flee the country. From 1966 to 1972 under President Michel Micombero a series of purges removed the Hutu from high office and the army. These and other excesses by the ruling Tutsi were the background to a Hutu uprising of April 1972 aimed at overthrowing Tutsi domination. The uprising did not succeed and systematic massacres of the Hutu followed with the educated Hutu as particular targets. Depending upon the estimates used, between 80000 and 250000 Hutu lost their lives while 500000 were rendered homeless and 40000 became refugees in Zaire and Tanzania. A period of relative stability followed but in 1988 another upheaval occurred which cost between 5000 and 10000 lives although its relative smallness indicated more the grip which the Tutsi had on the country than any reduction in the ethnic hatreds which existed. In June 1993, under President Pierre Buyoya, Burundi's first ever multi-party elections were held and Buyoya was defeated by Melchior Ndadaye, the leader of the opposition Front for Democracy in Burundi (Frodebu) who was the first Hutu to become president of the country. Ndadaye was only to last until October when a bloody coup led to his death and this was followed by a renewed bout of Hutu–Tutsi violence whose estimated casualties ranged from 15000 to 200000. In February 1994 an international commission of inquiry reported that most of the army had been actively or passively involved in the coup attempt. The new President who was also a Hutu, Cyprien Ntaryamira, was elected by the National Assembly on 13 January 1994. Both President Ntaryamira of Burundi and President Habyarimana of Rwanda were killed on 6 April 1994 when travelling together in a plane which was hit by a rocket fired by extremist Hutu troops to spark off the wave of genocidal killings which then occurred in Rwanda.[1] From this point onwards into 1996 the signs multiplied that Burundi would follow Rwanda and deteriorate or erupt into a new series of massacres. In the immediate wake of the Rwanda catastrophe, for example, Burundi's Hutu extremists began to make contact with the armed Hutu beyond Burundi's borders (in the huge refugee camps in Zaire).[2] During 1995 Burundi could be described as being in a state of 'low-intensity civil war' with unofficial Tutsi militias and guerrilla groups of rival Hutu operating through the country and producing periodic explosions of violence.[3] During the year the UN High Commissioner for Refugees was encouraged by the Security Council to look at the situation in the refugee camps in Tanzania and in Burundi itself.

Burundi, at this stage, could be numbered with half a dozen other countries, wracked by civil war or near civil war, as a state whose structures had largely imploded, in which the international community did not wish to become involved and where the United Nations was, at most, carrying out peripheral activities. Approximately 800000 Burundians had fled the country following the events of 1993 to become refugees in neighbouring states (nearly 15 per cent of the entire population) and the UNHCR was responsible for emergency relief measures among them. Otherwise, though it was clear to intelligent observers that conditions would get worse without some form of intervention from outside, no one with the capacity to intervene wished to do so. Following the death of President Ndadaye the Security Council had 'confined itself to verbal condemnation of the coup, a tribute to the dead president and murdered ministers and a call on the Secretary-General to monitor developments, bring the murderers to justice and to assist the parties in returning the country to constitutional legality'.[4] The Secretary-General was also encouraged to continue using his 'good offices' and to consider sending a small fact-finding team to facilitate the efforts of the Burundi government and the OAU. Just how, in such circumstances, the Secretary-General was going to be able to bring the murderers to justice was not explained. All the signs pointed to a determination on the part of the major powers, the permanent members of the Security Council, to keep as clear of Burundi entanglements as they possibly could, no matter what might take place on the ground.

Following attacks by the army, which is almost exclusively Tutsi, on Hutu areas in Bujumbura at the end of March 1995, in which about 500 people were killed, President Sylvestre Ntibantunganya described the events as the beginning of genocide. Meanwhile, Hutu extremists from Burundi and Rwanda were linking up with each other as were Tutsis from the two countries so that a further conflagration could engulf them both, and should that happen a strong case could then be made for United Nations intervention. Meanwhile, the British Labour Party foreign affairs spokesman, Robin Cook, urged European countries to help the new government in Burundi provide the means to dispense justice.

In January 1996 the US ambassador to the United Nations, Madeleine Albright, warned Burundi's Tutsi-dominated army that there was real danger of another coup and that Burundi was in danger of sliding into full-scale civil war. She said: 'I think that what has happened is genocide. I think we have to make sure that what happens in the future is not genocide.'[5] She went on to say that the United States would not support any government that came to power by force though she did not say what it would do. The UN Special Rapporteur for Human Rights in Burundi condemned torture, arbitrary detention and massacres in the country and said the situation revealed 'an increasing genocidal trend'. Tanzania, meanwhile, appealed for international help as thousands of Hutus poured into the country after the Burundi army had killed about 20 in a refugee camp. The extent of Tutsi-organized terror against Frodebu (the Hutu dominated political party) since the coup of 1993 until 1996 included the assassination of 48 senior members of the party and the detention of more than 5200 of its members – teachers, engineers, drivers. Although moderate Hutus periodically expressed the hope that the international community will intervene on their behalf there were few signs of any such intention.

Foreign ministers of African countries meeting in Addis Ababa under the auspices of the Organization of African Unity (OAU) in February 1996 considered the establishment of a military force in order to prevent further

bloodshed in Burundi. Intervention plans had already been devised by the
UN Secretary-General, Boutros Boutros-Ghali, and were then under
consideration by the Security Council. However, the auguries were not
good. A proposal to station a Rapid Reaction force in Zaire had been opposed
by the United States. Under the Secretary-General's second plan an
international intervention force would be placed on standby while the
situation in Burundi was monitored and the troops which had been assigned
to the force would remain in their home countries but be ready for deployment
at short notice. Should the force be sent to Burundi and be faced with
resistance from the warring factions it would need to be expanded to at least
25 000 soldiers. The United States, France and Britain each refused to
earmark troops for Burundi although Washington signalled its willingness
to assist with logistics. Belgium, the former mandatory and trusteeship
power, also refused to make troops available.

The main problem, however, was the opposition of the government in
Burundi to any foreign intervention and its refusal even to accept UN guards
for aid workers in the country. Given the ethnic divisions which dominate
Burundi, such a refusal is understandable since intervention, if it means
anything, must eventually produce a more equitable political settlement that
will derogate from Tutsi dominance. Such a situation requires a major United
Nations reappraisal. Should the United Nations first consider whether to
intervene anyway, whatever the government says, in order to pre-empt
further genocide? Then, having done so, should it insist upon staying to impose
a political solution? Given the kind of problem to be found in Burundi (and
elsewhere) such an approach to intervention is probably coming closer to
the realities of future UN operations.

Burundi was top of the OAU summit agenda when it opened in Cameroon
during July, at a time when an estimated 1000 people were being killed in
Burundi every month. After resisting the idea of intervention for months
Burundi's leaders had finally accepted the concept of 'security assistance'
at a peace summit in Tanzania attended by the Prime Minister, Antoine
Nduwayo (a Tutsi), and the President, Sylvestre Ntibantunganya (a Hutu).
However, the possibility of a coup by the Tutsi-dominated army to block
foreign involvement now became more likely. As it was, the army could no
longer contain the situation and some parts of the country had become 'no-
go' areas for the government. In the plan which had been drawn up at Arusha
under the chairmanship of Tanzania's former President, Julius Nyerere, an
East African force of Ugandans, Tanzanians and Ethiopians would protect
politicians, civil servants and strategic installations and help retrain the
security forces which by then were locked in conflict with the Hutus. The
Prime Minister's own party, Uprona, denounced the plan as high treason and

Tutsi extremists and Hutu rebels found themselves in accord in denouncing any peacekeepers as a hostile invasion force.

The OAU in Cameroon endorsed the idea of sending a regional intervention force to Burundi; the force would be under independent command although Burundi's defence minister who had only reluctantly accepted the idea of such a force insisted it should come under the control of the national army. By late July the crisis had moved significantly closer to an all-out explosion following the massacre of 300 Tutsis at Bugendena in central Burundi. By this time an estimated 150000 people had been killed since the assassination of President Ndadaye in October 1993. In Bujumbura demonstrating Tutsi students opposed any international peacekeeping force from the OAU although outsiders saw this as the last hope of avoiding even greater bloodshed.

The Tutsi Prime Minister, Antoine Nduwayo, now reversed his in any case reluctant agreement to an OAU force and announced instead his resolute opposition to any multinational peacekeeping operation in Burundi, claiming that such a force would make the situation worse and would not be able to prevent massacres such as that at Bugendena. The Prime Minister's change of mind signalled the end of the peacekeeping intervention force. At what was supposed to be a memorial service for the massacred Tutsis at Bugendena the Prime Minister did nothing to quell a demonstration that erupted as soon as the President arrived and the latter was forced to retreat into his helicopter for his life. He then went into hiding as the country teetered on the edge of new anarchy and later took refuge in the US embassy. In New York the Security Council warned against a military coup while the Under-Secretary-General for Peacekeeping, Kofi Annan, said that with the necessary political support a force could be deployed within a week. He said, plaintively: 'The dilemma that the international community faces is can it sit back and allow the genocide to continue? Can it allow that in all conscience and sit back and do nothing?'[6] Such hand-wringing was not going to produce the troops. A UN force would need to be 20000 strong but few pledges of troops had been forthcoming from nations willing to contribute forces and the major powers remained unwilling to do so. The US ambassador to the United Nations, Madeleine Albright, once more reiterated Washington's view that 'under no circumstances would we tolerate a government installed by force or intimidation in Burundi. And we would work to isolate such a government.' She added that the United States would not be prepared to offer any fighting forces to support a UN intervention. The Burundi government now disintegrated following an announcement by the Tutsi Uprona party that it had withdrawn from the National Convention of Government while the Tutsi-dominated military found itself engaged in an increasingly desperate effort to suppress Hutu insurgency.

The long-expected coup duly took place on 25 July and the army installed former President Pierre Buyoya as President. Belgium put paratroopers on standby to evacuate the hundreds of its citizens living in the capital, Bujumbura, and the United Nations ordered all non-essential UN personnel to leave the country. Announcing the coup, the Defence Minister, Firmin Sinzoyiheba, said: 'In consideration of the fact that President Ntibantunganya has effectively resigned, in consideration of the genocide prevailing in the country and given that no solution has been found among the politicians the army has decided to introduce the new measures.'[7] Parliament and political parties were dissolved, demonstrations and strikes made illegal, the airport and borders closed. Since repeated calls by the United Nations for a peacekeeping force had gone unanswered by the international community, it seemed the world was ready to stand by and wring its hands while yet more genocide was perpetrated. The Security Council continued to agonize over the fate of Burundi but, mindful of its disastrous showing in Somalia and neighbouring Rwanda, did not come up with any new initiative. Without the involvement of at least one of the major Western military powers (the United States, Britain or France) the chances of a successful peacekeeping initiative appeared remote. As a Western diplomat said: 'Nobody in Burundi wants outside intervention, so do you impose yourself? And if you do, what is your mission when you get there?'[8]

Unsurprisingly, it was revealed in a UN document that the new President, Pierre Buyoya, had been implicated in the coup of October 1993 which led to the assassination of President Ndadaye and the subsequent deaths of 100000 Burundians. Despite this revelation and earlier condemnations of any army takeover, within a few days the West appeared ready to accept the new Buyoya government. At least African leaders from neighbouring countries – Kenya, Tanzania, Uganda, Ethiopia and Zaire, as well as Cameroon as current chair of the OAU – decided to impose sanctions upon Burundi. Then the world waited to see what would happen next.

RWANDA

Rwanda, like Burundi, falls into the category of a collapsed state whose problems are primarily internal and, as Britain's Anthony Parsons points out, 'There is of course no *prima facie* reason why the Council should engage itself with any of these problems.'[9] At the same time such devastating, genocidal problems did, in fact, face the United Nations with a new category of crisis which it could not ignore. When the explosion of April 1994 occurred in Rwanda, the United Nations was already involved in the country and, therefore, was faced with the question of whether it should stay and expand its operations in an attempt to stop the genocide or whether it should clear out. In the event it did a little of each with disastrous results to its reputation.

In 1990 fighting began between the Hutu-Rwandan armed forces and the Tutsi-Rwandese Patriotic Front (RPF) which operated from bases across the border in Uganda. A series of ceasefires were made but quickly broken and following a renewal of serious fighting in 1993 both Rwanda and Uganda requested the Security Council to station observers along their joint border. A UN Observer Mission Uganda–Rwanda (UNOMUR) was deployed on the Ugandan side of the border in September 1993. Meanwhile, an OAU-Tanzanian initiative had produced a peace agreement between the Rwanda government and the RPF in August and the United Nations was asked to provide a peacekeeping force to guarantee public security. In October, therefore, the Security Council created the UN Assistance Mission in Rwanda (UNAMIR) which replaced UNOMUR with a mandate to assist the creation of a transitional government. UNAMIR had a force of 2500 military personnel at its disposal as well as civilian police and by the end of 1993, an apparent success, some 600000 displaced Rwandese had returned home.

Following the deaths of the presidents of Burundi and Rwanda (both were Hutu) on 6 April 1994, the presidential guard in Kigali went on the rampage to kill hundreds of people including the Prime Minister while the RPF began direct attacks upon government forces. Targets in Kigali included UN peacekeeping forces; Belgian and French troops stood ready to evacuate foreign nationals (principally their own) and casualties reached thousands. The rebel RPF forces now moved on the capital and their leader, Paul Kagame, said they would restore law and order. On 10 April 800 Belgian paratroopers arrived to evacuate foreigners who were estimated at 3000. A majority of those killed in the capital at this time were Tutsis but on 12 April the Tutsi rebel RPF fought its way into the capital to cause panic among both government and foreigners. A week after the death of the two presidents an estimated 10000 people had been killed in the capital alone. A week later, amid growing chaos, UN peacekeepers began to quit the country, some in obvious panic. They did so, they claimed, because the government had refused to hand over control of the airport to them. On 19 April the UN special envoy to Rwanda, Jacques-Roger Booh-Booh, said that if the warring parties did not reach an agreement on a ceasefire 'it must be very clear we shall not stay here'. He added, in answer to a question as to whether the United Nations was about to abandon Rwanda, 'We came to assist Rwanda, but we cannot impose any solution on the Rwandan people, who have to help us to help them.'[10]

In the course of the next ten weeks perhaps as many as one million people, mainly Tutsis, were to be massacred. On 21 April, 17 May and 8 June the Security Council adjusted its mandate of UNAMIR to make it an effective instrument for protecting civilians. On May 25 the Secretary-General, Boutros-Ghali, condemned the killings as genocide and said the world's unwillingness to stop it was 'a scandal'. However, states which had burnt their fingers over Somalia or were involved in Bosnia were reluctant also to become involved in Rwanda and offers of troops or materiel were simply not forthcoming. The United States refused to sanction the despatch of 5500 troops to Rwanda; the Security Council then accepted a French offer of 2500 troops for one month to provide temporary security and humanitarian aid for the hundreds of thousands of refugees. This non-UN French force arrived in late June but was regarded with suspicion by the government because of France's earlier role in training and equipping the Rwandan army. The French withdrew in late August to be replaced by UNAMIR forces to which African countries were pledging contingents. On November 8 the Security Council authorized the creation of an international tribunal to try persons accused of genocide and other crimes committed in Rwanda during the previous months. On 21 November the Secretary-General asked the Security Council to send 12000 troops to stem violence in the refugee camps in Zaire and Burundi and protect the relief workers.

Early in 1995 the main problem facing the UNHCR was how to persuade nearly one million refugees in the camps in Zaire and Tanzania to return home. It was then apparent that extremists of the former Hutu regime had seized control of the distribution of aid in the camps and were intimidating or killing refugees who wanted to return to Rwanda. The UN Secretary-General called on the Security Council either to back an international force to police the camps or support the efforts of local countries to restore law and order in the refugee centres. But according to the UN special envoy to Rwanda, Shaharyar Khan: 'There's no positive response to providing forces on the ground to form the contingents that would address the law and order issue in Zaire.'[11] Meanwhile, the former government had embarked upon a low-level insurgency campaign to destabilize the new government. By March 1995, moreover, evidence had accumulated that arms were being flown to eastern Zaire to equip the exiled Rwandan Hutu forces in preparation for an invasion of Rwanda from neighbouring countries. In August 1995 the Security Council lifted its 1994 arms embargo on Rwanda while a month later it established an international commission of inquiry to collect information about the supply of arms to former Rwandan government forces in the Great Lakes region of Africa.[12] In December 1995 the Security Council adjusted the UNAMIR mandate and reduced its contingent from 5600 to 1800 troops.

Meanwhile, in March 1995, the Security Council had passed Resolution 978 which recalled Resolution 955 of November 1994 that set up the International Tribunal for Rwanda and called on all states to arrest and detain persons suspected of genocide. Most of the leading Rwandans known to be responsible were free and unmolested while the only advocate of genocide who had been arrested in Canada – Leon Mugesera – had been released on bail! In November of 1995 it transpired that senior officials at the United Nations had been warned three months prior to the April outbreak that Hutu extremists were planning to exterminate the Tutsi minority in Rwanda. The information was sent by cable on 11 January by the UN Force Commander in Rwanda, General Romeo Dallaire, to his superior in New York but nothing had been done about it.

These and other post facto activities and revelations demonstrated clearly enough that the international community had not wished to be involved in Rwanda and continued to evade any commitment to become involved there. Perhaps most damning of all for the so-called 'New World Order' had been the absolute determination of the United States to resist all pressures for action: 'American diplomats were ordered not to describe the mass killings as genocide but as "*acts of genocide*", thus avoiding any legal obligation to do anything under the 1948 UN Convention.'[13] The general message to Africa, the world's poorest continent, was to expect a minimum of assistance from the international community when major disasters struck.

SOMALIA

It is especially ironic that Somalia, one of the most ethnically homogeneous states in all Africa should, nonetheless, have collapsed into a bitter clan-based civil war. Formed in 1960 of British and Italian Somalilands it held together remarkably well for its first 20 years which included the Ogaden War of 1977–8 against Ethiopia. During the 1980s, however, the Somali National Movement (SNM) and the Democratic Front for the Salvation of Somalia (DFSS) rebelled against the government of Siad Barre though for years without any striking successes. In 1988, however, the SNM-led rebellion turned into a full-scale civil war and at the beginning of June Western governments, backed by the United Nations, evacuated their personnel from northern Somalia. This fighting of mid-1988 reduced towns to rubble, killed an estimated 50000 people and made refugees of a further 400000 people. The SNM then reverted to guerrilla tactics.

The government, though apparently in general control, was far from secure and its position did not improve during 1989 when there was a steady exodus of influential Somalis who clearly believed that Siad Barre's rule was coming to an end. In January 1990 the American human rights group, Africa Watch, claimed that Somali forces had killed between 50000 amd 60000 civilians over the previous 19 months and that 500000 had been driven into exile. The government position deteriorated throughout 1990 with various rebel groups gaining control of different regions of the country while the SNM controlled most of the north. By January 1991 anti-Barre unrest was so severe that he was forced to flee the country and an interim government was proclaimed by the United Somali Congress (USC) which named Ali Mahdi Mohammed as President. However, differences soon emerged between Mohammed and the USC chairman, General Muhammad Farah Aideed, and by September a power struggle had broken out in Mogadishu between the followers of the two men. The situation was to deteriorate rapidly through 1992. General chaos and famine followed as numerous armed bands, taking advantage of the collapse of law and order, acted as independent authorities and held to ransom both people and relief supplies of food which were being provided by a range of international agencies. Various international organizations and non-government relief bodies then called upon the United Nations to restore order and ensure the safe passage of relief supplies to the rapidly growing numbers of people in need of assistance.

The Security Council had imposed an arms embargo on Somalia on 31 January 1992 when it also called for a ceasefire and requested the UN Secretary-General to contact all parties to end hostilities and bring about a political settlement. But though the Secretary-General did negotiate a ceasefire and 40 UN observers arrived in Mogadishu to supervise it, large numbers of Somalis continued to flee to Kenya while the first ship with World Food Programme supplies to arrive at Mogadishu was fired upon and returned to Mombasa fully loaded. In April the Security Council created a United Nations Operation in Somalia (UNOSOM) to facilitate the cessation of hostilities and promote reconciliation between the warring factions as well as safeguarding humanitarian aid. By May, while only a small amount of relief was getting to those in need, about 3000 people a day were crossing the border into Kenya as refugees. The Security Council then authorized an increase in UNOSOM strength to escort humanitarian supplies. The first 500 troops were to arrive in September, and a further four units of 750 each were authorized, as well as 700 logistics personnel, to guard supplies at the ports, bringing the total strength of UNOSOM up to 4000.

Prior to taking office as Secretary-General, the Egyptian Boutros Boutros-Ghali had compared the readiness of the West to intervene in Yugoslavia, the 'rich man's war', with its reluctance to do anything about Somalia. In May 1992 the Algerian diplomat, Muhammad Sahnoun, was appointed the Secretary-General's representative in Somalia and between that month and October he endeavoured to persuade the Somali warlords, as well as regional countries, to permit outside troops to protect humanitarian food supplies from looters. In October, however, Sahnoun resigned, accusing the United Nations as well as relief agencies (although he excepted the ICRC and some NGOs) of unnecessary bureaucracy and lethargy while they allowed Somalia to descend into a 'hell' where some 300000 people, mainly women and children, had died over 18 months. On 25 November, after one of its ships had been attacked, the United Nations suspended its Food Programme of relief shipments. On 30 November, following this incident, the Secretary-General requested the Security Council to launch a military operation to safeguard relief workers although this was not formally agreed until 30 December. It was now that President Bush of the United States authorized the use of 28 000 American troops in Somalia (under UN auspices) to act as guards for the relief columns taking food and other supplies to the large numbers of starving or near-starving people at risk from the acivities of the rival warring clans.

The first US troops, part of the multinational United Nations Task Force (UNTAF), landed in Somalia on 9 December 1992, with the immediate objective of securing airfields, ports and roads. Early in 1993 UNTAF began to search for weapons in Mogadishu and elsewhere, and on 7 January the US commander, General Robert Johnson, said his troops had opened up supply routes to famine afflicted areas and that a 'new phase' was about to begin. The US troops in Mogadishu were soon subject to sniper fire from the supporters of General Aideed who, meanwhile, had formed the Somali National Alliance (SNA) with its Somali Liberation Army (SLA). Early in January US marines destroyed an SLA arms cache and killed 30 Somalis in the process. On 13 January the marines suffered their first casualty and the US policing operation then became more aggressive. US and Belgian (UN) troops killed a further 42 Somalis in the southern town of Kismayu on 25 January. By the end of January there were 24000 US troops in Somalia and a further 13600 from other countries under UN control.

Tensions arose during February between the United States and the United Nations about how the US-led intervention should be handed over to the world body: Washington hoped its forces could be withdrawn within two months, the United Nations wanted them to stay longer. A Security Council resolution of 4 May 1993 gave operational command in Somalia to UNOSOM II;

under Chapter VII of the UN Charter it was empowered to use force to disarm
Somali warlords so that relief supplies could get through to their targets. This
new UN body faced bitter opposition during June. A battle betwen UN
Pakistani troops and members of Aideed's SNA on 5 June resulted in 23
Pakistani deaths and 50 wounded; the Somalis suffered comparable casualties.
Pakistan then called for punitive action against Aideed and the Security
Council ordered the arrest and punishment of those responsible. US
reinforcements were sent to Somalia from the Gulf and UNOSOM launched
a series of operations against the SNA. US aircraft attacked SNA targets in
Mogadishu and Aideed then accused the US government of attacking civilian
targets. On 13 June Pakistani troops fired on demonstrators to kill 20 and
wound 50 and the Security Council then ordered the arrest of Aideed. A huge
but unsuccessful manhunt through Mogadishu followed and 31 UN soldiers
were killed during the month. Following the death of three Italian soldiers
the opposition in Rome demanded the recall of the Italian contingent and
blamed US belligerency for their deaths. A further US operation on 12 July
led to the deaths of another 54 Somalis and the wounding of 174.

In a bungled operation mounted during August the elite US Ranger troops
managed to take prisoner French and UN aid workers instead of Aideed. They
had targeted the wrong house. By this time the Americans had come to see
the arrest of Aideed and the neutralization of his forces as a precondition of
their withdrawal. On 12 August Italy withdrew its contingent of troops from
Mogadishu to deploy them elsewhere in Somalia. There was now growing
criticism of what was seen as a 'macho' US attitude and of the US Special
UN representative, former admiral Jonathan T. Howe. On 9 September, 200
Somalis were killed when a US helicopter fired on a crowd in Mogadishu
which, allegedly, was taking part in a gun battle on behalf of the Somali militia
against UN troops. The United Nations claimed that the militia were using
the crowd, many of whom were women and children, as a human shield. UN
casualties included seven Nigerians. On 22 September the Security Council
adopted Resolution 865 to end UNOSOM II by March 1995.

At the beginning of October a battle in Mogadishu resulted in the deaths
of 18 US soldiers and 300 Somalis; later, a US helicopter pilot and Nigerian
soldier were taken prisoner. The United Nations now abandoned its policy
of hunting down Aideed and on 19 October the US Rangers were withdrawn
from Somalia. On 7 November Aideed warned that if US troops returned to
the streets of Mogadishu he would break the ceasefire to which he had
agreed on 9 October. On 16 November the Security Council accepted an
Aideed suggestion that it should appoint a special commission to examine
the charges against him – this, in effect, was a face-saver for the world body
which allowed it to abandon its June resolution to arrest him. It was after

the events of October, when the bodies of dead Americans were shown being dragged through the streets of Mogadishu on television, that President Clinton announced the withdrawal of US forces by 31 March 1994 at the latest, which was a year earlier than planned under the UN authorization of 22 September 1993.[14]

The failure of the US forces to capture Aideed and the subsequent American decision to withdraw from the Somalia operation may well have marked a turning point in the relations between the United States and the United Nations. There were indications that Boutros-Ghali believed the United States wanted to make both him and the United Nations scapegoats for the failure to capture Aideed although the October operation had been a purely American affair. Following this debacle, the United States showed marked reluctance to be further involved in Somalia, was unwilling for its forces to come under a UN commander and later, in relation to Rwanda (see above) did not wish to be involved at all.

The departure of the Americans signalled the run-down of the UN operation in Somalia although this took a further year to accomplish. In January 1994 the Secretary-General reported that the international community was suffering 'unmistakable signs of fatigue' over Somalia. In February the Security Council renewed the UNOSOM II mandate but it now had fewer than 19 000 troops for its peacekeeping and food delivery safeguarding operations as the US contingents were rapidly reduced. On 1 June 1994, a commission of inquiry investigating attacks on mission personnel noted that member nations were not prepared 'to accept substantial casualties for causes unrelated to their national interests', a finding that had major implications for future UN operations.[15] Efforts to bring about an end to hostilities between the warring factions continued, without success, through the year while UNOSOM forces were mainly confined to fortified compounds in Mogadishu and might as well not have been there at all. On 4 November 1994, the Security Council decided to recall UNOSOM II by 31 March 1995, one year after the departure of the Americans, even if no political settlement had been reached, and this is what happened. On 2 March 1995, the UN peacekeepers were all withdrawn from Somalia under the protection of a 'United Shield' of troops provided by seven countries and the UN operation in Somalia was over without having achieved its objective, although some 50 international staff remained, with other aid agencies, to assist with humanitarian operations in 14 regions. The civil war in Somalia continued.

On 2 August 1996, Muhammad Farah Aideed, the man who had successfully defied and humiliated both the Americans and the United Nations, died of gunshot wounds received during continuing clan fighting in Mogadishu.

LIBERIA

President Samuel Doe, who seized power in a coup of April 1980, became progressively more unpopular through the decade; over Christmas 1989 fighting erupted in Nimba county on the border with Cote d'Ivoire and within ten days about 10000 people had fled across the border to escape the violence. The majority of the rebels came from the Gio tribe in Nimba and they made members of the Krahn tribe from which Doe came the particular objects of their attacks. The rebels called themselves the National Patriotic Front. Their leader was Charles Taylor, a former minister who had fled the country in 1984 following corruption charges; he was hardly seen as a liberating hero by other Liberians.

The rebellion rapidly escalated and by the end of January 1990 about 50000 people were thought to be in hiding in the bush in Nimba county to escape retribution from government forces. At the end of April 1990, as the rebels advanced on Monrovia, the United States advised its 5000 citizens in Liberia to leave and British Airways laid on special flights from Monrovia for British and Commonwealth citizens. The rebels now had an army estimated at 3000 with alleged support from Libya facing a Liberian army of 7000. The President, with a Krahn bodyguard of 1000, established himself in the Executive Mansion. The US human rights group, Africa Watch, claimed in May that there were 300000 refugees from what had now become savage intertribal fighting and that most of the casualties were among the Gio or Mano people. Africa Watch said that Doe's ten-year rule had been a reign of terror.

At the end of May Charles Taylor, whose forces had increased to 10000, captured Robertsfield, the capital's airport, while, early in June, government troops began to turn against members of their own side who belonged to different ethnic groups. Taylor would not talk with other exile groups and was clearly bent upon power for himself. The United States and Britain now sent warships to lie off Monrovia ready to evacuate their citizens and the US ships were said to carry 2100 marines. Half the capital's population of 750000 fled as the forces of the Patriotic Front closed in on Monrovia and President Doe annnounced he had authorized the US marines to come ashore to help end the fighting. He also said he would welcome an international peacekeeping force. Government forces now began to disintegrate.

By the end of July the rebels were reported to have split with a new faction emerging under Prince Yormie Johnson; government forces massacred 600 people who had taken refuge in a church; and an estimated 375000 Liberians had fled into neighbouring countries. The ambassadors of the EC countries called for an emergency session of the Security Council while in the first week of August the United States landed 200 marines to evacuate 59 US citizens. A number of West African governments belonging to the Economic Community of West African States (ECOWAS) under Nigerian leadership coordinated plans to intervene and end the civil war. This group consisted of The Gambia, Ghana, Guinea, Nigeria and Sierra Leone. It prepared a military force under the command of Lieutenant-General Arnold Quainoo of Ghana but requested US assistance to fund the operation.

The civil war now became a three-cornered fight between Doe and his supporters, Taylor and Johnson who each held part of Monrovia. The West African multinational force said it would not intervene until the three had agreed a ceasefire. However, on 9 September 1990, Doe and 60 of his followers were intercepted on their way to the headquarters of the ECOWAS Monitoring Group (ECOMOG) and Doe was first tortured and then killed. The country then descended into anarchy which continued throughout 1991. The key to peace through 1992 was Charles Taylor and his National Patriotic Front of Liberia (NPFL) and some of the worst fighting of the war took place in October–November 1992 when his forces were besieging Monrovia while the Nigerians bombed his positions outside the capital and ECOWAS ordered a trade embargo on NPFL-controlled parts of Liberia. On 19 November the UN Security Council called for a 'general and complete' arms embargo on Liberia.

Under the terms of its 1992 Security Council Resolution 788 which called upon the factions in Liberia to respect the provisions of the peace process, the UN Secretary-General sent his special representative, Trevor Gordon-Somers, to assess the situation; then, on the basis of his findings, the Secretary-General submitted a special report to the Security Council on 12 March. On 26 March the Council adopted Resolution 813 of 1993 reaffirming its belief that the Yamoussoukro IV Accords reached by the contending factions in Cote d'Ivoire represented the best chance for peace. The Council demanded that the parties refrained from actions that would prevent the delivery of humanitarian aid. In August 1993 the Security Council authorized the despatch of 30 military observers to Liberia to monitor the ceasefire agreement of 25 July which had been reached at a summit in Benin held under the tripartite auspices of ECOWAS, the OAU and the United Nations and by Resolution 866 of 22 September established the UN Observer Mission in Liberia (UNOMIL). The UN peacekeeping mission in Liberia was only the second (following the UN–OAS cooperation in the Dominican Republic in 1965–6) to be undertaken in collaboration with another organization (ECOMOG)[16] and set a possible precedent for the future.

The United Nations played a secondary role in Liberia, whose civil war represented a major African tragedy, leaving the main effort at peacekeeping

and then peace enforcement to the Economic Community of West African
States (ECOWAS) in which Nigeria took the lead. The United Nations,
indeed, showed no disposition to involve itself and, instead, the Security
Council threw 'its weight unequivocally behind ECOWAS/ECOMOG'. The
relationship between ECOMOG and UNOMIL

> distinguishes the Liberian operation from all others mounted by the
> Security Council and may well constitute a precedent for international
> involvement in future civil wars. In the debate leading to the adoption of
> Resolution 866, speakers mentioned the unique nature of this joint effort
> involving the Council and a regional organization.[17]

Should this combined approach – the United Nations and a regional
organization, each with its own command structure – work, it could well
provide a pattern for dealing with civil wars elsewhere in the world. In this
case, 'since ECOWAS represents a far from rich part of the world, the
Council has established a voluntary Trust Fund to defray part of ECOMOG's
expenses'.[18]

CONCLUSIONS

A number of lessons for the future emerge from the study of these four crises
– Burundi, Rwanda, Somalia and Liberia. First, the international community
will not willingly become involved, even in a major crisis, simply because
the United Nations asks for its commitment to finding a solution. This was
made very clear in the cases of both Burundi and Rwanda. Second, American
reluctance to undertake responsibilities under the United Nations, for
whatever reasons, could cripple the organization in the future for no other
country has anything approaching US resources or the capacity to deploy
them anywhere in the world at speed. Third, is a major UN operation possible
if it is not supported by at least one of the major Western military powers
– the United States, Britain or France? The above three examples concern
the willingness of the international community or individual states to become
involved in crises.

Fourth, these particular crises have each, in their different ways, raised a
fundamental issue: should the United Nations intervene in civil wars and, if
it does so, what ought to be its aims? When is pre-emptive intervention either
permissible or desirable and should it be attempted (for example in Burundi)
even against the wishes of both sides to a confrontation if it is clear that the
alternative will be genocide or something similar?

When Kofi Annan, the Under-Secretary-General for Peacekeeping, posed his rhetorical question: 'Can the international community sit back and allow the genocide to continue?', he must have known that the answer, in certain circumstances, would be 'Yes, it can.' The core issue here is that of interest: major powers will be prepared to intervene if their interests are at risk; if not, their intervention is far more problematic and certainly cannot be taken for granted. Moreover, if as in Burundi neither the Tutsis nor the Hutus wish for international intervention ought the United Nations to interfere? Or should it wait until, for example, genocide is clearly taking place before it acts?

More generally, several other lessons have emerged from these four cases. First, sadly, Africa has learnt that its troubles rate low on the international scale. Second, peacekeepers ought always to try to be impartial and not turn the operation into a vendetta as the Americans were perceived to do in Somalia as they sought to capture Aideed. Third, no UN operation can ignore the presence and influence of the media whose instant images have an enormous capacity to sway public opinion in those countries upon whose assistance any UN operation must rely. Fourth, the United Nations and its Secretary-General must expect to be made scapegoats for the failures of the major powers while the same powers will always claim credit for any UN operation in which they are involved. Fifth, major powers who provide military forces will relate casualties to their interests and only allow a relatively high casualty rate among their own forces when an operation is seen to be essential to their own world influence.

6 The United Nations in Africa (2): Southern Africa

Given the long years of growing confrontation with South Africa, with the General Assembly condemning apartheid every year from 1949 onwards, it is, perhaps, astonishing that the changes which came so suddenly in the 1990s were accomplished so smoothly. Over the years the United Nations played a particular role in relation to South West Africa (Namibia) because this was regarded as a UN Trusteeship territory from 1946 onwards even if the Republic of South Africa refused, for many years, to recognize UN jurisdiction over it. Nationalists demanding independence had fought the Portuguese in Angola and Mozambique from the early 1960s; following the Lisbon coup and revolution of April 1974 which toppled the Portuguese dictator, Marcello Caetano, these two territories became independent the next year under leftwing Marxist-oriented governments and both, subsequently, were to experience years of civil war betwen rival factions. In the case of Angola both the United States and South Africa joined in supporting the rebel movement, the National Union for the Total Independence of Angola (Uniao Nacional para a Independencia Total de Angola) (UNITA), against the Popular Liberation Movement of Angola (Movimento Popular de Libertacao de Angola) (MPLA) government. In the case of Mozambique, first Rhodesia under the Smith regime from 1975 to 1980 and then South Africa provided weapons and money to support the Resistencia Nacional Mocambicana (Renamo) in revolt against the Frente de Libertacao de Mocambique (Frelimo) government. In Rhodesia the government of Ian Smith had made a unilateral declaration of independence (UDI) in 1965 and held out, despite escalating guerrilla warfare, for 15 years until forced to come to terms with reality in 1979/80 when an independent Zimbabwe was born. During those years the United Nations had called for sanctions against Rhodesia and these had been made mandatory although South Africa ensured that they were not effective. The United Nations, generally, over these years supported the stand of the frontline states and the Southern Africa Development Coordinating Conference (SADCC) which opposed South Africa, while also recognizing the African National Congress (ANC) as a legitimate liberation movement. At the time of Zimbabwe's independence in 1980 the South African Defence Minister, General Magnus Malan, reckoned (accurately) that South Africa could hold on to Namibia for another ten years and the policy of destabilization – cross-border raids into its weak neighbour states to discourage them from providing aid to the ANC – was adopted. Constant protests and condemnations through the United Nations had little impact on this policy through the 1980s although, in the second half of the decade, mounting demands for UN sanctions against South Africa began to have an effect with, for example, a significant number of US corporate investors disinvesting, or partially disinvesting, from South Africa. International pressures undoubtedly played an important part in the South Africa story but it was internal events which forced the changes that came in the first half of the 1990s. When F. W. de Klerk became President in 1989, despite his own 'hardline' credentials, he soon saw that maintaining the apartheid system he had inherited (and helped create) would no longer work and that the only hope for the future of South Africa (and its white community that he represented) was to come to terms with the ANC and the black majority. Once these momentous changes got underway in South Africa and it was clear that the apartheid system was to be scrapped, there was a role for the United Nations: it could assist the period of transition – from white minority to black majority rule – to take place as smoothly as possible.

ANGOLA

After the departure of the Portuguese in 1975, the MPLA formed the government of the new state but was to be opposed over the next 15 years in an escalating civil war by UNITA. The war became inextricably tied into the worldwide confrontation of the Cold War and, for example, in 1986 the US House of Representatives voted to provide UNITA with US$15 million in aid (seen by President Reagan as crucial to stemming Soviet expansion in Africa). South Africa, over these years, had made numerous military forays into southern Angola, supposedly in search of ANC or SWAPO (South West African People's Organization) military camps but in reality in support of UNITA. Cuba, on the other side, had committed increasing numbers of troops to assist the MPLA government and by the late 1980s there were an estimated 50000 Cubans in the country. A major battle at Cuito Cuanavale in the southeast of Angola was fought in 1988: it involved a force of 6000 (later increased to 9000) South African troops supporting UNITA and large numbers of the Cubans who had introduced superior air defences into Angola in support of the government. The battle was a decisive turning point since the South African troops were cut off and in danger of being destroyed; as a result of this changed military situation both sides were prepared to talk.

Negotiations were carried on throughout 1988: the United States insisted upon linkage – that any settlement of the Angolan war or independence for Namibia depended upon the withdrawal of the Cuban troops; the Soviet Union under Gorbachev wanted to disengage from confrontations worldwide with the United States and was prepared to accept this US formula. After a year of negotiations a final agreement was signed by the various parties to the war on 22 December in New York. South Africa, Angola and Cuba formally signed agreements whereby the Namibian independence process would begin on 1 April 1989, and all Cuban troops would be out of Angola by July 1991. The agreement, however, did not cover the war between the Angolan government and UNITA and the United States maintained that its aid to UNITA was a separate issue; nor was it clear whether South Africa would continue its aid to UNITA or not. The ANC, however, withdrew its forces from Angola to other frontline states.

Following the December 1988 agreement in New York, the United Nations Security Council established the UN Angola Verification Mission (UNAVEM) to monitor the redeployment of the Cuban troops away from the Namibian border and then their withdrawal over the succeeding 18 months. The Cuban withdrawal was disciplined and went according to plan and the UNAVEM team of 70 unarmed military observers and 20 civilian staff had no problems so that the Secretary-General was able to report to the Security Council in June 1991 that all 50000 Cubans and their equipment had been withdrawn one month ahead of the agreed schedule. In the meantime the United States, the USSR and Portugal had worked out a ceasefire between the MPLA government and UNITA which came into effect on 31 May 1991 and it was agreed that elections should be held between September and November 1992. This ceasefire was to be jointly monitored by the United States, the USSR and the United Nations. The land forces of the two sides were to be merged prior to the elections. Although the agreement of May was hailed as a triumph of superpower cooperation, in fact the 'seeds of disaster' had been sown.

> First, the accords were a victory for UNITA. Armed to the teeth by South Africa and the United States, cossetted by Washington, including a photo-call reception by President Reagan, Savimbi had succeeded in being accepted not as a rebel making terms with a government but as an equal with the government.[1]

Moreover, the United States refused to recognize the MPLA government until May 1993.

In March 1992 the Security Council mandated UNAVEM to observe and monitor the elections and increased its numbers to 450 unarmed observers plus another 100 when it was agreed to monitor the elections with a further 400 being sent to the country for the month of the elections. Such numbers were absurdly inadequate for a country the size of Angola where democratic elections had never been held before. The elections were held on 29–30 September and were contested by 18 parties while 12 candidates stood for president. The MPLA government party won 128 seats, UNITA 71. However, neither President Jose Eduardo dos Santos nor Jonas Savimbi received 50 per cent of the presidential vote so that a run-off was required. Savimbi now claimed that the elections had been fraudulent and returned to the bush and fighting between the two sides was renewed in October. By the end of November UNITA controlled about two-thirds of the country. When the new Assembly met on November 30 the UNITA members did not take their seats. During January 1993 a government offensive succeeded in driving UNITA forces out of most of the towns they then held. On 18 January the UN representative in Angola, Margaret Anstee, said there was now 'full-scale civil war' and that the UN mandate in Angola was 'increasingly irrelevant'.

The renewed fighting was on a savage scale. The UN mandate had been due to expire on 31 January1993, but both sides pressed the United Nations to remain in Angola. The new Secretary-General, Boutros Boutros-Ghali, advised a reduction of the UN presence to 60 who should be withdrawn to Luanda and then withdrawn entirely on 30 April unless peace had been achieved by that date. The United States, which had been a steadfast opponent of the MPLA and supporter of UNITA now shifted its position and said that UNITA's return to the use of force was 'unacceptable' and on 25 March the US Senate and House of Representatives passed a joint resolution condemning UNITA and calling for US recognition of the Angolan government. On 2 June the United Nations again extended the mandate for UNAVEM. In July the new UN representative in Angola, Alioune Blondin Beye, claimed that more that 1000 people a day were dying from the direct and indirect consequences of the 'world's worst war'. The United Nations again extended its mandate and called on UNITA to end the fighting. On 9 August Britain lifted its arms embargo on the MPLA government which it had maintained since 1975, arguing that the government had a 'legitimate right to self-defence' and on 26 September the United Nations implemented a mandatory oil and arms embargo against UNITA. On 6 October UNITA announced it would accept the election results of the previous year and at the end of the month talks were resumed in Lusaka between UNITA, UNAVEM and the three observer countries (Portugal, Russia and the United States). An estimated 100000 Angolans died as a result of the fighting between October 1992 and October 1993. Substantial progress was reported in the Lusaka talks by December 1993 in terms of demobilization and subsequent military integration. The United Nations again extended its mandate to 16 March 1994. But, as Anthony Parsons says of this period: 'The Security Council had adopted what I think of as the Arab/Israel posture, pumping out forlorn resolutions of which the offending party takes no notice.'[2] There was no disposition on the part of the Security Council to send troops on the scale needed to escort humanitarian supplies or to break the sieges of the towns. Indeed, it could be said that Angola was a victim of the end of the Cold War. Once the United States and Russia had resolved their differences Angola no longer mattered to them and despite the fact that the two superpowers had provided levels of support over the previous years which had made possible the scale of the war, now they left Angola to its own devices, with a weak and totally ineffective UN mission on the ground as a useless gesture of world concern.

During 1994 the Angolan government and UNITA approved a new mandate for UNAVEM and the Security Council then decided not to strengthen the existing oil and arms embargo against UNITA. On 21 November the Security Council welcomed the signing of the Lusaka Protocol by the government and UNITA. At the end of the year UNAVEM II was restored in strength to 476 observers. In February 1995 Security Council Resolution 976 established UNAVEM III 'to help the country's factions to restore peace and achieve national reconciliation'.[3] By the end of 1995 the Security Council was expressing its concern that the implementation of the Lusaka Protocol of 1994 was progressing slowly and that no agreement had been reached on integrating the armed forces. Such resolutions merely served to disguise the reality: that the country remained hopelessly divided and in a state of war. In June 1996 President dos Santos sacked his government and called upon the leader of the National Assembly, Franca Van Dunem, to form a new government. The President was fighting for political survival, hoping to start a new initiative in a desperate situation while Jonas Savimbi of UNITA continued to threaten to turn Angola, one of the continent's richest countries, into 'another Somalia'. In the years since UNITA resumed the war, despite periodic renewals of the UNAVEM mandate,

> the infrastructure of the state has virtually disappeared. A ceasefire at the beginning of this year [1996], while political negotiations continue, has left UNITA in control of most of the North and the East – though in many places the population fled to zones controlled by the government, despite its inability to look after them.[4]

Angola represents a prime case of a country where massive peace enforcement by the United Nations would be justifed but those with the means to make such enforcement possible – the major Western powers and Russia

– are uninterested. The country's Cold War importance has evaporated so that by the mid-1990s it was left to join the ranks of Somalia, Rwanda and Burundi, a failed state whose potential for the future, let alone the condition of its people, was of insufficient importance to warrant a peacekeeping effort on the scale required. According to Anthony Parsons:

> In multilateral diplomacy, there is a powerful impetus towards settling for any agreement as being better than none so that the file can be closed and the next problem on the agenda addressed. Even so, Angola must stand alone as the quintessence of how not to do it.[5]

MOZAMBIQUE

Mozambique might have gone the same way as Angola. By 1990 it had suffered an equally devastating three decades of warfare – first the struggle against the Portuguese and then the civil war between the Frelimo government and Renamo – and the country was in ruins with approximately a quarter of its population refugees either inside or outside Mozambique. Early in 1990, faced with growing unrest and a collapsed economy, President Joaquim Chissano announced major constitutional changes which represented the introduction of democracy along Western lines rather than a one-party state structure. At the end of January the United States government formally declared that it no longer regarded Mozambique as a communist state, opening the way for US economic support. However, the abduction by Renamo of a British scientist and a Zimbabwean businessman travelling in the Beira Corridor in February emphasized that the war continued.

In July 1990 the two sides met in Rome for the first of a series of peace talks that had been brokered by Zimbabwe's President Robert Mugabe and the churches. In November the government announced its abandonment of Marxism-Leninism and said it would run the economy according to market forces. Renamo agreed a ceasefire with the government in December. On-off talks and sporadic fighting continued throughout 1991 until, on 4 October, a ceasefire agreement was finally signed in Rome by President Chissano and the Renamo leader, Afonso Dhlakama. It owed much to the efforts of Zimbabwe's President Mugabe, the British businessman Tiny Rowland and the Roman Catholic Church – as well as war exhaustion on both sides. By that time, according to the World Bank, the war had reduced Mozambique's standard of living to the lowest in the world with a per capita GNP of only US$80.

On 16 December 1992, the UN Security Council decided to send a peacekeeping force (UNOMOZ) of 7500 troops, police and civilians to Mozambique to oversee the disarming of the rival forces and to organize free elections. The force would also protect the vital railway 'corridors' to Beira and Maputo which were so essential to Mozambique's inland neighbours and would allow Zimbabwe to withdraw its own troops which had guarded the corridors over the preceding years. At the beginning of 1993 there were renewed fears that the civil war might be resumed; the first 100 of the proposed 7500 UN force arrived in Mozambique on 15 February. April was a nerve-wracking month during which Renamo withdrew from the ceasefire and control commissions, halting the process of demobilization, while the Zimbabwe troops all withdrew. However, during May some 4721 UN troops from five countries as well as unarmed units from three others arrived in Mozambique; in June, under the auspices of the UNHCR, the task of repatriating 1.3 million refugees from neighbouring countries began. International donors, meanwhile, had pledged US$520 million for humanitarian aid. Agreement on an electoral commission was reached on 20 October when the Secretary-General, Boutros-Ghali, visited Maputo to hold talks with Chissano and Dhlakama, and October 1994 was set as the date for elections while the completion of the demobilization process was to be carried out between January and May 1994. The Security Council then extended the mandate for UNOMOZ for a further six months and requested the Secretary-General to report to the Security Council by 31 January 1994, and every three months thereafter, on progress towards implementation of the peace agreement.

Security Council Resolution 898 of February 1994 authorized the establishment of a UN police component of UNOMOZ prior to the holding of elections and by March, with troops coming into 40 demobilization centres, and 6000 UNOMOZ troops deployed throughout the country, it appeared that the peace process was working. At this stage UNOMOZ was costing Western donors £600000 a day. The elections were held between 27 and 29 October and there were many fears that Mozambique could go the same way as Angola when Savimbi had returned to the bush on hearing adverse results. At least in Mozambique UNOMOZ had a full complement of troops and police and was headed by an extrmely shrewd special representative, the Italian Aldo Ajello, who paid particular attention to ensuring the participation of Renamo in each stage of the elections. A UN trust fund was created to provide the means for Renamo to organize itself as a political party. Moreover, the process of demobilization was far more thorough than in Angola and by the end of July, well ahead of the elections, 80000 Frelimo troops and 20000 Renamo guerrillas had passed through demobilization centres. In the elections for President, which the UN representative declared to be free and fair, Chissano won 53 per cent of the votes while Dhlakama won 33 per cent out of 4.9 million votes cast. In the elections for the National Assembly Frelimo just won a majority – 129 out of 250 seats, while Renamo won 112 and the Democratic Union nine seats. The victor, President Chissano, refused to follow the South African example of creating a coalition government and Dhlakama accepted the role of leader of the opposition.

In the case of Mozambique, in marked contrast to Angola, the United Nations had played a leading role in supervising the peace and monitoring the elections and had sufficient forces on the ground to do an adequate job. By November 1995 when a newly peaceful and slowly recovering democratic Mozambqique was warmly welcomed as the fifty-third member of the Commonwealth at Auckland, New Zealand, this period of transition from civil war to peace, with the guerrilla leader Afonso Dhlakama now in the role of leader of the opposition, could be seen as a distinct success for the United Nations. A combination of circumstances had contributed to this success: these included war weariness, a more vulnerable and weaker opposition in Renamo and Dhlakama than was the case with Savimbi and UNITA in Angola, and more skilful and determined peace brokers. At the same time, the Security Council had been willing to vote greater resources for UNOMOZ than in Angola where, perhaps, it had been mesmerized by the apparent readiness of the two superpowers to oversee the peace, a readiness that evaporated once the United States and Russia lost their strategic interest in Angola.

NAMIBIA

South West Africa was colonized by imperial Germany during the Scramble for Africa and brought under German control by 1890. It was overrun by South African forces during World War I and made a mandate of the new League of Nations in 1920. The administration of the mandate was entrusted by the League to the Dominion of South Africa. In 1946 the mandates of the defunct League of Nations became trust territories of the United Nations but the Pretoria government refused to recognize UN jurisdiction over the territory and embarked instead upon more than 40 years of defiance of the world body. Over no other issue of decolonization has the United Nations played so central a role. From 1946 onwards South African control of the territory was to be challenged on an annual basis in the General Assembly.

In 1949 South Africa virtually incorporated Namibia into the Union as a province and ceased providing annual reports of its administration to the United Nations. Gradually, from the late 1950s onwards, nationalist opposition to South African occupation crystallized under the South West African People's Organization (SWAPO) which in 1966 launched an armed struggle from the Caprivi Strip in the north of the country while maintaining bases across the border in Angola and Zambia.

Constant and gradually increasing pressures were mounted against South Africa through the United Nations during the 1960s and 1970s. In 1964 the United Nations voted to end South Africa's mandate over Namibia; in 1968 it voted to change the name from South West Africa to Namibia; in 1969 the Security Council voted 13–0 (with two abstentions) to withdraw its administration from Namibia; in 1971 the International Court at The Hague reversed its earlier decision and ruled that South Africa's presence in Namibia was illegal. After South Africa's Prime Minister, B. J. Vorster, had refused to allow the UN 11-nation Council for Namibia to visit the territory in 1968, the UN passed Resolution 283 requesting all states to refrain from any action that implied a recognition of South African authority in Namibia. In 1972 the UN Secretary-General, Kurt Waldheim, visited Namibia as part of a new UN initiative. In December 1973 the Security Council voted 15–0 to halt further talks with South Africa over Namibia; it appointed Sean MacBride as Commissioner for Namibia and recognized SWAPO as the 'authentic representative of the people of Namibia'. Little, however, came of these initiatives since the major Western powers were unwilling to have any real confrontation with South Africa.[6]

Following the Portuguese withdrawal from Angola and that country's independence at the end of 1975 the northern border of Namibia, including the 300-mile-long Caprivi Strip, became an increasingly embattled South Africa's frontline with major troop concentrations stationed there. Periodically these forces were used to launch raids into Angola, ostensibly to 'take out' ANC and SWAPO camps, and though this was done the wider strategic objective was to provide support for UNITA in its war against the MPLA government of Angola and so destabilize the new state. In 1978 the Security Council adopted Resolution 435 which set out a framework for the achievement of Namibian independence and followed this by creating a UN Transition Assistance Group (UNTAG) to help its Special Representative achieve the independence of Namibia through free elections. At the same time, the Security Council declared null and void any unilateral measures taken by South Africa in relation to the electoral process.[7]

A Western Contact Group of five nations (the United States, Britain, France, Germany and Canada) was formed to assist the Secretary-General's

Representative, Martii Ahtisaari of Finland, to negotiate with South Africa but any progress they might have made was destroyed by Washington which, under the new Reagan administration which came to power at the beginning of the 1980s, insisted upon linking any advances towards independence in Namibia with the withdrawal of Cuban troops from Angola. This gratuitously brought Cold War considerations to the forefront of the Namibian question while also giving South African intransigence a new lease of life with the result that no further progress was to be made through the 1980s until the battle of Cuito Cuanavale in 1988 had transformed the situation in Southern Africa (see above, p. 59).

On 16 February 1989, the Security Council unanimously agreed to create a Transition Assistance Group (TAG) of 4650 troops at a cost of US$416 million to help prepare Namibia for independence. African objections that TAG should have had 7500 troops – the original proposal – was overruled by the Security Council (partly for reasons of cost), with the United States, the USSR and China voting together, which was a first for the three countries. Despite the cutback, it was the largest UN force of this nature to be voted since the Congo operation of 1960–4 which had been 19000 strong. The South Africans kept to their side of the agreement and on 6 June 1989, President Botha ended apartheid in Namibia and granted an amnesty to SWAPO guerrillas returning to the country from Angola. On 12 June a six-week UN airlift got underway to bring back 41000 refugees including the leader of SWAPO, Sam Nujoma, soon to be president of an independent Namibia. Elections for a Constituent Assembly to draft a constitution were held on 7–11 November 1989; they were monitored by 1695 UN-trained supervisors as well as South African observers. Over 90 per cent of the 700000 registered voters participated in the elections and SWAPO obtained 56.3 per cent of the votes cast. The United Nations declared the elections to have been free and fair. Despite a brief and bloody setback in April 1989, when hundreds of SWAPO fighters poured across the Angolan border to set up bases in Namibia and ended up being shot down by the South Africa armed forces, the transition process had otherwise gone remarkably smoothly and could be regarded as a distinct UN success story. American insistence upon linking Namibian independence to events in Angola did neither Namibia nor the United Nations a service. Even so, the achievement of independence by Namibia represented a major shift in the balance of power in Southern Africa by removing South Africa from Angola's doorstep so that the government in Luanda, at least in theory, had a better chance of coping with the UNITA insurgence. Namibia achieved its independence after 100 years of colonialism; in September 1993 South Africa agreed to transfer sovereignty of Walvis Bay to Namibia on 1 March 1994.

SOUTH AFRICA

The subject of race discrimination and apartheid in South Africa was to be discussed in the General Assembly of the United Nations almost from its inception but for many years it was no more than a discussion: nothing was done. South Africa itself was a founder member of the United Nations and when pressures did begin to mount was able to count upon the protection – and if necessary the veto – of the leading Western powers, especially Britain and the United States. As the Cold War polarized the world, South Africa came to be seen as strategically vital to Western interests so that attacks upon its race policies from the Soviet Union or its allies simply ensured a closing of Western ranks in support of the Pretoria regime. Year after year, it is true, condemnations of apartheid were ritualistically made but they were never followed by any meaningful actions. At first, therefore, the United Nations could do little more than act as the conduit of opposition to apartheid which for the most part was voiced by the weak and powerless; in any case, for the greater part of the world, apartheid was a remote problem. Only four countries on the entire African continent had been independent in 1945 – Egypt, Ethiopia, Liberia and South Africa itself – and it was not until the late 1950s when Morocco, Tunisia, Sudan and then Ghana became independent, and then 1960 – the so-called *annus mirabilis* of African independence – when 17 African countries achieved their freedom, that a sizeable African bloc in the United Nations (soon to be the largest single bloc) began to change the nature of the debates.

In 1960, in the wake of the Sharpeville massacre, the Security Council called upon South Africa to abandon apartheid. In 1962 the General Assembly called upon member states to break diplomatic relations with South Africa, boycott its goods and refrain from exports including arms to South Africa. This year saw the establishment of the UN Special Committee against Apartheid. In 1963 the Security Council instituted a voluntary arms embargo against South Africa. In 1965 the Smith government in Rhodesia, against the wishes of South Africa, declared independence unilaterally from Britain; the crisis which followed drew world attention to Southern Africa where two liberation struggles had also broken out against the Portuguese in Angola and Mozambique. Slowly but surely a world spotlight was being turned upon a region whose escalating violence arose from the same cause of white racialism. In 1966 the General Assmbly proclaimed 21 March (Sharpeville Day) as International Day for the Elimination of Racial Discrimination which was to be observed annually. In 1967 a UN Educational and Training Programme for Southern Africa was established: it provided scholarships for students from Namibia, South Africa, Rhodesia and the Portuguese colonies of Angola and Mozambique (by 1980 the scholarships would be confined to students from South Africa and Namibia). Most of these actions, taken during the 1960s, were symbolic and made little difference to South Africa where the government, presided over by Hendrik Verwoerd and then Balthazar Vorster, applied its apartheid laws relentlessly to every aspect of life in total defiance of world opinion.

The anti-apartheid tempo was to rise significantly during the 1970s with boycotts of South African cricketers, student campaigns in the United States and Britain to penalize companies that dealt with South Africa and a more coherent African policy towards the apartheid state as growing support for the liberation struggles in Angola, Mozambique and Rhodesia helped crystallize opposition to South Africa. In 1970 the United Nations strengthened the arms embargo against South Africa and urged member states to terminate diplomatic and other official relations with South Africa. In 1971 the International Court at The Hague ruled that South Africa's presence in Namibia was illegal. In 1972 the Security Council, meeting symbolically in Addis Ababa, recognized the legitimacy of the anti-apartheid struggle and requested all nations to adhere strictly to the arms embargo. In 1973 the General Assembly adopted the International Convention on the Suppression and Punishment of the Crime of Apartheid and established a Trust Fund for Publicity against apartheid. In 1974 the General Assembly invited representatives of South African Liberation Movements recognized by the OAU to participate as observers in its debates on apartheid; the General Assembly then rejected South Africa's credentials so that from this year onwards South Africa ceased to participate in the deliberations of the General Assembly. In 1975 the General Assembly proclaimed that the United Nations and the international community had a special responsibility towards the oppressed people of South Africa.

South Africa became the object of world attention during 1976, first, because of its highly publicized military intervention in Angola and then, 16 years after Sharpeville, as a result of the Soweto uprising and subsequent deaths of up to 1000 young students shot by the security forces. It was another turning point. During the year the General Assembly condemned South African aggression in Angola and rejected as spurious the so-called independence of the Transkei (Homeland). In 1977 the Security Council made the arms embargo against South Africa mandatory and in 1978 the General Assembly proclaimed an international Anti-Apartheid Year. The end of UDI in Rhodesia and the emergence of an independent Zimbabwe in 1980 meant that only Namibia remained as some form of buffer betwen South Africa and independent black Africa to the north; however, the climate of international politics also changed at this time with President Ronald Reagan in power in Washington and Prime Minister Margaret Thatcher in London. Both leaders showed positive sympathy for South Africa: under President Reagan the concept of linkage meant that independence for Namibia was now tied to the withdrawal of Cuban troops from Angola which was to give the South African presence in Namibia a new lease of life while the United States was to join with South Africa through the decade in supporting the rebel UNITA in Angola; and under Prime Minister Thatcher Britain was to set its face resolutely against the application of sanctions to South Africa, so much so that Margaret Thatcher isolated Britain on this issue in relation to the Commonwealth. Yet, if there was an easing of international pressures at least from the two major Western powers, events inside South Africa were building up to a crisis which, by the middle of the decade, made apartheid increasingly unworkable.

In 1982 the General Assembly proclaimed an International Year of Mobilization of Sanctions against South Africa. In 1984 the General Assembly rejected the new South African racially segregated tricameral constitution. By 1985, as violence was escalating in the South African townships, the Security Council condemned the Pretoria regime for killing defenceless Africans. This was the year when President Botha made his 'Rubicon' speech in which reforms had been anticipated; none were announced and over the following weeks the withdrawal of short-term international loans led by the US Chase Manhattan Bank resulted in a collapse of the rand. In 1989, with South Africa in deep crisis, the General Assembly adopted a Declaration which listed the steps the South African government should take to create the climate necessary for negotiations. By this time the end of the Cold War signalled massive changes in world attitudes and priorities; Pretoria would no longer be able to advance its strategic usefulness to the West as a reason for support.

The new South African President, F. W. de Klerk, recognizing the inevitable, inaugurated the end of apartheid with his speech unbanning the ANC and 33 other banned organizations followed by the release of Nelson Mandela during February 1990. Later that year the UN Secretary-General sent a mission to South Africa to report on progress in the implementation of the Declaration (of 1989). On 13 December 1991, the General Assembly, in recognition of its progress towards abolishing apartheid, called unanimously for all nations to begin restoring sporting, cultural and academic ties with South Africa. In 1992, in what many must have seen as a triumphant vindication of the long years of mounting pressures that never appeared to bring results, Nelson Mandela addressed the United Nations and called upon it to lift sanctions as a result of the progress that had been made inside South Africa in abolishing apartheid. In June 1992 the OAU called for a meeting of the Security Council to consider violence in South Africa to which both the Pretoria government and the ANC were invited. The Secretary-General appointed the former US Secretary of State, Cyrus Vance, as his special representative for South Africa to make recommendations for a peaceful transition to democratic, non-racial rule there and, following his report, the Security Council adopted Resolution 772 which authorized the deployment in South Africa of 30 observers to help implement the National Peace Accord which the various parties in South Africa had agreed the previous year. Thus, after the long years of condemnations, the United Nations had finally established a presence in South Africa with the agreement of the government. A further ten observers were added to the mission – the UN Observer Mission in South Africa (UNOMSA) – and the number had risen to 100 by late 1993. In January 1994, under Resolution 894, the mandate of UNOMSA was expanded to allow 2840 observers (including personnel from the OAU, the Commonwealth and the European Union) to monitor the April elections. In the meantime sanctions against South Africa had been lifted with the exception of the Security Council arms embargo. It is difficult to say just how effective these United Nations pressures had been over the years; apartheid was only brought to an end when the alternative facing the minority government was an explosion which it knew it could not control. As Anthony Parsons claims:

> There is no doubt that the UN anti-apartheid campaign helped to create a major shift in the international climate, which resulted in South Africa's almost total ostracism from participation in international activities.[8]

The fact that the United Nations was welcomed back into South Africa in 1992 by the de Klerk government was indication enough that renewed UN membership was seen as a valuable and necessary recognition of South Africa's acceptance once more by the world community.

CONCLUSIONS

The United Nations record of opposition to apartheid and racism was unwavering: although it could not force the major Western powers such as Britain and the United States to change their policies it never permitted them to forget the just demands of the peoples who suffered under the system. As the momentum of opposition to apartheid built up during the 1980s the United Nations came to the forefront as the natural instrument to assist the long-awaited transition to majority rule. Its record in relation to both Namibia and South Africa shows the world body at its persistent best. Nonetheless, a number of lessons emerge from the hectic period of changes which took place during the first half of the 1990s.

Angola was a disaster though not of the United Nations making. The blame for the renewal of the fighting by Savimbi's UNITA, following his defeat in the 1992 elections, lies squarely with the United States which had armed him for its own Cold War reasons and refused to disarm him at the time of the peace; secondly, it lies with Russia since, once they had obtained what they sought from the 1988 peace negotiations, both superpowers were prepared to leave Angola to its fate. The United Nations should have pulled out completely once the civil war began again, as Boutros-Ghali advised. In any case, the tiny size of UNAVEM spelled disaster from the beginning. Once it is clear that the parties to a dispute are determined to ignore the UN presence then either the United Nations should pull out or it should so increase its presence that the warring factions are obliged to take note of its actions. Neither of these options was followed and the continuing presence in Luanda of an impotent UN group merely ensured that the United Nations reputation was hurt without any achievements to counter-balance the damage.

In Mozambique, on the other hand, admittedly in slightly more favourable conditions, the United Nations acted decisively and sent a large enough mission under an extremely able representative who was able to maintain the momentum for peace and achieve the settlement everyone sought. The difference between the two cases is striking and perhaps the most important lesson to be learnt is the need for the United Nations, always, to show boldness in execution on the ground. On the whole, the United Nations played a vital and successful role in Southern Africa and after many years of steadfast application had the satisfaction of seeing its past endeavours bear fruit.

7   Other Interventions: Cambodia and Central America

CAMBODIA

Cambodia has had a complex, troubled history since 1941 when it was invaded by the Japanese. By 1970, during the war in Vietnam, it was suffering from border incursions by the North Vietnamese and the Viet Cong, and bombing by the Americans. In the mid-1970s it was torn by civil war whose victors, the Khmer Rouge under their leader Pol Pot, imposed upon the country one of the most murderous regimes to be found anywhere in the world. This period ended in 1979 when the country was invaded and occupied by Vietnam although their occupation was resisted by the Khmer Rouge and other non-communist groups. The world community refused to give any legitimacy to the Vietnam-supported government in Phnom Penh. In 1989, following the withdrawal of Vietnam, it appeared that Cambodia would descend once more into civil war.

During the long years of the Vietnam conflict the United Nations had not been called into the region since the three major outside powers which were involved in the war – the United States, the USSR and China – preferred to keep their confrontations clear of UN entanglements. In international terms the issue of the Khmer Rouge was less important than the occupation of Cambodia by Vietnam, even though this had ended the infamous Pol Pot regime, because their invasion was seen (by the Americans) as an attempt, funded by the USSR, to annex Cambodia. Moreover, as long as the Vietnamese remained in Cambodia a rapprochement between the USSR and China was impossible since China supported the Khmer Rouge. At the same time, the United States was not prepared to restore relations with Vietnam. Throughout the 1980s, therefore, there was a 'stand-off' by these powers in relation to the future of Cambodia. By 1988, however, the government of Mikhail Gorbachev in Moscow desired to pursue its policy of *glasnost* and achieve an understanding with China; the USSR, therefore, exerted pressure on Vietnam to withdraw. By the end of 1988 a revitalized Khmer Rouge, apparently as fanatical as ever, had an estimated 40000 troops under its command while China made plain it would not cut off its military aid to the

Khmer Rouge until the Vietnamese had completely withdrawn. It seemed probable that any post-Vietnamese government in Cambodia would have to include the Khmer Rouge.

Early in 1989 it appeared that a solution was in sight. The Chinese indicated their readiness to phase out their support for the Khmer Rouge and the anti-Vietnam coalition if the Russians would end their support for Vietnam and the Vietnamese would complete their withdrawal from Cambodia during the year. The dominant, most enduring political figure in Cambodia remained Prince Sihanouk who wanted to ensure that all factions were disarmed. Negotiations came to a climax in September 1989 when the last Vietnamese troops were withdrawn from the country. At once the Khmer Rouge and their non-communist allies, the Khmer People's National Liberation Front (KPNLF) and the Armee nationale Sihanoukist (ANS), began a new guerrilla offensive against the Hun Sen government and it soon looked as though this, without Vietnamese support, was in trouble. Both Thailand and China alleged that thousands of Vietnamese had in fact been left behind; two of the coalition guerrilla groups – the KPLNF and the ANS – were receiving training from Thailand, the United States and Britain while the Khmer Rouge continued to receive Chinese arms and backing. All the signs pointed to a new and ugly civil war. When it became clear that, despite the accusations, the Vietnamese troops really had been withdrawn the West was shown to be in disarray, supporting the anti-Phnom Penh coalition which included the Khmer Rouge whom the West had consistently denounced for years. At this point the United Nations became involved.

In November 1989 the United Nations General Assembly, in a motion on 'the situation in Kampuchea', voted 124–17 (with 12 abstentions) to send a fact-finding mission to Kampuchea to examine ways to monitor a comprehensive settlement. The Assembly voted in favour of the coalition – the Khmer Rouge, the KPNLF and ANS – rather than the sitting government of Hun Sen which was opposed by the Americans for its communist leanings even more than they objected to the Khmer Rouge for its murderous propensities. There was heavy fighting in 1990 as the coalition forces attacked towns held by the Phnom Penh government and the fighting in the west was so severe that about 150000 villagers became refugees in their attempts to escape the fighting. The United Nations, in support of its policy of backing the coalition, proposed the creation of a Supreme National Council (SNC) to include both the Phnom Penh government and the three resistance groups. China, the USSR and the United States now worked together to produce a peace. The UN Security Council put forward its peace proposal in August 1990 and this was 'accepted' in September by the guerrilla factions although at first the Khmer Rouge held back. The plan envisaged placing

Cambodia under a UN Transitional Authority for a year or more until elections could be held under UN auspices. The plan was endorsed by the five permanent members of the Security Council. By December, although fighting continued, the four groups had partially accepted the UN plan. This was given a major boost by the collapse of communism in Eastern Europe and this shock to the Phnom Penh government was followed by a greater one when Moscow informed it that as of 1991 it would have to pay for Soviet imports at full market rates instead of receiving subsidies.

The fighting during the first three months of 1991 was very severe and increased the number of refugees inside Cambodia to 186000. A ceasefire was agreed by the four factions on 1 May; subsequent talks between them continued through to October before an agreement was reached. The four factions – the Phnom Penh government (which changed its name from the Kampuchean People's Revolutionary Party to the Cambodian People's Party), Prince Sihanouk's faction, the Khmer People's National Liberation Front (KPNLF) and the Khmer Rouge – signed an agreement on 23 October in Paris accepting a political settlement; 19 other countries also signed the peace treaty as guarantors thus finally bringing 12 years of civil war to an end. The advance mission of the United Nations Transitional Authority in Cambodia (UNTAC) arrived in Phnom Penh in November. Its task was to supervise the ceasefire, help demobilize 70 per cent of the various military groups, and assist a total of 350000 refugees to return home from camps along the Thai border. In addition, the United Nations had to work with the Supreme National Council (SNC) which now represented all the Cambodian factions and, where necessary, be responsible for certain government functions. Its longer-term objective was to help organize free elections for a Constitutional Assembly to be held in 1993 to draft a national human rights charter. The first UN personnel began to arrive in Cambodia in December 1991. Meanwhile, countries which had refused to recognize the Phnom Penh (communist) government now returned to resume diplomatic relations and in mid-November Sihanouk was made head of a transitional government. UNTAC became fully functional in Cambodia during January–March 1992 under its chief coordinator, the Japanese diplomat Yasushi Akashi. The Security Council approved a force of 16000 UN troops with an additional 3600 police and other civilian staff. UNTAC was expected to cost the UN US$2 billion.[1]

The following 15 months were dangerous and uncertain as the Khmer Rouge withdrew from the new arrangement and continued fighting against the government forces from the areas they controlled. UNTAC operated entirely within Chapter VI of the UN Charter – that is, by persuasion and consent of the parties and without coercion. The Khmer Rouge, however, would not cooperate and would not allow UNTAC personnel into the areas under its control. Nevertheless, the Secretary-General insisted that UNTAC should continue despite the non-cooperation of the Khmer Rouge. This meant that little progress could be made disarming the various groups since they were not prepared to lay down their arms unless the Khmer Rouge did so as well. The Khmer Rouge argued that the two million Vietnamese settlers in Cambodia were in reality troops and said it would not take part in the elections scheduled for May 1993. The Security Council, however, insisted that the elections would proceed with or without the Khmer Rouge. In December 1992 the Khmer Rouge took several dozen UN personnel hostage although they were all to be released later.

Despite these problems and much foreign criticism of UNTAC, in January 1993 the Secretary-General was able to report that 4.4 million Cambodians who represented more than 90 per cent of the electorate, had registered and that most of the 360 000 refugees had returned to their homes. The elections were held as planned during 23–28 May and there was a 90 per cent turnout of voters; UNTAC pronounced the elections to have been free and fair. The result gave Prince Sihanouk's FUNCINPEC 58 seats and Hun Sen's CPP 51 seats and after some allegations of fraud all the participants agreed to accept the results.[2] The Provisional National Government of Cambodia (PNGC) was established on 1 July, led by Norodom Anariddh and Hun Sen; the PNGC excluded the possibility of cooperation with the Khmer Rouge which had not taken part in the elections and later in the year the Cambodian National Army (CNA) launched an offensive against Khmer Rouge positions.

In August UNTAC began to withdraw its military personnel from the country (there were then more than 20 000 UN troops in Cambodia) and the whole UNTAC exercise was brought to a conclusion by 15 November 1993, ending one of the largest operations in the history of the United Nations. A small UN presence remained in Cambodia; it consisted of military police, medical personnel, a mine-clearing unit and a military liaison team.[3] 'But the UNTAC operation, whatever the future may bring, must be accounted a notable success against heavy odds. It had cost fifty-two UNTAC lives and $1.5 billion.'[4] That judgement, however, raises questions about what happens as opposed to what is supposed to happen after such a UN operation is concluded and its personnel withdrawn. By the end of 1995, two years after the withdrawal of UNTAC, the government was dominated by Hun Sen and the former communists rather than Prince Sihanouk's party and was becoming increasingly authoritarian while opposition was being intimidated or persecuted. But there was peace, of a kind.

CENTRAL AMERICA

The United States, which for nearly two centuries has treated Central and South America as its 'backyard' and warned off other powers from interference, has shown itself equally anxious to prevent the United Nations from involvement in the region, even though many of the problems of instability, poverty, violence and civil war that have characterized Central America since 1945 have been the obvious concern of the United Nations elsewhere in the world. American readiness to intervene, when it has believed its interests to be at stake, has been matched by its lack of finesse: the exercise of power has been absolute and crude – as in Guatemala, Cuba, the Dominican Republic, Nicaragua, Grenada or Panama. In the case of Cuba, which actually did manage to turn communist before the United States could prevent it, their enmity has come close to paranoia. Washington has either acted unilaterally, through the Organization of American States (OAS) which it dominates or by means of friendly governments in the region. This, arguably, is doubly ironic since the 20 countries of Latin America formed the first major bloc in the United Nations at the time of its inception and many of them have long resented American interference in their affairs.

The 1980s witnessed widespread violence in Central America, particularly in Guatemala, Nicaragua and El Salvador; the decade also saw Washington use its veto eight times against resolutions relating to Nicaragua. More encouraging was the development of a regional consensus about peacekeeping with the formation in 1983 of the Contadora Group of countries consisting of Colombia, Mexico, Panama and Venezuela that did not wish to leave all the peacemaking initiatives to the United States. The region, in Maoist terms, was 'ripe for revolution' but Washington was determined to prevent a second Cuba. The next move towards a regional consensus came in 1987 when, under the leadership of President Arias of Costa Rica, the five Central American heads of state from Costa Rica, El Salvador, Guatemala, Honduras and Nicaragua reached what became known as the Esquipelas Agreements dealing with the subjects of national reconciliation, the ending of hostilities, democracy and free elections, ending aid to insurrections and not allowing rebels from one state to operate from the territory of another. The five then asked the OAS and the United Nations to be ready to verify elections by participating in an International Verification and Follow-up Commission (CIVS). On 12 December 1989, at San Jose, Costa Rica, the five presidents called upon the United Nations to extend its peacekeeping efforts to El Salvador. Less than three weeks later the General Assembly voted by 75–20 with 35 abstentions to 'strongly' deplore the US invasion of Panama which had taken place on 20 December. Despite Panama, however, the end of the

Cold War and the readiness through 1990 of the five permanent members of the Security Council to cooperate over the crisis in the Gulf, which had been sparked off by the Iraqi invasion of Kuwait, meant that Washington was marginally more receptive to UN initiatives in the region than ever before. Over the next few years, in relation to Nicaragua, El Salvador and Haiti, the United Nations did become involved in the region and perhaps more important than its limited achievements was the creation of what in essence was a virtually new precedent that, as with other trouble-spots worldwide, the United Nations ought to be called in to assist in finding solutions instead of being sidelined by a power-jealous Washington.

In 1989, at the request of Nicaragua and the OAS, the United Nations despatched a civilian observer group and a military mission to supervise the elections of 25 February 1990. This was the first UN Observer Group to supervise an election in an independent country and the the first in Latin America. The Secretary-General's personal representative, Elliott Richardson, reported that the campaign and election of Violeta Barrios de Chamorro as President of Nicaragua was generally fair. On 27 March the Security Council then enlarged the UN Observer Group in Central America so that it could supervise the disarmament and demobilization of the Nicaraguan rebel groups (Contras) before the inauguration of Chamorro. The group consisted of 260 unarmed observers equipped with helicopters and light planes to monitor the Central American governments' commitment not to aid the 11 000 Nicaraguan Contra forces then based in Honduras. Given that these had been funded and armed by the United States, this represented a radical advance for the United Nations' Central American presence. As a result of the success of this operation, the government of Haiti requested both the United Nations and the OAS to send observers and provide aid to promote fair elections there the following December and the United Nations subsequently sent 130 observers to Haiti.

The United Nations also contributed to peace moves in El Salvador. Just before his term as Secretary-General came to an end, Perez de Cuellar persuaded the El Salvador government and the rebel Farabundo Marti National Liberation Front (FMLN) guerrillas to agree to end their 12-year civil war by 1 February 1992. Later, on 16 October 1992, the government and the rebels agreed to accept a UN proposal to redistribute 163 000 hectares of land to 47 500 peasants and fighters from both sides, a move which saved the peace accords. In 1993 the UN 'Commission on the Truth' found that active and retired military officers had been responsible for killing thousands of civilians during the 12-year civil war. The Commission called on the government to dismiss them and ban them from leadership posts for ten years. Further, the Commission considered 22 000 cases of alleged violence. It suggested that the former US UN ambassador, Jeanne Kirkpatrick, and the former US Secretary of State, Alexander Haig, both of whom had denied such claims, defended the El Salvador government and justified providing it with aid, were either cynical or badly misinformed. The importance of these accusations lies less in their justification than in the fact that they were being made on the ground in Central America by a United Nations Commission on the Truth in what, traditionally, had been a 'closed area' for political interference apart from the United States itself. These UN interventions in Central America had, at best, a marginal effect upon actual policies taking place on the ground. What gave them significance was the fact that here the United Nations was clearly engaged in one of its primary tasks: that of protecting the rights of the weak against more powerful nations.

HAITI

Haiti, the first independent black state, has had a troubled history. Under the Duvalier family – 'Papa Doc' and 'Baby Doc' – and their much feared *Tontons Macoutes* police the state was run by a corrupt oligarchy from the 1950s until the overthrow of 'Baby Doc' in 1986. But little seemed to change until widespread demonstrations in 1990 forced the 19-member Council of State to promise free elections for December of that year and it was to monitor these that the Haiti government requested a UN observer group. A young, charismatic Roman Catholic Priest, Jean-Bertrand Aristide, won the elections. The former supporters of Duvalier mounted a coup attempt in January 1991 but this failed when the army refused to back it and Aristide became President of Haiti on 7 February 1991.[5]

Like other reformers of the left, Aristide succeeded in annoying and threatening too many interest groups too quickly without first ensuring that he had the power (in the form of army backing) to be able to make his reforms stick and in September 1991 rebel troops seized Aristide and persuaded the army chief of staff to take power. Aristide was expelled from Haiti. He appealed to both the Organization of American States and the United Nations to help restore him. He warned the Security Council in October that illegal takeovers could 'murder democracy' and thanked the international community for its support. At this stage the UN Security Council supported OAS efforts to restore democracy in Haiti. On 11 October the General Assembly unanimously demanded Aristide's return to office, the restoration of constitutional rule and full observance of human rights. A new problem had arisen, meanwhile, as thousands of Haitian 'boat people' fled the island; the

UN High Commissioner for Refugees attempted to resettle them in other Caribbean islands.

Aristide was to remain an exile through 1992 while Marc Bazin, a presidential candidate in 1990, was sworn in as prime minister of Haiti in June with a mandate to negotiate a settlement with the exiled Aristide. The figurehead president, Joseph Nerette, resigned once Bazin had been sworn in so as to leave the post vacant for Aristide. Only the Vatican recognized this new regime. In September representatives of this army-backed regime met with Aristide and it was agreed that 18 members of the OAS should go to Haiti to monitor human rights violations. Meanwhile, tens of thousands of Haitians applied for US political asylum and headed for Florida by boat. The United States, however, claimed that they were economic refugees and repatriated them. The army commander, General Raoul Cedras, continued as the effective ruler of Haiti at this time.

Efforts to restore Aristide to power were pursued through 1993. After the joint representative of the OAS and the United Nations, Dante Caputo (a former Argentinian Foreign Minister), warned that they would not be recognized, the 18 January elections for the Senate were boycotted by the opposition parties. On 8 June Prime Minister Marc Bazin resigned having failed to replace four ministers. Then, on 12 June, the Congress formally recognized the legitimacy of the deposed Aristide but made his return to Haiti as President conditional on his acceptance of the acts of the military government since his overthrow. On 27 June 'proximity talks' were held on Governor's Island, New York, between Father Aristide and General Cedras who signed an agreement to permit Aristide to return to Haiti. UN personnel were now supposed to assist the return to democracy by separating the police force from the army but when a US troop ship carrying 194 American and 25 Canadian instructors and military engineers arrived at Port-au-Prince on 11 October thugs protected by the police prevented the instructors from landing. The United States and the United Nations then said they would not return until the military authorities in Haiti guaranteed their safety. When Cedras made plain that he would not resign, the Security Council, under Resolution 841, instituted a worldwide arms and oil embargo which was to be enforced by an international fleet from 16 October. On 28 October Aristide addressed the General Assembly; he asked the United Nations to impose a total trade embargo on Haiti until Cedras had been forced from power. On 6 December the General Assembly called for Aristide's restoration to office and a return to democracy in Haiti.

On 6 May 1994, the Security Council adopted Resolution 917 which increased sanctions against Haiti; the Council said these would not be lifted until the military had created the proper environment for the deployment of the proposed UN Mission in Haiti (UNMIH). On 31 July the Security Council adopted Resolution 940 authorizing member states to form a multinational force and to use all necessary means to bring about the departure of the military and the reinstatement of Aristide as president. On 19 September, US troops landed unopposed in Haiti; they were followd by 60 UN observers. The OAS/UN representative, Dante Caputo, then resigned on the grounds that the United States had acted unilaterally. On 29 September the Security Council lifted sanctions. Despite the presence of US troops in Haiti, attacks upon pro-Aristide demonstrators were made by the Haiti military, virtually unhindered by the occupying forces. However, the junta leaders whom Aristide had pardoned under amnesty left Haiti on 10 October and Aristide arrived aboard a US aircraft on 15 October. On 15 November the UN Secretary-General, Boutros-Ghali, visited Haiti to discuss the multinational force that was to take over from the US troops preparatory to elections in 1995. Under Resolution 975 of 30 January 1995, the Security Council authorized the transfer of military responsibility for Haiti from the US-led multinational force to the UN Mission in Haiti by 31 March. The Security Council claimed that a secure and safe environment then existed for the deployment only of UNMIH. By June, 1996, the Secretary-General proposed to cut the UNMIH force to 1200 troops and 300 police.

Throughout the Haiti crisis the United Nations had to step warily because of American susceptibilities. Although there could be no argument about the unconstitutionality of the military coup or of President Aristide's legitimacy, he was not a political figure who garnered much sympathy in Washington where he was seen as too left wing. Moreover, any military intervention in Haiti, other than by the United States, would be regarded with extreme reserve in Washington since the country had always been seen as totally inside the US sphere of influence and control. As a result, the UN operation was carefully geared to allow the United States to take the lead, which it did to the extent that the Argentinian UN representative, Dante Caputo, saw fit to resign. Nonetheless, Aristide was restored to power and the United States was then prepared to step back and allow UNMIH to take a central position of responsibility. In UN terms the Haiti exercise provided an object lesson in how to work through the regional powers – in this case the OAS and the United States.

*   *   *

All-pervasive American power and influence dominate crises in the Western Hemisphere. In this respect Cuba provides the acid test of Washington's tolerance levels. Fidel Castro's successful defiance of Washington for more than 30 years, the abortive and humiliating Bay of Pigs invasion attempt, the fact that through the last three decades of the Cold War Cuba proudly proclaimed itself a communist state, the 1962 missile crisis that brought the world as near as it has ever been to a nuclear war, the justification of the US invasion of Grenada in 1983 on the grounds that the Cubans were turning it into an anti-American base and Cuba's highly successful military intervention in Angola have, between them, shaped US attitudes towards Havana and led Washington to maintain a ruthless, internationally illegal blockade of the island for more than 30 years. For most of this period the Central and South American states have accepted, with varying degrees of protest or reluctance, US rigidities over Cuba although periodically they have revolted. In a debate of 24 November 1992, the General Assembly voted 59–3 (the US, Israel and Romania), with 79 abstentions, for the United States to end its 30-year embargo against Cuba. The exercise was repeated on 26 October 1994, when the voting was 101–2 with 48 abstentions. Aware of its isolation on this issue, the United States continues to demonize Castro and Cuba and in February 1996, for example, called an emergency meeting of the Security Council after the shooting down by the Cuban airforce of two Miami-based private light aircraft flown near the Cuban coast. While US Secretary of State Warren Christopher described the incident as a 'blatant violation' of international law, the Cuban government insisted the planes had been shot down over its territorial waters after ignoring warnings from Havana airport.[6] Later in the year the United States provoked its European allies over the issue of Cuba when it proposed to prosecute foreign businessmen who traded or invested in Cuba. Whatever the provocations, the United States has persistently ignored international law in its treatment of Cuba and behaved like a major bully, yet the United Nations, which ought to have adopted far stronger attitudes towards Washington over its Cuba policies, has as a general rule remained muted if not silent. It is a question of power.

What is most interesting and encouraging about these United Nations interventions in Central America is the fact they have taken place at all. The big powers like to act without the United Nations and, historically, this has been especially true of the United States which, at best, has been a lukewarm supporter of the UN idea. Again, certain lessons can be learned. The most obvious one is that deadlocks can best be broken when it suits a major power to alter its stand or policy. The end of the Cold War made it easier for the United States to accept UN interventions in Central America because it no longer saw the crises there solely in terms of Moscow-backed communism against American interests. The result, at the beginning of the

1990s, has been a slow if reluctant American acceptance of a growing UN role in the region. The United Nations, from long experience, has shown an increasing capacity to walk on a knife-edge between two conflicting, though not necessarily incompatible, sets of interests: those of the United States in a region which it has always seen as its own exclusive zone of influence and those of its own (UN) responsibilities.

8   Compromises

Politics, the art of the possible, is about compromises and nowhere is this more true than in the United Nations. Essentially, of course, the compromises are always about power and convenience: how much can those with more power be persuaded to make concessions to those with less power and what arguments are most persuasive and why? When the five permanent members of the Security Council insisted upon awarding themselves the power of veto at the San Francisco deliberations which brought the United Nations into being this was a double-edged acknowledgement of power: on the one hand, the big five – the United States, the USSR, Britain, France and China – had emerged the victors in World War II to become the arbiters of the new world – their authority (and military might) were unique and extraordinary and no one was in a position to deny their demand; on the other hand, their insistence upon the right of veto was also a tacit admission of their fear of the majority, the fact that in the coming years their apparently overriding power would, inexorably, be whittled down and reduced.

Given the circumstances of the time and the big-power rivalries which then existed the veto was probably inevitable but much of the subsequent UN story has concerned the struggle by the General Assembly to wrest more decision making powers from the Security Council to compensate for the powers of veto held by the five permanent members. Between 1945 and 1985, the membership of the United Nations grew from the original 51 to 158 and the great majority of these new members, especially after 1955, belonged to what came to be called the Third World, later the South. They were, in other words, predominantly poor developing countries, newly independent nations of the former European empires, and their independence had been greatly assisted and accelerated by the United Nations. These new nations, almost automatically, saw themselves as members of the Third World and so sought to strengthen Third World influences in the United Nations which they regarded as the natural forum where the weak majority could put its case to the big powers. They were to be so successful at using the General Assembly and the various specialized agencies as instruments for advancing their views that they created a backlash among the old-established nations: Britain and France, as the leading imperial powers, found themselves constantly on the defensive in an age in which empires were in retreat; while the United States, which had taken upon itself the burden of defending the 'free world' against the communist 'threat', found the endless criticisms and pinpricks of the non-aligned especially irksome. Thus, right from the beginning, there has been a division between the interests of the great powers and the interests of the rest. The consequence of this division has been to foster a tendency on the part of the big powers to see the United Nations as an irrelevancy or at best an irritant to be overruled or ignored rather than as an instrument of policy through which to achieve results.

The weak majority, on the other hand, have seen the United Nations in a very different light. Apart from acting as a forum for their views, the General Assembly has enabled them to exert pressures upon the big powers, over issues such as decolonization or apartheid, in ways that became increasingly difficult to bypass or ignore. Slowly yet relentlessly, a kind of 'drip drip' approach across the years, the majority gradually converted the United States and the European Union to the need to apply sanctions against apartheid South Africa. Similarly, in relation to Rhodesia, it seems likely, in the retrospect of history, that had there been no United Nations (and no Commonwealth), Britain, after suitable hand-wringing protestations against racism and pleas of incapacity, would have allowed the Smith regime to get away with its illegal declaration of independence. The United Nations could not force Britain to send troops to Rhodesia to resume imperial control but it could, with its relentless and often subtle pressures, shame her into not actually relinquishing responsibility and this is what happened. Later, when the white minority was losing the guerrilla war, Britain was forced to take more positive action. Such pressures are almost impossible to quantify but without them the story of imperial decolonization over the years 1950 to 1980 would have been very different and probably a good deal more sanguinary as well.

The long stalemate of the Cold War blinded people to the importance of the United Nations even when it appeared least effective. The fact that the United Nations was unable to solve the world's most dangerous problems; that the Soviet Union, in a permanent minority position, was forced constantly to cast its veto; that confrontation rather than consensus characterized the activities of the Security Council; or that Soviet Premier Nikita Khrushchev could bang his shoe on his desk while Britain's Prime Minister, Harold Macmillan, addressed the General Assembly, convinced many people that the world body was no more than a useless talking shop. This was not true for the talking was far from useless and the constant airing of Cold War problems in New York familiarized the world with the obstacles to peace and development that needed to be overcome. That alone was an achievement as it was also an achievement to keep the two sides talking since, to quote Winston Churchill's famous aphorism, 'to jaw jaw is better than to war war'. By the mid-1980s even the superpowers found they could not ignore the activities and opinions of the United Nations and by the early 1990s, with the end of the Cold War, it had been given a new lease of life.

As the Cold War recedes into the past there is a real danger that the major powers will simply revert to the older pattern of behaviour in pursuit of their interests that they followed prior to World War I and ignore, or attempt to ignore, the United Nations altogether. Alternately, they might use the United Nations only when they believe it can be manipulated to their advantage. These possibilities are immediate and real and there is a consequent danger that the United Nations Secretariat and Secretary-General will be tempted to fudge, ignore or play down issues so as not to offend powers whose backing they seek for other more important policies or, indeed, simply to keep the world body alive and working. It may be tempting to accept a *fait accompli* that is unjust instead of insisting upon a confrontation with an influential member state. Or, it may seem more practicable to acquiesce in sanctions against a maverick state like Libya, even when the evidence no longer justifies such action, rather than go against the wishes of the United States, Britain and France. Politics may be the art of the possible; it should not also be reduced to such a level of pragmatism that the United Nations ceases to stand for any principles. On a number of issues since 1990 overt pragmatism has replaced principle; if the process continues it will do irreversible damage to the United Nations.

WESTERN SAHARA

This bleak stretch of desert on the Atlantic seaboard of North Africa may seem an unlikely candidate for United Nations fudging with its tiny population and limited resources yet, too often, it is precisely such irritating and seemingly unimportant problems that lend themselves to injustice since the world at large is uninterested in their fate and a neighbouring power on the spot is most likely to triumph through perseverance, whatever the justice of the case.

Spain had assumed full colonial control of the territory of Rio de Oro or Spanish Sahara in 1934. In 1956, on becoming independent from France, Morocco claimed both Spanish Sahara and Mauritania to its south. In the years that followed Moroccan forces were to enter Spanish Sahara; representatives of parts of Spanish Sahara would pledge allegiance to Morocco; and Mauritania, which became independent in 1960, repudiated Moroccan claims to its territory. In 1967 Spain announced that it favoured self-determination for its territory and the United Nations then urged Spain to hold a referendum (in consultation with Morocco and Mauritania) as to the territory's future. Fighting against the Spanish colonialists broke out in 1970 at El Aaiun when many people were killed and the United Nations again called for a referendum. When, in 1973, the United Nations passed a resolution calling upon Spain to grant independence to its Sahara territory the resolution suggested that both Morocco and Mauritania should be involved in a referendum upon its future, a tacit admission that both had claims upon the region. King Hassan of Morocco then attempted to pre-empt an impartial referendum by saying he would only agree if it did not include the question of independence which would have made the exercise pointless. In November 1975 Spain set up a tripartite administration for the territory with Morocco and Mauritania and announced it would cease to administer it on 28 February 1976, thus setting the stage for Morocco and Mauritania to take over.

In the meantime a number of nationalist movements emerged in the territory itself and of these the Popular Front for the Liberation of Saguia al-Hamra and Rio de Oro (Polisario) was to become the most important and lasting. Their demands for an end to Spanish rule led Spain to declare a state of emergency in 1972. A ruling of the World Court of October 1975 laid down that when the territory became a Spanish colony it belonged to the people who lived there although the clarity of this judgement was spoiled by an addition which stated that legal ties also existed between the territory and its two neighbours. On 6 November 1975, King Hassan of Morocco launched his famous 'Green March' of 350000 Moroccans who marched peacefully into Western Sahara as far as El Aaiun before being halted by Spanish troops. Spain, by this time, simply wished to extricate itself from an embarrassing colonial problem and pressured the Djemaa (Assembly) to approve a joint Moroccan-Mauritanian takeover. On 27 February 1976, the day before the Spanish departure, the Polisario proclaimed the Saharan Arab Democratic Republic (SADR) and the stage was set for 15 years of warfare.

At first the Polisario found itself fighting the Moroccans in the north and the Mauritanians in the south; over the years it was to obtain assistance from Algeria and Libya. In 1979, however, Mauritania withdrew from the contest: it was too weak and had too many internal problems of its own, leaving Polisario to fight the far more formidable forces of Morocco. By 1982 Morocco had gained control of the principal centres of population – El Aaiun, Smara and Bojador – as well as the huge phosphate deposits at Bou Craa and by 1984 had built more than 600 km of defensive walls round much of the territory including as far south as the border with Mauritania. By the mid-1980s this intensive little desert war had taken on Cold War dimensions with Morocco accusing both Algeria and Libya of providing Polisario with Soviet-made missiles and suggesting that East German or Cuban advisers were assisting the Polisario, an accusation calculated to obtain US sympathy for the Moroccan cause, especially as Morocco was seen in Washington as one of the very few stalwart pro-Western Arab states in a largely unreliable Arab world.

In August 1988 Morocco and Polisario accepted a UN plan for a ceasefire and referendum which would give the people of Western Sahara the choice between independence and integration into Morocco but this first UN effort broke down and fighting was resumed in 1989. After further negotiations at Geneva during June 1990 the United Nations announced that a referendum would be held in 1991 at an estimated cost of US$250 million. Renewed fighting led to another postponement until January 1992 and 1700 UN monitors were sent to the territory to prepare the referendum. However, in January 1992 the referendum was again postponed at Moroccan insistence. On 16 October 1992, after flooding the territory with new settlers, Morocco held elections in it. Morocco effectively defeated the UN plan for a referendum by objecting to the voting lists (even though it had accepted the presence of MINURSO, the UN peacekeeping force) because it argued that an additional 120000 names should be added to the 74000 derived from the 1974 Spanish census. When the United Nations warned that it would withdraw at the end of 1992 if no agreement had been reached this was tantamount to ceding a Moroccan victory. In February 1993, however, Polisario threatened to renew the fighting to prevent a UN legitimization of the Moroccan claim to the territory and this threat forced the Security Council to pass a new resolution, number 809 of 2 March 1993, again calling for a referendum.[1]

In his report of 24 November 1993, to the Security Council, the Secretary-General, Boutros-Ghali, said the referendum would again have to be postponed to mid-1994 as deadlock between Morocco and the Polisario as to the eligibility of voters in the referendum still persisted. Thus, for 1993, the UN Mission for the Referendum in Western Sahara (MINURSO) was reduced to monitoring the current ceasefire; in September Britain withdrew its personnel from MINURSO. Almost no progress was made through 1994, due to delaying tactics by Morocco, and by November the Secretary-General was obliged to state that the referendum would (or perhaps might) be held in October 1995. The Algerian President, General Zeroual, angered Morocco when he referred to Western Sahara as 'an illegally occupied country', a bluntness of language avoided by the United Nations.[2]

In world terms the story of Western Sahara hardly rates headline news but it does illustrate a potentially fatal failing of the United Nations and one it is important to understand. Given the huge problems it constantly faces, there is a growing tendency on the part of the United Nations to allow the more powerful, influential members of the world body to get away with claims, if only by default, that would not be permitted in other circumstances. Morocco has behaved with blatant opportunism over Western Sahara and whenever a possible solution that it did not favour was in sight, has changed the rules. It has made it absolutely plain that it will only abide by a UN resolution that works in its favour and since the Polisario now has no major world backers – not because its cause is necessarily unjust but because the advantages of supporting it are so manifestly less attractive than those of not offending Morocco – there is a real possibility that its claims will be overlooked in order to appease Rabat. If the United Nations will behave in such a manner in relation to Morocco, a minor actor on the world stage, how much more will it bend the rules and its principles on behalf of the big powers?

LIBYA

Libya's leader, Colonel Muammar al-Gaddafi, has long been regarded with suspicion by the leading Western powers, and most notably the United States which has constantly searched for ways to humiliate Gaddafi or force him from power. Western anger at Gaddafi goes back to the time when he came to power in 1969 as the result of a coup. It was his determination to take effective control of Libya's oil resources which gave the Organization of Petroleum Exporting Countries (OPEC) 'teeth' and persuaded the other Arab oil states to follow suit, thus setting off the oil crisis of 1973. Gaddafi's oil revenues enabled him to support a wide range of nationalist and more dubious causes round the world to the consistent embarrassment of the West. Moreover, he always acted as though Libya had as much right to intervene in world affairs as did the United States and for this he was not forgiven. He came, instead, to be regarded as a permanent thorn in Washington's flesh and was also demonized, though to a somewhat lesser extent, in Britain.

An excuse to strike at Gaddafi occurred in 1986 when a terrorist bomb killed a US serviceman in a Berlin discotheque. The bomb was blamed on Gaddafi terrorists and the air raid which the United States then mounted against Libya was the culmination of a long period of US frustrations at Gaddafi's tactics in support of terrorists. On the night of 14–15 April 1986, US bombers flying from bases in Britain and from aircraft carriers of the US Sixth Fleet in the Mediterranean bombed targets in Tripoli and Benghazi in Libya. Total casualties (dead) came to 130, both civilian and military, and included Gaddafi's adopted daughter. If the purpose of the raid had been to topple

Gaddafi it failed; instead, it enabled the Libyan leader to describe President Reagan as the world's number one terrorist. A majority of states, including all those of the Third World, condemned the raid which raised awkward questions about US behaviour and use of its power. It was also suggested that the United States had attacked Libya – as opposed to Syria or Iran (which Washington also regarded as 'terrorist' states) – because Libya was a 'soft target' and not able to retaliate. The United States, in any case, had claimed that the bombing was precise, aimed at military targets, when in fact it damaged civilian targets and killed civilians. In the event, the raid did more damage to the image of the United States than to Libya while the setback to American prestige by such a failed exercise of power possibly explains later US attitudes in relation to the Lockerbie bomb.

On 21 December 1988, a terrorist bomb on Pan American flight 103 over Lockerbie in Scotland killed all 270 people aboard the plane, including the crew. Western outrage was justified but the subsequent determination to pin the blame on Gaddafi outran the evidence. By November 1991 three Western governments – the United States, Britain and France – had combined to present a package of demands to be made upon Libya, the principal of which was the handover of two Libyans believed to be responsible for planting the bomb on the Pan American flight. The Western powers made plain that if their demands were not met they would have recourse to 'all necessary means' which clearly implied the threat of force. They also demanded compensation for the crash victims and a Libyan renunciation of terrorism. The United Nations was now requested to make the already existing EC embargo against Libya worldwide. At the same time the Western nations decided to ask for a UN resolution demanding that Libya should comply with these Western requests. At that stage in the Lockerbie drama, when the two Libyan suspects had only been indicted for the crime in the West, such a demand for their handover would not for a moment have been tolerated by other more powerful countries while neither the United States nor Britain would have contemplated for a moment handing over their nationals to Libya, had the positions been reversed; instead, they would have argued that their nationals could not expect a fair trial. As the British newspaper, the *Independent*, asked in a leader: 'Ought great powers to threaten diplomatic and ultimately military sanctions to enforce what are only indictments, not convictions, in their domestic courts? ... What is needed is a sense of proportion in the enforcement of national law abroad and a new respect for international law.'[3] What was becoming increasingly apparent was the disproportionate response of the United States and Britain in particular; they appeared to be focusing all their anti-Gaddafi grudges upon the Lockerbie case and expecting the United Nations to act as a policeman on their behalf.

By the middle of 1992 Libya had not complied with these Western demands and the West applied sanctions to it. The Libyan parliament, however, did say it would allow the Lockerbie bombing suspects to be heard by a 'fair and just' court chosen by the United Nations or the Arab League and agreed by Tripoli. The Western action now had more the appearance of a crusade against a particular Arab leader rather than a reasonable demand for justice while Western pressures upon the United Nations to act as a justifying cloak for these demands placed the world body at risk of losing any appearance of impartiality. On 15 April 1992, the Security Council imposed sanctions upon Libya for failing to hand over the two Lockerbie suspects; the following September Gaddafi called for direct talks with the United States and urged the Libyan legislature 'to negotiate directly with America' without going through the United Nations, a deserved snub to the world body in the circumstances. By and large, throughout its history, the United Nations has done its best to stand up for the rights of small nations against the arrogance of the great powers. There was no sign of this in relation to Libya and Lockerbie. The application of international law must be the same, and be seen to be the same, for everybody but as the Lockerbie dispute unfolded there were increasing signs that the three Western powers were prepared to twist and bend international law for their own convenience and, in relation to Gaddafi, for revenge as well while there were no signs of any UN effort to redress the balance.

The Lockerbie affair dominated Libya's external policies throughout 1993 with the United States demanding a general expansion of sanctions against Libya. In April the Security Council renewed the original sanctions for a further 120 days but although Washington attempted to impose an oil embargo on Libya this was resisted by Germany, Italy and Spain which are the main European importers of Libyan crude oil. In July France demanded tougher sanctions; then in August, after the Security Council had decided to maintain sanctions at their existing level, the United States, Britain and France issued an ultimatum to Libya that if the two Lockerbie suspects had not been handed over for trial by 1 October they would table a Security Council resolution to impose sanctions covering oil-related, financial and technical sectors in the Libyan economy. Libya did not comply with these Western demands and on 11 November the Security Council adopted Resolution 883 freezing all Libyan assets abroad, banning the sale of equipment for the downstream oil and gas sectors and placing further restrictions on Libyan civil aviation. The sanctions meant new hardships for the Libyan people.

During 1994 new evidence emerged in both Britain and the United States which threw doubt on the alleged responsibility of Libya for the Lockerbie bombing;[4] these doubts raised fundamental questions about the justifications for continued UN sanctions against Libya. During 1995, despite renewals of sanctions by the Security Council, it became increasingly plain that the case against the two Lockerbie suspects was dubious at the very least and that it would be possible to make out equally strong cases against both Syria and Iran for responsibility for the bomb. But it was not in the interests of the West, and most notably the United States, either to reassess the case against Libya which had taken on the nature of a vendetta or to make accusations against Syria or Iran, and so the deadlock continued. The United Nations, however, showed no inclination to champion the rights of Libya (admittedly an unpopular state) since this would mean a clash with the United States, Britain and France. In respect to the Lockerbie case, United Nations compromises, which pander to the wishes of the big three Western powers, have done less than justice to Libya's case and, in consequence, have damaged rather than enhanced the image of the United Nations.

JUSTICE AGAINST WAR CRIMINALS

Justice against the perpetrators of inhuman cruelties in the wake of a war is as desirable as its implementation normally turns out to be both impracticable and unpragmatic. During August 1996 members of the NATO forces responsible for peacekeeping in Bosnia carefully avoided meeting the Bosnian Serb leader, Radovan Karadzic, who had been cited as a war criminal and was to be handed over to the United Nations tribunal in The Hague by anyone who apprehended him; they did not want to be embarrassed with the necessity of arresting him. Pragmatic political reasons dictated that he should be left at liberty whatever might be required by more abstract notions of absolute justice.

The United Nations did not fall into the trap of proclaiming Saddam Hussein of Iraq a war criminal to be arrested once Kuwait had been liberated or it would also have been saddled with the necessity of pursuing the war until all Iraq had been laid waste. In Somalia, by demonizing General Aideed, one of the principal actors in the civil war, the United Nations destroyed its ability to act impartially or to be seen any longer to occupy an impartial position. If adequate justice were to be done in relation to the terrible massacres that have rent Rwanda and Burundi apart, half the populations of those two desperate countries would qualify for investigation. President Aristide of Haiti was only returned to power, courtesy of US troops acting for the United Nations, after the coup-makers had been granted an amnesty and been permitted to leave the country unscathed. Inevitably, in these varying circumstances, the United Nations finds itself on the horns of a dilemma. The delivery of peace in the former Yugoslavia probably demands that such brutal figures as Radovan Karadzic and Ratko Mladic are allowed to continue free despite their known responsibility for ethnic cleansing brutalities and murders. It is a question of pragmatism versus principle and though many will raise their voices in anguish at the suggestion that such men should not be pursued and punished, the ultimate question is whether peace for everyone in a region that has suffered such terrible war horrors is not more important than the satisfaction of punishing guilty men.

The precedent for war crimes tribunals was set in the aftermath of World War II with the Nuremberg trials but, as Goering described the process of retribution, it amounted to 'victor's justice', and though the punishments handed out to the leading Nazis may indeed have been just, the principle was tarnished at once in Japan where the Emperor was excluded because of a political deal – he was seen as necessary for the victors' control of his conquered country. The United Nations, therefore, has to decide what precedents it should set in an age of apparently endless civil conflicts in which brutalities and war crimes are as monstrous as they have ever been. If it places pragmatism before principle as circumstances have dictated it should do in most of the cases cited here, then it must lay itself open to constant accusations of not caring about justice. If, on the other hand, it insists upon the principle of retribution for war crimes at any price it must ensure, first, that it commands the means to bring such men as Karadzic to book and, second, that it has the will. It becomes an obvious and damaging hypocrisy if the United Nations calls upon anyone with the means to arrest such figures (as with the NATO forces in Bosnia) if they deliberately ignore their responsibility for pragmatic reasons. Here is one of those many dilemmas for the United Nations which pits abstract principle against working pragmatism. There are no easy answers and in many such circumstances the United Nations will probably have to put up with accusations of hypocrisy while it pursues the most practicable solution available at the time.

9 Unfinished Business: Israel and Palestine

The creation of Israel in 1948 meant the destruction of the Palestinian Arab state and for that the United Nations must take full responsibility. Britain was the responsible authority in Palestine, having received the mandate for the territory from the League of Nations after World War I, and Britain retreated unilaterally from its responsibility in 1948, leaving Palestine to its warring factions. The United States, responding in part to its new role as the world's leading power and still more to its powerful Jewish lobby, became the champion of the new state of Israel, as it has remained ever since. If the deliberate intention of the powers in 1945 had been to destabilize the Arab Middle East for the next 50 years they could not have come up with any more effective means to that end than the creation of Israel. To place the problem in its starkest terms, the world community wanted to do justice by the Jews in restitution for centuries of anti-Semitism and the more recent and awful persecutions under Hitler which had culminated in the Holocaust; the only way they found of making such restitution was at the expense of the Palestinian Arabs and no amount of special pleading about the claims of Zionism or the fact that Palestine had once been the historical home of the Jews before the second diaspora under the Roman Emperor Hadrian in 135 AD can alter that fact. As Britain's post-war Prime Minister, Clement Attlee, said at the time, he could not understand how 2000 years of absence constituted a claim. He was never, as he put it, 'a great enthusiast for the idea that Palestine was the one place for the Jews'.[1] Over the next 50 years the Palestinian Arabs were to be treated as second-class citizens in their own land and as refugees or terrorists outside it; Israel was to behave as the 'Sparta' of the region, constantly using one of the world's most efficient war machines to destabilize its neighbours. There can be no lasting peace until a fully independent Palestinian state has been re-created and that remains the responsibility of the United Nations.

Despite the secret agreements reached by Israel and the PLO in Oslo during 1993 and the subsequent peace process which had all but foundered by 1996, the key to the conflict remains the Arab denial of the legitimacy of the claims upon which the state of Israel was founded in 1948: that historical possession of the territory up to the diaspora of 135 AD under the Romans justified the repossession of Palestine by the Jews 1800 years later. The fact that Palestine had first been occupied by the Arabs in 635 AD and was an entirely Arab land at the end of the nineteenth century when Zionism began to grow, was for Jews beside the point. The Austrian Jew, Theodor Herzl (1860–1905), became the leader of Zionism and the chief advocate of a modern Jewish state of Israel (in Palestine) and from 1880 onwards, as Jewish Zionist immigration into Palestine began to gather pace, so too did Arab hostility. In 1880 there were an estimated 25 000 Jews in Palestine; by 1914 the figure had risen to 90 000. Up to this point, however, Zionism remained a relatively slow-growing concept. It was to be given a major boost during World War I.

The Zionists, who had begun by appealing to Istanbul for permission to settle in Palestine, turned to Britain and France for a sympathetic hearing and it suited British considerations of *realpolitik* in 1917 (the worst year of World War I) to attract the support of the international Jewish community to the British war cause. The result was the Balfour Declaration of 2 November 1917, in the form of a letter from the British Foreign Secretary, Arthur Balfour, to the head of the Zionist Federation and leading British Jew, Lord Rothschild, in which Balfour made his famous and contradictory promise:

> His Majesty's Government view with favour the establishment in Palestine of a national home for the Jewish people, and will use their best endeavours to facilitate the achievement of this object, it being clearly understood that nothing shall be done which may prejudice the civil and religious rights of existing non-Jewish communities in Palestine, or the rights and political status enjoyed by Jews in any other country.

Balfour never explained how his promise to the Jews could possibly be made good without prejudice to the existing rights of the non-Jewish peoples of Palestine (the Arabs) who then constituted the overwhelming majority of the Palestinian population and had already made plain their opposition to further Jewish immigration.

The British mandate over Palestine, which was approved by the League of Nations on 24 July 1922, committed Britain to secure the establishment of a Jewish national home in Palestine, again, 'provided it did not prejudice the civil and religious rights of non-Jewish communities'. This condition was clearly unworkable and indicated right from the beginning the double standards that the League, Britain as the mandatory power and, later, the United Nations were to apply to this question, for at the time the mandate was applied 92 per cent of the inhabitants of Palestine were Arabs and they owned 98 per cent of the land. During the years of the mandate these ratios were to be changed fundamentally to the advantage of the Jews and to the

detriment of the Arabs. As early as 1920, two years before the mandate, Arabs
in Palestine had begun to attack Jewish settlements.

Arab–Jewish hostility mounted throughout the years of the mandate and
Britain failed at every attempt to obtain any kind of Arab–Jewish cooperation
since the two sides did not share any common ground. By 1928 there were
150000 Jews in Palestine as opposed to 600000 Arabs. The advent to power
in Germany of Hitler accelerated the rate of Jewish emigration to Palestine;
in response, the Arabs formed an Arab High Committee to oppose further
immigration. In 1936 a British Royal Commission recommended partition.
In 1937 the Arabs launched the Arab Revolt against both Jews and British
in Palestine and remained unswerving in their opposition to any legitimization
of Jewish control of Arab land. When World War II began there were
445000 Jews in Palestine, equivalent to 30 per cent of the population, against
more than one million Arabs. In Nazi-occupied Europe the extermination
of the Jews, the Holocaust, proceeded unchecked.

In 1937 the more extreme Jews who believed Britain had betrayed the
Zionist cause formed the Irgun Zvai Leumi (National Military Organization)
and when the war came to an end they turned to terrorist tactics against the
British in Palestine. The Stern Gang, another Jewish terrorist organization,
was also formed at this time. Meanwhile, leading Zionists who met at the
Biltmore Hotel in New York issued on 11 May 1942, what became a
fundamental statement of Jewish principle, the Biltmore Programme. In it
they demanded that Palestine should be opened to unrestricted Jewish
immigration, that the Jewish Agency should be in control of immigration
(and not the British), and that Palestine should be turned into a Jewish
Commonwealth. Any form of cooperation with the Palestinian Arabs was
not considered or mentioned even though they still formed the majority of
the people in Palestine. By 1945 the Jews had obtained influential and in the
end crucial American support for the creation of a Jewish state.

As World War II came to an end and revelations about the Holocaust
became widely known, sympathy for the Jewish cause greatly increased while
the Jews themselves determined to create a homeland at any cost. By 1945,
moreover, the British had come to accept that no compromise between Jews
and Arabs in Palestine was possible. Britain, therefore, gave way to mounting
Jewish and American pressures to allow unfettered Jewish immigration into
Palestine; by 1946 the Jewish population had reached 608000, equivalent
to 40 per cent of the total and would be up to 650000 on the eve of the birth
of Israel. Britain now found itself maintaining major forces in Palestine at
a time when war weariness and demands for demobolization made this
extremely politically unpopular at home. These forces were fighting both
Jewish and Arab terrorists and were under increasing international pressure,

primarily from the United States, to allow unlimited Jewish immigration, and though they attempted to control this more Jews continued to arrive illegally.

In 1947 Britain decided to refer the question of Palestine to the United Nations; it also made plain its intention to bring its mandate to an end and withdraw its troops from Palestine by 15 May 1948. The United Nations Special Commission on Palestine (UNSCOP) proposed partition or a form of federation; a modified form of partition was agreed by 29 November 1947, between Arabs and Jews and passed by the General Assembly. Under this plan 56 per cent of what had been an entirely Arab state was reserved for the new Jewish state while Jerusalem, home to three religions, was to be international and administered by the United Nations. Britain (as the mandatory power) objected that it would not accept a solution that had to be imposed by force. Escalating violence between Arab and Jew and between the Jews and the British then followed and the Arabs said they refused to accept the UN solution which they intended to oppose by force. The United Nations solution represented a victory for the Jews: it affirmed their right to establish a Jewish homeland in Palestine and it assigned to them over half the territory. By January 1948 Arab volunteers were arriving in Palestine to assist the Palestinian Arabs to fight the Jews; in April 1948 the Jews went on to the offensive forcing 400000 Arabs to evacuate Palestine as refugees. By 13 May the Zionist forces had occupied all the areas of Palestine that had been assigned to the Jews as well as capturing important positions in the Arab areas. Irgun Zvai Leumi then stormed the Arab village of Deir Yassin and massacred part of the population in a deliberate act of terrorism which produced a mass exodus of Arabs. At midnight on 14 May Britain brought its mandate to a close and the state of Israel was proclaimed. Both the United States and the USSR recognized the new state at once. On 15 May the regular forces of Egypt, Transjordan, Iraq and Lebanon moved into Palestine and the war of 1948 – the first Arab–Israeli war – was underway.

In terms of Jewish history, the centuries of anti-Semitism and the Holocaust, it could be argued that the creation of the state of Israel represented restitution for past wrongs. In terms of the Arab people of Palestine the creation of the state of Israel represented a total injustice imposed upon them by outside powers and sanctified by the newly created United Nations for reasons of world *realpolitik*. Nowhere else in the world have past wrongs been rectified in such a manner; in no other case have the majority people in a particular country seen their rights steadily eroded in order to placate incomers until they found themselves replaced in their own land or turned into refugees. The 1948 solution to the world Jewish problem gave rise to a new Middle East confrontation which not only ranged the new state of Israel against its

Arab neighbours but did so in such a way as to cast the Jews in the role of an extension or vanguard of Western power, backed primarily by the United States, in the centre of the Arab world. The result has been 50 years of grief and there is still no solution in sight.

In the years 1948 to 1990 there were four major Israeli–Arab Wars – that of 1948, the Suez War of 1956, the Six Day War of 1967, and the Yom Kippur War of 1973; there was also the Palestinian uprising in Jordan of 1970, the invasion of Lebanon by Israel in 1982, the 15-year civil war in Lebanon which began in 1975 and included both Israeli and Syrian interventions and then, towards the end of this period, the eruption of the *Intifadeh* in the West Bank from 1987 to 1990.

The war of 1948 produced eight months of fighting and ended in January 1949; only Jordan of the Arab states acquitted itself well militarily and the United Nations, having just created the state of Israel, condemned the Arab action from the outset. The Suez War of 1956 was really an 'end of empire' problem for Britain and France (Nasser was providing support for the FLN in Algeria) and Ben Gurion's Israel was happy to act in collusion with the two European powers in order to strike a blow at the Arab states whose resentment against Israel had grown steadily stronger since the defeat of 1949. Suez, in any case, became inextricably interwined with the Cold War. Israel, under pressure from both the United States and the USSR, for it had intended to hold on to the Sinai Peninsula which it had overrun, agreed to withdraw once the UN Emergency Force (UNEF) had been put in place. In summary, the Suez War resulted in a decline of British influence in the Middle East, the growth of Franco-Israeli ties, an increase of Soviet influence in the Arab world and a corresponding growth of American support for Israel. Nothing had been solved.

The Six Day War was the culmination of growing Arab determination to assist the Palestinians who had established a Palestine National Council (PNC) in 1964 which in its turn set up the Palestine Liberation Organization (PLO); the PNC charter stated that 'Palestine is the homeland of the Palestinian Arab people', and argued that the territory of Palestine under the old mandate was indivisible. Arab border violations of Israel escalated during 1966. By May 1967 Egypt, Jordan and Syria were in alliance preparatory to an attack upon Israel (while Iraqi forces had been moved into Jordan to support the proposed war), and so the Israeli military then carried out a brilliant series of pre-emptive strikes which destroyed the Arab air forces on the ground and gave Israel control of the Sinai Peninsula, the whole of Jerusalem, the West Bank of Jordan, the Gaza Strip and a strip of the Golan Heights of Syria. Israel now controlled 27000 square miles of territory as opposed to 8000 square miles in 1948 and in order to strengthen its hold on these newly acquired lands embarked upon a policy of creating Jewish settlements in them. On 22 November 1967, the UN General Assembly accepted Resolution 242 which became the basis of UN policy thereafter. Only Syria of the Arab states which had fought Israel rejected the idea of any compromise and the scene was set for a return match.

Resolution 242 was a compromise between supporters of Israel, which principally meant the United States, and supporters of the Arabs. Its most important clauses were the following: withdrawal of Israeli armed forces from territories occupied in the recent conflict; termination of all claims on states of belligerency and respect for the acknowledgement of the sovereignty, territorial integrity and political independence of every state in the area and their right to live in peace within secure and recognized boundaries free from threats or acts of force; and for achieving a just settlement of the refugee problem. This last statement in relation to the refugee problem did not, remotely, go far enough; rather, it was a lukewarm admission that the United Nations had some responsibility in relation to the Palestinians who wanted, and had the right to, a state of their own.

In mid-1973 there was no sign of any solution to the Arab–Israeli confrontation: not only had Israel not returned any of the territories it had taken in 1967; it had established some 50 civilian or paramilitary settlements in them. The Yom Kippur War which followed served several purposes. First, it broke the myth of Israeli invincibility, even though at the end the Israelis were in the ascendant, and it reduced Israel to more manageable proportions. As a result a more troubled Israel was prepared, at least in theory, to concede land to the Arabs in return for a working peace. Second, the war revealed the total commitment of the United States to Israel – they had flown massive supplies of munitions to Israel at a crucial point in the war to save the day for the Israeli military – while subsequently they built up Israeli strength to give it 'an edge over all Arab states in combination'.[2] Third, following from the US military commitment to Israel, the war inaugurated a period in which US policy became so bound up with providing support for Tel Aviv that by the 1990s (after the Gulf War of 1991) the United States found itself close to being execrated throughout the Arab world and this appeared increasingly to be the case even in countries such as Saudi Arabia with which it was supposedly in close alliance. Just before the Security Council Resolution 338 of 22 October 1973, calling for a ceasefire, the USSR had alerted airborne forces to fly to the battle zone and the United States had alerted its airborne forces in Europe. The United Nations, therefore, provided a way out of this confrontation for the two superpowers as it had provided one for Britain and France at the time of Suez.

The period from the Yom Kippur War to 1990 witnessed compromises on the part of the Arab states (or some of them) as they moved reluctantly towards acceptance of the *fait accompli* of Israel, and the growth of terrorist activity by the PLO and its offshoots on the one hand, and by the Israeli state, especially in southern Lebanon, on the other. From 1975 onwards Egypt worked to recover all its Sinai territory and achieved this by means of the Camp David Accords of 1978 which had been brokered by US President Jimmy Carter. At the same time, the 1970s witnessed the rise of the PLO, after the 1970 uprising in Jordan which forced it to move to Lebanon. At the 1974 Rabat Arab summit 20 Arab states recognized the PLO as the sole legitimate representative of the Palestinians, a position that King Hussein of Jordan was reluctantly compelled to accept although, up to that time, he had acted as spokesman for the Palestinians since the West Bank had been incorporated in Jordan from 1949 to 1967. Subsequently, he relinquished Jordan's claim to the West Bank.

Through the 1970s and 1980s Syria emerged as the Arab state which held the key to peace in the Middle East. Its interventions in Lebanon over these years and its switches of policy (from backing to opposing the PLO wing controlled by Yasser Arafat) always had the same object in view: to prevent Lebanon falling under Israeli domination. Similarly, Israeli interventions in Lebanon were part of a balancing act to offset Syria, whose armed forces had been completely re-equipped by the USSR following the Yom Kippur War, and to punish the PLO, the Hizbollah (Iranian-backed 'Party of God') or anyone else deemed to be collaborators with Israel's enemies. As the 1990s began Lebanon seemed set for increasing violence as Israel repeatedly launched attacks upon guerrilla targets in southern Lebanon and Syria remained in place, a sullen presence with an army of 25 000 troops. This was the situation when the Cold War came to an end and political parameters everywhere began to change.

By the time the Cold War came to an end the United States had so entrenched itself in the position of defender of Israel that any moves to break the Middle East deadlock could equally be seen as moves to make Washington change its stance. Until 1970, for example, the United States had never once used its veto in the Security Council; between 1970 and 1987 it cast 56 vetoes, mainly in relation to Palestine and South Africa and, according to Parsons, its second veto of July 1972 (of the moderate Egyptian motion deploring Israel's continued occupation of the territories seized in 1967) was a contributory cause of the Yom Kippur War since President Sadat, who had just expelled about 15 000 Soviet advisers from his country, had set out to test Washington's impartiality which he found totally wanting.[3] Throughout the Cold War the United States had come to regard Israel as an ally to be supported in all circumstances in a troubled region where Soviet influence was strong; in addition, its responses to Tel Aviv or the pressures of the Jewish lobby in the United States suggested that Israel rather than Washington actually made their joint policies. Certainly, by the end of the Cold War the general Arab expectation was that the United States would support Israel in virtually any circumstances.

On 17 February 1989, the United States vetoed a resolution approved by the other 14 members of the Security Council which deplored Israel's treatment of the Palestinians (by then the *Intifadeh* uprising was well underway) and later in the year (6 October) a General Assembly resolution condemning Israel's persistent violations of Palestinian rights was passed 140–2 (the United States and Israel) with six abstentions. By this time it was plain that if the United States stood by Israel almost no one else did. In 1990, with an astonishing display of subservience to Washington, the Security Council met in Geneva so that the United States was spared the need to decide whether or not to grant Yasser Arafat a visa to visit the United Nations. At Geneva Arafat accused Israel of 'waging a war of extermination on all fronts' against Palestinians; he asked the United Nations to require Israel to withdraw from the occupied territories. However, on 31 May the United States vetoed a Council resolution to send an investigating team to Israel following an upsurge of violence in which seven Gaza workers had been killed near Tel Aviv. Later in the year, following the killing of 17 Arabs at the al-Aqsa Mosque in Jerusalem, the Security Council twice requested Israel to allow a UN mission to investigate the incident but Israel refused. In May 1991 the Security Council called on Israel to stop deporting Palestinians from the occupied territories. On this occasion, the United States joined in a condemnation of Israeli actions for the third time in six months, since even Washington found Tel Aviv's tactics hard to defend at this time.

In September 1991 the United States embarked upon a major campaign on behalf of Israel to persuade the Assembly to repeal its resolution of November 1975 which had equated Zionism with racism. The Arab members wanted to delay the repeal until Israel had revealed good faith in the peace negotiations then being sponsored jointly by the United States and the USSR but American pressures were successful and on 16 December the Assembly voted 111–25, with 13 abstentions and 17 not participating, to revoke the resolution.

Despite this continuing, all-important American support, Israel probably felt less secure and more uncertain of its future in 1991, as world priorities were daily changing, than at any time in the previous several decades. Although the Gulf War witnessed the firing of Iraqi missiles into Israel to threaten its physical security, of far greater moment was the realization that

Israel was no longer a strategic necessity to the United States as Cold War absolutes receded. On 18 October Israel and the USSR resumed diplomatic relations after 24 years and Tel Aviv agreed, after a year of shuttle diplomacy by US Secretary of State James Baker, to a peace conference with its Arab neighbours to be held in Madrid. Washington, at this time, was taking a tough line with Israel and, for example, opposed further funding for new immigrants unless Israel ceased planting new settlements in the occupied territories. Israel showed no inclination to compromise, however, and on 17 December 1991, incurred major international censure by first expelling 415 Palestinians to a bleak buffer zone in southern Lebanon and then refusing to allow aid to be taken to them. The United States now appeared to be tying further aid to Israel to the peace process.

Israel stalled the peace process through 1992 while settling more Jews in the occupied territories; the June elections brought Labour under Yitzak Rabin to power. By this time the population of Israel consisted of 4.4 million Jews representing 85 per cent of the total. During the first half of 1993 violence in Gaza and the West Bank increased and the peace talks in Washington stalled; then on 30 August the world was startled by the news of the secret Oslo talks and on 13 September Israel and the PLO signed a peace agreement. The peace plan envisaged a total Israeli withdrawal from the Gaza Strip and the Jericho area by 13 April 1994 and the beginning of a five-year interim period of Palestinian self-government with a target of a more permanent settlement in 1999. The agreement met with mixed receptions: hardline Israelis saw it as the beginning of a 'sell-out' and hardline Palestinians saw it as a compromise that defeated their claims for full independence. The more general world reaction was one of hope that at last real progress was being made towards a full settlement. Subsequent violence on both sides and the assassination of Prime Minister Yitzak Rabin by an Israeli hardline fanatic on 4 November 1995, combined to bring the peace process into doubt though both sides insisted that it would continue.

The United Nations, which ought to have been at the centre of any peace process, had been largely sidelined. In 1993 the Secretary-General had welcomed the prospect of limited Palestinian self-rule by 1994 and then said that the United Nations was ready to assist with the implementation of the peace accord and that this would involve liaison with the World Bank, the IMF, the donor community and other organizations through a special coordinator.[4] A task force on development assistance for Gaza and Jericho was then established in response to requests from the PLO and Israel. UN inability to influence Israel had been illustrated earlier in 1993 when the Security Council avoided a head-on clash with Israel over the (415) deportees in Lebanon.

Although Yitzak Rabin, Shimon Peres and Yasser Arafat were the joint recipients of the Nobel Peace Prize for 1994, implementation of the peace process was another matter altogether as extremists on both sides sought to derail it. On 25 February a Jewish extremist, Dr Baruch Goldstein, opened fire on worshippers in the Ibrahimi Mosque in Hebron to kill 29 and wound 60, while Islamic militants killed about 100 Israeli civilians during the year so that support for the peace process among Israelis was steadily undermined. The UN response to this violence was Resolution 904 to establish a temporary contingent of observers, the Temporary International Presence in Hebron, which was deployed from May to August.

No one had expected the peace process to be easy and hardliners on both sides made sure it was constantly put in jeopardy. The January 1996 elections among Palestinians of the West Bank, the Gaza Strip and East Jerusalem were held in the aftermath of the Rabin assassination of the previous November. Yasser Arafat received overwhelming endorsement from the 750000 voters (75 per cent of those eligible to vote) as President of the Palestinian Council. A Paris donors' conference pledged US$865 million in economic assistance to the Palestinian people for 1996. In February further suicide bomb attacks upon Israelis led the government of Shimon Peres to put the country on a virtual 'war footing', closing off the West Bank and Gaza Strip so that 60000 Palestinians were unable to travel to their work in Israel. The United States, in the meantime, continued to broker talks between Israel and Syria but these were broken off by the Israelis following further suicide bomb attacks on 3–4 March. President Hafez al-Assad of Syria refused a personal telephone request by US President Bill Clinton to condemn the suicide attacks, maintaining that the bombers were exercising their right to liberate their occupied land. In April Israeli forces launched a major military action into southern Lebanon, claiming this was to protect its citizens from rocket attacks by the Hizbollah. On 18 April, as part of this exercise, Israeli artillery hit the Fijian headquarters of the UN Interim Force in Lebanon (UNIFIL) at Qana to kill 110 Lebanese civilians sheltering there. International outrage followed and, while Prime Minister Peres blamed the Hizbollah, opponents of Israel suggested it was calculated terrorism. The United States appeared reluctant, as always, to censure Israel yet reaction to the Qana masssacre was so great that it effectively forced the United States and the international community to adopt a more lively diplomatic role.[5] By then it had become an unfortunate fact that only an event such as the Qana massacre would galvanize the international community – for a time – into some kind of more active role.

The Israeli elections of May 1996 brought the hardliner, Binyamin Netanyahu of the rightwing Likud Party, to power as Prime Minister. His party had explicitly ruled out the eventual establishment of an independent Palestinian state. By mid-1996, therefore, nearly 50 years after the creation of Israel, the situation that existed could be summarized in the following terms: a new hardline Israeli government which explicitly opposed a Palestinian state had just come to power; Yasser Arafat (showing an increasing tendency towards authoritarian rule) was precariously entrenched in the West Bank where his position depended as much upon the goodwill of Israel as it did upon Arab support; the Hizbollah and other Arab guerrillas were as determined as ever to disrupt the peace process and seek full independence; the United States remained committed to maintaining Israel whatever policies it might adopt; and the United Nations remained ineffectively on the sidelines.

What was desperately needed was a new United Nations initiative and this was most likely to occur if Europe – especially Britain and France – were to break the deadlock by opposing the monopoly of the Middle East debate by the United States which by this time behaved as though it alone had the right to dictate or control the Middle East peace process. If a lasting peace is ever to be established a programme along the following lines will have to be adopted and enforced. First, Israel must be persuaded to withdraw from Lebanon as must Syria; this will only happen when Israel has also withdrawn from the Golan Heights and restored these to Syria. Second, Israel must withdraw completely from the West Bank and such a withdrawal must include the withdrawal of the Israeli settlements. Third, a fully independent Palestinian state comprising the Gaza Strip and the West Bank must be established and guaranteed by both the United Nations and the major powers. Fourth, Jerusalem must be returned to the status of an international city guaranteed by the United Nations. The United States remains the key to such a change and the United States must be persuaded to use its authority with Israel to force that state to come to terms with its Arab neighbours. Unless and until a settlement along these lines is established there will be no lasting peace at all. The United Nations created Israel and in consequence must guarantee its future; but the United Nations also effectively deprived the Palestinians of their rights in the land of their birth and it is its absolute responsibility to make restitution to them as in 1948 it made restitution to the Jews for the wrongs they had suffered in the past.

In the case of no other international problem has a solution depended so singly upon the attitude of one power, the United States, and since throughout the relevant years it has always been the most powerful nation it is understandable that the United Nations has bowed to American *force majeure*.

At one level the United Nations had no alternative since the combination of American power and the American veto meant that Washington would always have its way. In the 1990s, however, following the end of the Cold War, the situation has altered sufficiently radically for it to be possible to enforce a lasting solution (as outlined above); but that will only happen when the United Nations reasserts itself in relation to Washington and is supported in such a stand by the major European powers.

10 Combating World Poverty

The United Nations has had an economic role to play from its inception although this was not seen as its primary responsibility. Through the International Monetary Fund (IMF) and the World Bank, as well as various specialized agencies such as the United Nations Development Programme (UNDP), the Food and Agricultural Organization (FAO) or the United Nations High Commissioner for Refugees (UNHCR) the United Nations has undertaken to assist economies in trouble (through the IMF), to channel development funds including special concessionary funds (through the World Bank and its soft arm, the International Development Association or IDA) and technical assistance (through the UNDP), or to provide relief assistance through such agencies as the FAO (and its subsidiary the World Food Programme or WFP) and the UNHCR.

These economic activities have become a major aspect of all United Nations work and many of the poorest countries now look to the world body for various forms of assistance. Yet, apart from the World Bank and the IMF, the UN agencies have only limited funds at their disposal; they act as conduits for aid from donor nations and they publicize the problems of the world's poorest countries. As with so many other areas of international politics, the end of the Cold War has changed both the expectations of what the United Nations might do and the willingness or interest of its more affluent members to provide the necessary funds to make it effective. By the mid-1990s, therefore, we are faced with a number of questions: How effective is the United Nations in fighting world poverty? How much are United Nations anti-poverty activities really only a matter of rhetoric? The United Nations may exhort the rich to do more to assist the least developed but what can it actually deliver? The end of the Cold War has witnessed a sharp diminution of interest on the part of the major donors in providing aid for the least developed countries (LDCs). Will the trend continue or can the United Nations persuade the advanced economies to provide at least a minimum of economic assistance – not necessarily in the form of aid – that will allow the LDCs to overcome some of the most difficult hurdles which they face?

One of the incipient tragedies of the 1990s is the growing polarization that is taking place between the advanced economies and the poorest nations even at a time when the possibility of a one-world society becomes increasingly practicable. While there is much talk of a global village or global partnership there are also many indications that the world is entering upon a new economic era in which the capacity to operate anywhere in the world makes the notion of national companies, and even national economies, appear increasingly obsolete. Such developments may be welcome but, it seems, will only be welcome to the rich or better-off economies while the poorest are far more likely to be marginalized by such developments than to be assisted by them, for although the increasing movement of men, money and ideas makes it harder for countries to maintain any form of genuine isolation, such movements appear to make little difference to the world's poorest people. The poorest are in real danger of being ignored and their greatest hope, therefore, must lie in the United Nations, one of whose tasks has always been to publicize the needs of the least developed and try to persuade the advanced economies to include them in the development plans of a global economy. This United Nations role is likely to be even more important in the aftermath of the Cold War than it was before.

The 1991 report of the UN Economic and Social Commission for Asia and the Pacific (ESCAP) pointed out that 'More than 800 million poor people, 72% of the world's total, reside in the Asia-Pacific region; of these 633 million are extemely poor.' Moreover, only a minority of the rural poor owned land and the majority subsisted as day labourers while few efforts had been made in the cities to narrow the gap betwen rich and poor.[1] At the same time, of the world's 41 poorest nations with a then population of 2948.4 million, 27 were in Africa with a combined population of 418.4 million (1989); 13, including China and India, were in Asia with a combined population of 2491.5 million; and one in Latin America (Haiti) with a population of 6.4 million.[2] All these countries then had per capita incomes below US$700.

What is needed is a reversal of approach. As the United Nations Development Programme (UNDP) has pointed out through its Human Development Reports, we must stop looking at the poor simply as those whose poverty requires to be relieved; instead, they must be equipped to develop on their own although that approach is not often achieved in practice even if lip-service is sometimes paid to it in theory. There now exists a real danger that the poor will only be assisted if they are seen to be of value to the advanced economies. As the UNDP asked at the begining of the decade: 'In a period of rapid economic globalisation, who will protect the interests of the poor?'[3] As the United States adjusts to the new challenge of the emerging Pacific Rim, and the European Union tries to come to terms with the challenge of expanding eastwards now that the Iron Curtain has disappeared, and Russia comes to terms with the end of its Soviet Empire and superpower status, and everyone eyes the rapdily developing Asian giant of China, there is little remaining interest for the world's poorest nations. If the United Nations does not champion their interests no one else is likely to do so. Moreover, its capacity to assist the poorest, through such institutions as the World Bank and the IMF or its various specialized agencies, will depend upon the willingness of the major economies, led by the Group of Seven, to provide the means and this they are only likely to do on their own terms.

Any consideration of the kind of world which the United Nations has to deal with in the 1990s brings us back, again and again, to the growing disparities that exist between the world's rich minority, the North, and the poor developing majority, the South. The gap betwen North and South was growing fast before the end of the Cold War; now there are signs that it will grow even faster. At the beginning of the present decade the North, which accounts for only 25 per cent of the total world population, nonetheless consumes 70 per cent of the world's energy, 75 per cent of its metals, 85 per cent of its wood and 60 per cent of its food while the rate of growth of the OECD countries collectively has been consistently above the world average by a margin of 0.5 per cent. Moreover, the prices paid for crucial exports from the South – principally raw materials and food commodities – have steadily declined; they dropped by 20 per cent between 1980 and 1990 and have continued to do so in the 1990s. In general terms, therefore, the imbalance between North and South is increasing; if it continues to do so it will either create even more dangerous divisions between North and South than those which exist already or it will marginalize a substantial number of the world's poorest countries entirely. The United Nations has the only real prospect of bridging this gap; whether it is permitted to do so effectively must depend upon the direction of international politics over the next decade.

The absolute majority in the General Assembly of Third World countries or members of the South means, at least in theory, that they can win their point. As a result, the General Assembly has often adopted resolutions favourable to Third World aspirations in the field of development. A typical example of this process occurred in the wake of the OPEC price rises of 1973 when on 1 May 1974, a special session on development (in the General Assembly) adopted the *Declaration and Programme of Action on the Establishment of a New International Economic Order*. Member nations declared their determination to work for 'the establishment of a new international economic order based on equity, sovereignty, interdependence, common interest and co-operation among states, irrespective of their economic and social systems' in order to 'correct inequalities and redress existing injustices, make it possible to eliminate the widening gap between the developed and developing countries and ensure steadily accelerating economic and social development in peace and justice for present and future generations.' Admittedly, this declaration came at a high point of new-found Third World confidence when the sudden rise of OPEC power in the immediate aftermath of the October 1973 Yom Kippur War had placed the OECD countries (the principal customers for Middle East oil) on the defensive, yet by the end of the 1970s, by which time the main Western oil consumers had adjusted to the new situation, the declaration had become a dead letter.

Such statements of principle illustrate both the strengths and weaknesses of the United Nations. The resolution may accord with the economic aspirations of the LDCs as a whole but the world economic climate is controlled by the handful of advanced economies, led by the Group of Seven, although this is increasingly being joined by a small number of thrusting newly industrialized countries (NICs) such as Malaysia, Mexico or the New China and though these latter countries may speak out against what they see as the selfishness of the advanced economies they are, in real terms, far too busy trying to overcome their own problems to undertake any collective responsibility for the South as a whole. During the 1970s the majority of Third World countries imagined that OPEC would act for them all; it soon became clear that it only acted for its members. Similarly in the 1990s, while a few countries – the 'Asian Tigers' – are posing substantial economic threats to the prevailing dominance of the advanced economies it is unrealistic to suppose that they will use what strengths they possess on behalf of the South as a whole. What this means in practice is that only through the United Nations can the weakest, least developed countries expect to alter their standing. It is, therefore, very much in their interest to subscribe to such resolutions even if there is little prospect of their immediate implementation. The leading economic powers – the United States, the European Union, Japan (and, no doubt, Russia once it has sorted out its post-USSR problems) – will not alter the thrust of their economic policies because of such resolutions even if they pay lip-service to the general principles embodied in them. On the other hand, in political terms even the United States does not wish to be seen too often and too obviously to go against the South. As a result such declarations will not be opposed even if the advanced economies have no intention of doing anything to implement them. Nonetheless, and though this is perfectly understood, it is part of the South's strategy to get such declarations approved and on the UN 'statute book'. Then, later, they can be used as points of reference in the ongoing struggle between North and South to bring about adjustments, bit by bit, to a world economic system which is still dominated overwhelmingly by the North.

The converse of this process can be seen in the way the major Western countries dominate the policies of the World Bank and the IMF. A World Bank policy research report *Adjustment in Africa* (published in 1994) examined recent policy reforms in Africa. It focused upon 29 sub-Saharan countries with a population of 500 000 or more at mid-1991 that enjoyed reasonable social stability and were implementing economic adjustment programmes during the years 1987–91. The World Bank, it should be remembered, started out as a *bank* to lend money for reconstruction and development purposes, and though it was the creation of the United Nations, it was at once given an independent role of its own. Today it is pertinent to ask whether the World Bank acts impartially on behalf of its members, which include those that are economically weakest, or whether it proposes and then imposes economic policies which are less the brainchild of the United Nations acting for all its members than the economic guidelines of the advanced economies whose interest it is to control the developing world to their own advantage?

The report is cautious and does not claim too much but its general conclusion is that those countries which follow World Bank prescriptions have done better than those which do not, although the prescriptions are almost always geared in terms of increasing exports to the more advanced economies. A typical entry in the report is the following:

> In agriculture, two-thirds of the adjusting countries are taxing their farmers less. Despite huge declines in real export prices, policy changes have increased real producer prices for agricultural exporters in ten countries. Of the fifteen governments that had major restrictions on the private purchase, distribution, and sale of major food crops before adjustment, thirteen have withdrawn from marketing almost completely.[4]

The nub of the problem for so many poor agricultural countries is to be found in the second sentence above: 'Despite huge declines in real export prices, policy changes have increased real producer prices for agricultural exporters in ten countries.' Here the World Bank strategy is merely compensating for a growing imbalance of prices that works to the advantage of the advanced economies. If the World Bank were interested in a more equitable economic order of the kind envisaged in the proposals for a New International Economic Order (referred to above) it would be less concerned with the adjustment of producer prices and, instead, would be examining ways in which to increase absolutely the prices paid for agricultural commodities by the advanced economies.

Part of the problem is the sheer dominance of World Bank thinking by economists from the advanced (market force) economies and this is true despite the national composition of its various teams. During the 1980s Britain's Prime Minister, Margaret Thatcher, adopted privatization as a major plank of her economic policies, though whether the process actually improved the performance of the British economy is open to question. Other countries, more or less willingly, have followed the British example which became a fashion and the World Bank has pushed privatization as one of the adjustment policies which would attract new assistance or investment from the major donors. Thus, in *Adjustment in Africa*, we find the following appraisal of the privatization approach:

> African governments have sold off only a small share of their assets. The value of privatisations in Nigeria between 1988 and 1992 was less than 1 per cent of that in Argentina, Malaysia, or Mexico, even after adjusting for Nigeria's smaller GDP. Explicit and implicit financial flows to public enterprises are still high. But one encouraging trend is that governments have stopped expanding their public enterprise sectors.[5]

The advantages of privatization in Britain are far from clear and their value has been widely disputed; why, then, should privatization be advanced as a necessary policy adjustment for some of the world's poorest countries? In many respects privatization can be seen as an overtly political act by rightwing governments rather than a necessary prescription for economic advance yet, too easily, the World Bank adopts policies which come out of the Western political stable and it does so, essentially, because the major Western economies (the Group of Seven) effectively control the thrust of all World Bank policies.

Although Africa is generally regarded as the world's poorest, least developed region, its numbers, nonetheless, are only half those of China whose overall poverty on a per capita basis is as great. China, however, has a powerful modern sector whose potential for growth is so great that economists are now predicting that its overall economic performance will come to equal that of the United States by about 2020. Moreover, China's vast potential market acts as a magnet to outside investors who are willing to take risks in order to obtain a share of it in a way they are not willing to do in the small markets of Africa. As a result, China will generate – and be expected to generate – the means to deal with its own problems of poverty although this should not exclude external assistance if Beijing asks for it. However, as a permanent member of the Security Council and a putative superpower of the near future China is unlikely, for reasons of political pride, to seek assistance except at what might be described as the margins of development. Africa falls into a different category entirely.

The small size of most African economies is itself a bar to rapid development and exacerbates all the other problems of limited trained manpower, inadequate industrial base, poor infrastructure and political instability. In too many cases, therefore, the point of economic take-off as envisaged by the American economist W. W. Rostow in the early 1960s has never been achieved. Recognizing these factors both the United Nations in general and the World Bank in particular have paid extra special attention to development problems in Africa. At the beginning of the 1980s, for example, the World Bank produced its *Accelerated Development in Sub-Saharan Africa – An Agenda for Action* which examined the problems peculiar to this region. As the World Bank President A. W. Clausen said in his Foreword to the report:

> The report accepts the long-term objectives of African development as expressed by the Heads of State of the Organization of African Unity in the *Lagos Plan of Action*. It emphasizes that if these objectives for the year 2000 are to be achieved, actions must be taken to reverse the stagnation and possible decline of per capita incomes which are projected for the 1980s.[6]

The intention to provide the assistance might have been there; the performance of Africa through the 1980s was, on the whole, abysmal. The continent was troubled by a number of brutal civil wars – Angola, Ethiopia, Mozambique, Sudan; it suffered from a high level of natural disasters; the terms of trade went against it; potential investors became increasingly wary of risking their capital; it came to be seen by the outside world as a 'basket case' for constant injections of aid; and in a number of countries negative growth was recorded for the decade. The question that this performance raises is how much should the United Nations take on a responsibility to raise Africa out of this development trough and how much will the world community be prepared to assist such a UN policy?

Another World Bank report of 1989, *Poverty, Adjustment, and Growth in Africa*,[7] confirmed the troubled state of the continent's economies and argued that: 'Despite the profound difficulties – economic, social, and political – involved in economic reform, there is now a strong consensus within Africa and within the donor community on the need for adjustment.' That statement may be true enough; the question it raises is what kind of adjustment – a programme worked out in Washington by economists imbued with Western 'market forces' answers to development problems and then 'sold' to governments desperate for any kind of economic assistance; or a programme worked out inside Africa in conjunction with the political leaders on the spot who will subsequently have the responsibility of implementing it and persuading their people to accept the hardships that such programmes normally involve. Almost always it is a Washington (World Bank) plan that is offered with the result that even if the recipient government accepts it in theory, in pactice such a government constantly drags its feet over implementation. This raises another vital issue for the future of the United Nations. In the coming years, just as it is being suggested that regional military forces should be used for peacekeeping operations, so it is worth considering how regional organizations should undertake economic adjustment programmes to ensure that these bear the imprint of the region and achieve real consensus. In the case of Africa the obvious regional economic instruments (apart from the United Nations' own Economic Commission for Africa – ECA) are first (on a macro-level) the Organization of African Unity and then, at sub-regional levels, the Economic Community of West African States (ECOWAS), the Southern Africa Development Community (SADC) and so on. One way for the United Nations to ensure its own survival and growth in the coming years will be for it to become more integrated with such regional organizations as a principal source of support for their initiatives rather than as the lead agency – and this should apply, perhaps especially, to the World Bank which has come to be seen as too monolithic and too ready to instruct from on high.

Despite formidable economic problems in the developing world, the picture is by no means all gloom and the 1995 World Bank *Annual Report* had this to say about overall achievements:

> The case for development is compelling, however. Over the past five decades, average per capita incomes in developing countries have more than doubled. The GDPs of some economies have quintupled. Life expectancy has increased by more than 50 per cent. There has been a 'green revolution' in South Asia, an 'economic miracle' in East Asia, Latin America has largely overcome its debt crisis, and substantial gains in health and literacy have taken place in Africa.[8]

If we are to move towards the goal of a single world community problems of extreme poverty must be tackled and overcome and while the advanced economies of the North possess the capacity to deal with such problems it is the United Nations which has to act as both the coordinator and the 'voice' of the dispossessed. As yet another report states:

> The entrenchment of poverty is borne out by the fact that the number of people falling in the World Bank's category 'the absolute poor' had climbed to 1.3 billion in 1993. This level of poverty spells acute destitution; it is life at the edge of existence. For the absolute poor, for example, a nearby source of safe drinking water is a luxury; in several countries – Bhutan, Ethiopia, Laos, Mali, Nigeria – less than half the population has even this.[9]

It is in response to such conditions that the United Nations periodically holds one of its special events – a year or decade devoted to upgrading a particular aspect of the human condition. Moreover, today no one can plead ignorance of conditions elsewhere in the world. Television has now become a global phenomenon and neither wars nor disasters nor extremes of misery in one part of the world can be ignored in another: not, at least, in the sense that we are made aware of them. What we choose to do is another matter. It is, perhaps pre-eminently, the task of the UN Secretary-General to speak out about these global distortions in an effort to persuade the world community to take action.

The globalization of the world economy has far outstripped world structures. Trade has grown faster than output, capital flows are now on a phenomenal scale and many industries are global rather than national operations yet, despite these rapid changes in the world economy, in other respects we behave as though we are still separate national entities without responsibility for what takes place in another such entity. The rapid movement of industries from one place to another or the transfer of capital may have a devastating impact upon a small weak economy which loses what it thought was a major source of employment but while an advanced economic grouping such as the European Union operates compensating mechanisms to assist its underdeveloped regions, and has the financial means to make these effective, there is no such mechanism to assist the weakest developing countries which is why in the next decade we are likely to hear a good deal more about marginalization.

A major problem faced by the United Nations, as it tries to persuade the world community to meet the needs of the poorest, is compassion fatigue. This was clearly a factor, though only one, in the reluctance of some UN members to become involved in peacekeeping operations in such places as Bosnia, Somalia or Rwanda. Similarly, as many donor organizations have discovered, too many images of starving children can be counter-productive. Nonetheless, the stark facts of overwhelming poverty must be constantly addressed:

> One fifth of the world lives in countries, mainly in Africa and Latin America, where living standards actually fell in the 1980s. Several indicators of aggregate poverty – 1.5 billion lack access to safe water and 2 billion lack safe sanitation; more than 1 billion are illiterate, including half of all rural women – are no less chilling than a quarter-century ago. The conditions of this 20 per cent of humanity – and of millions of others close to this perilous state – should be a matter of overriding priority.[10]

And if it is not a matter of overriding priority it is the business of the United Nations to make it so. As this same report points out, it is one of the great ironies of the present time that just as the former communist countries as well as many developing countries are discovering the benefits of openness and liberalization, the rich countries of the West may turn in on themselves. Should that happen existing divisions will become even greater than they are at present. Again, it should be the task of the United Nations to prevent such polarizations from taking place or, at the least, to work to minimize regional divisions. There is an irony within the irony for the very businessmen from the most advanced economies who speak most readily about a single global market are also often in the vanguard of those who seek protection for their own economies and express fears about the encroachment of the poor majority from the South upon the settled affluence of the North.

One of the most difficult problems to overcome lies in the concentration of economic decision making – on a global scale – in the hands of the United States, Europe and Japan, largely reflected through the Group of Seven. Moreover, these few economic powers dominate the decision making process in all the major world organizations such as the World Bank, the IMF, GATT and, indeed, in the United Nations itself. According to the authors of *Our Global Neighbourhood* it is necessary to shift the centre of gravity of the world economy:

> Taken as a whole, developing economies have been growing more rapidly than Western industrial ones during the last three decades, with Asian developing countries growing much more rapidly. The share of output accounted for by members of the Organisation for Economic Co-operation and Development (OECD) has shrunk to barely half, once we take account of the underlying purchasing power of economies measured at comparable prices. The world's ten biggest economies on a purchasing power parity basis include China, India, Brazil, and Russia, with Mexico, Indonesia, and the Republic of Korea not far behind.[11]

None of the above-mentioned countries are members of the Group of Seven which is still seen as the absolute pace-setter for global economic decisions. Truly global institutions have not kept pace with other global developments, while the end of the Cold War and the disintegration of the USSR between them have destroyed a system of balances without putting anything in its place, so that the world now faces the very real danger that the most powerful nations will simply try to control world events by acting unilaterally, which represents a return to the politics of the nineteenth and early twentieth centuries. The need for a system of strong international rules has never been greater; how they are to be effectively put in place remains to be seen.

Part of the present problem resides in the fact that whereas the Group of Seven now only represents 12 per cent of the world's population and, by excluding both China and India, cannot any longer claim to speak for the world's leading economies, the United Nation's economic work 'is fragmented and regrettably does not at present carry great authority. Evidence that the UN system is willing radically to rationalize and focus its activities would add greatly to its credibility and to the willingness of member-states to have international economic issues discussed within the system.'[12] At present, for example, meetings of the Group of Seven give little attention or priority to development issues despite their importance to the vast majority of the world's people and when, occasionally, pressures from below have forced the major powers to hold economic summits, as for example the 1981 North–South development summit at Cancun in Mexico, the 'one-world' rhetoric common to such occasions has rarely produced any subsequent actions of substance.

There is no lack of information about the problems the world economy faces. The United Nations and its various agencies are strong in their statistics and the wealth of information they make available and the proposals advanced for new attacks upon specific problems, annually for example by the World Development Reports, provide excellent guidelines for what ought to be done. The 1994 *World Development Report*, for example, focused upon the need to improve infrastructure to achieve better development. And the same report provided a wealth of information about differing standards worldwide and then reminded its readers of what the US Secretary of State had said to the 1945 San Francisco Conference which created the United Nations:

> The battle of peace has to be fought on two fronts. The first is the security front where victory spells freedom from fear. The second is the economic and social front where victory means freedom from want. Only victory on both fronts can assure the world of an enduring peace ... No provisions that can be written into the Charter will enable the Security Council to make the world secure from war if men and women have no security in their homes and jobs.[13]

Unfortunately we do not seem much closer to realizing that ideal in the mid-1990s than in the more hopeful mid-1940s. The same report advanced the idea of an Economic Security Council whose task would be to review threats to global human security and address such issues as global poverty, unemployment, food security, international migration and a new framework for sustainable human development.

Food aid needs for 1995 highlighted some of the worst problems faced by the poorest countries which the US Department of Agriculture estimated would require a minimum of 14 million tons of food aid during 1995–6 while the FAO estimated that 36 million people faced severe food shortages and that more than 23 million of them live in sub-Saharan Africa. These chronic problems were greatly exacerbated by civil strife in such countries as Somalia and Rwanda, while in Asia, Afghanistan and Bangladesh accounted for most of the food-aid needs for that region. Such food-aid requirements have been part of an accepted provision made by the food surplus rich countries for decades as problems have grown at least as fast as aid efforts to deal with them. What rang alarm bells for the United Nations in 1994–5 was the fact that food-aid shipments fell by a third compared with the previous year and that the United States, which is by far the largest source of food aid, was responsible for almost the entire drop in supplies. Shipments in 1994–5 as well as aid commitments for 1995–6 were not only the lowest since the mid-1970s but also fell well below the minimum target of 10 million tons of food aid set by the World Food Conference in 1974.

Almost all the world's population increases now take place in the LDCs; in 1995 they accounted for 98 per cent of the additional 88 million births worldwide. In Africa, which has the highest regional birthrate, the life expectancy is the lowest at 53 years for males and 56 for females. The United Nations has long concerned itself with population problems and regards control of population growth as a vital prerequisite for more manageable sustainable development. Africa, with the greatest general level of poverty and underevelopment has the highest world average rate of population increase at 2.8 per cent a year.

In March 1996 the United Nations Secretary-General, Boutros-Ghali, launched the world body's biggest ever campaign for the development of Africa, 'the world's foremost development challenge'. 'Now is the time for the United Nations and the international community as a whole to stand together with Africa, now is the time for us to forge a new partnership', he said. 'We want today to tell Africa solemnly it isn't alone, it isn't abandoned, it is more than ever in the sight of the world ... I'm not appealing to the generosity of the international community, I'm appealing to its conscience.' His rhetoric, unfortunately, hardly matched the world mood and there was little evidence that Western governments would provide very much of the additional US$25 billion required over the ten-year period of the planned initiative. The objectives of the UN programme were sound enough – the expansion of basic education and health care, the promotion of peace and better governance, the improvement of water and food security. The Secretary-General was vague as to where the money for this programme would be found. Much of the cost would have to be met by redirecting existing UN resources and by African governments themselves readjusting their expenditure plans; but it would also require Western financing equivalent to 20 per cent of their current (1996) aid flows to Africa, though whether these additional resources would be forthcoming was unclear.[14]

The need for such a programme was unquestioned: Africa in 1996 was the only world region where, according to UN criteria, poverty was on the increase and after three decades of economic, social and political crises there were few signs that these would diminish. Indeed, the state of crisis of much of Africa was itself a reflection of the continent's deep poverty, reinforcing the need for such a rescue programme, but whether the United Nations' initiative made sense at this particular time was another matter entirely. The programme was launched with more rhetoric than hard promises of aid in the bank at a time when the world body itself was in deep crisis and the question of Boutros-Ghali's re-election for a second term as Secretary-General was under critical discussion (his bid for a second term was clearly opposed in the United States). Launching such a programme (however much it may be required) at so critical a juncture in the history of the United Nations may well have been a mistake. If it does not take off and the required finances are not forthcoming the failure can only do the United Nations damage; it will be seen as yet another of the vague well-meaning UN initiatives that provide endless material for criticism to the hard-headed politicians in the advanced economies who argue that the United Nations tries to do too much and that it should only undertake what it is certain of being able to complete. Such arguments, in their turn, give rise to an opposing thesis: that the United Nations must continue to launch such initiatives since, even if their chances of success are minimal, the need to demonstrate the world's concern and, hopefully, to shame the rich nations into at least some form of action, is imperative if the United Nations is to continue in its role as the champion of the least developed nations. In such circumstances the United Nations is in a 'catch-22' situation: if it acts and the initiative fails it lays itself open to the criticisms of both incompetence and delusions of grandeur which play into the hands of those critics who want to see the world body's influence diminished; if, on the other hand, it does not take such initiatives it loses credibility with the countries which look to it most for support.

11 Social and Environmental Development

Under Article 55 of the Charter the United Nations is required to 'promote higher standards of living, full employment and conditions of economic and social progress and development'. What this has meant in reality is that historically the United Nations has spent a great deal of its time and energy devising, launching and subsequently maintaining programmes whose economic and social content is designed to assist the countries of the developing world where a majority of the world's population is to be found, often living in conditions of great poverty, hunger, disease or ignorance. Both during and after the Cold War the world has remained divided into rich and poor, advanced and developing or North and South, and the fact of this division colours most aspects of international affairs and is a dominant consideration in the way the United Nations works. The General Assembly may pass resolutions or proclaim a Development Decade but the success of these programmes which are designed to assist the LDCs or the Third World at large must depend upon the willingness of the advanced economies of the North to provide the means to implement them properly as opposed merely to supporting them with lip-service.

Political cynics in the advanced economies may ask what is the point in proclaiming a Development Decade: after all, everyone wants development and proclaiming such a decade is not of itself going to make anything happen which was not going to occur anyway. Similarly, the discussions which led to the Declaration and Programme of Action on the Establishment of a New International Economic Order (NIEO) by the General Assembly in 1974 might set out the principles of economic behaviour that would be most desirable in an equitable world but they were unlikely, remotely, to bring these about. The voting on this issue – 120 for and 16 either against or abstaining – made absolutely plain the fact that the advanced economies had no intention of being told that they should make sacrifices on behalf of the majority. Nor, of course, was there any mechanism to make them do so. The Charter of Economic Rights and Duties of States which the General Assembly adopted in 1974 in furtherance of the NIEO idea stipulated that every state has the right freely to exercise full permanent sovereignty over its wealth and natural resources within its national jurisdiction. This stipulation may have been conceived primarily on behalf of the developing countries which so easily find themselves subjected to exploitation by the transnational corporations

119

from the North yet the stipulation was a double-edged sword. It also meant that the advanced economies have the right to exercise absolute control over their own resources as they see fit and not necessarily in compliance with any principles advanced under such concepts as a NIEO.

If we examine the social and environmental activities of the United Nations over the years, all such activities being related, more or less, to development, we should do so in the light of the following questions: How much do such initiatives achieve? How much, once launched or proclaimed, are they ignored or allowed to become dead letters? How much do they emphasize, with potentially divisive results, the gaps in both wealth and poverty and, still more, in objectives between North and South?

The proclamation of Development Decades – in 1960, 1970, 1980 and 1990 – was a device to focus attention upon the development needs of the Third World while, under the umbrella of these decades, more precise initiatives were undertaken. In 1969, for example, the General Assembly adopted a Declaration on Social Progress and Development which, in its turn, led on to the adoption in 1970 of an International Development Strategy for the Second United Nations Development Decade (1971–80) which, again in its turn, was followed by the adoption in 1974 (admittedly in circumstances which were greatly assisted by the rise of OPEC power in 1973) of a New International Economic Order or NIEO. At the end of the 1970s, in deteriorating economic conditions, the General Assembly called for global negotiations on international economic cooperation for development and though these negotiations achieved nothing the General Assembly, nonetheless, adopted an International Development Strategy for the Third United Nations Development Decade (1981–90). It is possible to admire the determination of the General Assembly in passing such resolutions in the face of indifference from the advanced economies; otherwise, it might be asked, what is the point?

The 1980s was a gloomy decade for development. After the excitements of 1973 and 1974 the West did agree to a series of talks or dialogue in Paris during late 1975 but the Conference on International Economic Cooperation and Development (CIEC) which was attended by 19 representatives of the Third World and eight representatives of the capitalist West produced nothing concrete – only the idea of a continuing North–South dialogue – and though at first consideration the initiation of a dialogue may have appeared to represent an advance for the Third World, in retrospect its principal achievement was to emphasize the divide between North and South. During these Paris talks the skilful diplomacy of the US Secretary of State, Henry Kissinger, first diffused demands for a NIEO and then deferred any decisions by demanding more discussions in depth, a device that ensured no action was taken when OPEC power was at its height. Then, as the third UN Development Decade was proclaimed, came the Brandt Report.

The North no doubt felt the need to make some gesture towards the South after the failure of the CIEC talks in Paris and, following a suggestion of the President of the World Bank, Robert McNamara, the former West German Chancellor, Willy Brandt, was appointed chairman of an Independent Commission on International Development Issues. The object of the Commission was stated as to 'present recommendations which could improve the climate for further deliberations on North–South relations'. What the South wanted was action; what the North wanted was action deferred by discussion. Leading figures from the international establishment – Britain's Edward Heath, Sweden's Olof Palme, Tanzania's Amir Jamal – sat on the Commission whose report was finally published in 1980. As the Report said: 'Mankind has never before had such ample technical and financial resources for coping with hunger and poverty. The immense task can be tackled once the necessary collective will is mobilized.' As the Third World was to discover through the ensuing decade, the collective will was the principal ingredient which the Report lacked. And though few would object to the sentiments expressed in the Brandt Report, nor to its analysis of the problems which beset the South, the Commission had no powers of implementation and like its predecessor, the Pearson Report of 1969, the Brandt Report was soon collecting dust on bookshelves.

The Cancun Summit of 1981, in the immediate wake of the Brandt Report, saw 22 representatives of North and South meet to discuss 'Cooperation and Development' but times had changed markedly since the Paris summit of six years earlier. OPEC was no longer seen as the formidable organization it had been in the 1970s, the new governments of the United States under President Reagan and Britain under Prime Minister Thatcher had each signalled a sharp move to the right as they proclaimed their faith in market forces while mounting debts put many Third World countries on the defensive. Then, in 1982, the international debt crisis was sparked off by Mexico and Brazil declaring their inability to meet their debt obligations. The implied threat that some leading Third World countries might renege on their debts ensured that a massive rescheduling operation followed and the crisis passed. The lesson of the crisis, however, was in line with much else that affected North–South relations and was not lost on either side of the divide: when the South threatens action – as its oil states did in 1973 or its most indebted Latin American states did in 1982 – the North will act with speed to avert damage to its interests; when, however, action is simply called for as, for example, in the Brandt Report such appeals meet with no more than pious approval.

The fourth United Nations Development Decade to cover the last ten years of the twentieth century was launched at a time of unprecedented change when the international structures that had been more or less fixed throughout the years of the Cold War were being dismantled: the Soviet Empire was about to disintegrate, Russia was – apparently – coming in from the cold, the European Union was looking to expand its membership into Eastern Europe, the former Soviet Republics as well as Russia itself were suddenly open to Western investment and crying out for it while the advanced economies of the West (which for real purposes were synonymous with the rich North and alone had the means at their disposal to make any meaningful contribution towards economic changes in the South) were simply not interested in doing anything of the sort. Halfway through the decade the omens, if anything, were even less promising as the United Nations battled for its own survival against mounting pressures for its reform and growing signs of disunity among the major powers.

Between the demand for a NIEO in 1974 and the holding of the Rio Earth Summit in 1992 the United Nations mounted a wide variety of initiatives, usually launched by international conferences, that between them covered almost every aspect of development. These included the subjects of desertification (Nairobi 1977), water (Mar del Plata 1977), technical cooperation among developing countries (Buenos Aires 1978), science and technology for development (Vienna 1979), agrarian reform and rural development (Rome 1979), a Decade for Women (Copenhagen 1980), new and renewable sources of energy (Nairobi 1981), the least developed countries (Paris 1981) a world assembly on ageing (Vienna 1982), population (Mexico City 1984), an appraisal of the Decade for Women (Nairobi 1985), the promotion of international cooperation in the peaceful uses of nuclear energy (Geneva 1987), drug abuse and illicit trafficking (Vienna 1987), conferences on trade and development (UNCTAD) (Belgrade 1983, Geneva 1987, Cartagena 1992), the relationship between disarmament and development (New York 1987), a second conference on the LDCs (Paris 1990), and a world summit for children (New York 1990).[1] This impressive list shows the United Nations extending its involvement into all aspects of social and environmental activity worldwide. It raises two general questions. First, is the United Nations trying to do too much? Second, how effective are these initiatives?

It is, of course, easy to condemn the United Nations as a 'talking shop' and suggest that such conferences do little more than provide a 'gravy-train' for international civil servants and other personnel who spend their time moving from conference to conference, and there is no lack of people who undoubtedly fit this description. Apart from such critical considerations, however, this constant UN activity ought to be seen in the following light. It has steadily extended the realm of UN expertise until few areas of development have been omitted and the world body can claim pre-eminence (along with the World Bank) as the source of developmental knowledge and experience which is at the disposal of all its members. Second, by constantly extending the range of its involvement the United Nations has also gradually made itself indispensable in a number of development activities where, moreover, its participation is free of the bilateral limitations that are inherent in country-to-country aid programmes. Third, the comprehensive nature of this UN coverage provides the basis for a world development programme if and when the leading powers in the United Nations decide to tackle North–South relations on the scale they deserve. There is a fourth consideration. UN pronouncements on all these themes – water, health, population, the state of women, the needs of the poorest – provide a synthesis of agreement that has been accepted by all the members of the United Nations even if only in principle and such pronouncements can be referred to at some future date as the framework of a universal or world development policy. This may prove of crucial importance in the years to come.

More than five decades of United Nations activity have witnessed far-reaching changes whose most important aspects have been the rapid growth of population and increasing economic activity for, despite the huge problems of poverty which afflict wide regions of the world, living standards in many countries have been raised by improvements in health and education. It is as easy to be complacent as it is tempting to be cynical. The complacent approach – that of hope – has to be balanced against the self-interest of the powerful of the North who, too often, act as though the continuance of their own good fortune depends upon maintaining a distance between themselves and the developing world rather than assisting it to emerge from its poverty. In *Our Global Neighbourhood*, for example, the authors refer to the changes for the better which undoubtedly have taken place:

> As significant as these changes is the increasing capacity of people to shape their lives and to assert their rights. The empowerment of people is reflected in the vigour of civil society and democratic processes. These point to the potential of human creativity and co-operation, both vital to meet the many challenges – security, economic, environmental, social – that the world faces and that governments must address.[2]

Such a statement, with its faith in the empowerment of people, has to be considered alongside the terrible events which appear to have been given an extra lease of life by the end of the Cold War: these include developments in Burundi, Rwanda, Liberia, Sierra Leone, Somalia, Yugoslavia; the plight of the Kurds, the ruthless denial of human rights in Burma and Timor and in many other places, the growing world traffic in drugs and children, and what appears to be an escalating indifference towards poverty and suffering inside the advanced economies, let alone in their attitudes to the developing world. Empowerment of people can as easily mean the empowerment of the minority whose interests are opposed to a wider justice as it can mean the empowerment of a hitherto oppressed or neglected majority.

The size of the development problems we face can best be summarized in terms of population increases: the world population is now more than double what it was at the end of World War II and while in 1950 the global total increased by 37 million people a year, by 1993, that figure had more than doubled to 87 million a year, the overwhelming majority of whom were to be found in the Third World. Not only do developing countries contain 78 per cent of the present world population but about 94 per cent of all population increases also takes place in those countries where the main environmental pressures are linked to poverty.

Just as the United Nations has steadily amassed a vast storehouse of information on all the problems of development so also is it true that we both know how to deal with problems and possess the means to do so effectively:

> Population, consumption, technology, development, and the environment are linked in complex relationships that bear closely on human welfare in the global neighbourhood. Their effective and equitable management calls for a systemic, long-term, global approach guided by the principle of sustainable development, which has been the central lesson from the mounting ecological dangers of recent times. Its universal application is a priority among the tasks of global governance.[3]

Such statements are the stock-in-trade of the United Nations but does a knowledge of the problems or a clear idea of how they ought to be tackled make the slightest difference when the interests of major powers are at stake? The five permanent members of the Security Council (the United States, Russia, China, Britain and France) as well as leading industrial nations such as Germany and Japan or the other members of the OECD are well rehearsed in these arguments; there is little sign that they are prepared significantly to alter their policies of self-interest as a result. The Rio Earth Summit of 1992 illustrated very clearly how selfish motives on both sides of the divide operate first and foremost and the illustrations from that event are peculiarly apt since it was concerned with the resources of the whole world whose destruction or misuse must, in the end, hurt us all equally.

Over the three years prior to the Rio Earth Summit there were at least some signs of a willingness to cooperate over problems which affected the environment. On 22 March 1989, at Basel in Switzerland, 117 countries adopted an agreement to restrict shipments of hazardous wastes across international boundaries. On 2 May that year, at a meeting of the United Nations Environment Programme (UNEP) in Helsinki, 80 countries agreed to stop producing chlorofluorocarbons (CFCs), which threaten the ozone layer, by the year 2000. In the General Assembly 159 countries agreed a draft treaty to stabilize the earth's climate – the framework for Rio. At a London meeting of June 1990, in a follow-up to the Helsinki meeting of the previous year, 100 nations committed themselves to phase out by 2000 CFCs from aerosols, air conditioners and refrigerators which destroy the ozone layer. But when the World Climate Conference, held at Geneva during October–November 1990, urged countries to adopt strategies to limit 'greenhouse gases', the United States, which is responsible for 24 per cent of world carbon dioxide emissions, and Saudi Arabia, the USSR and Venezuela joined together to argue that it was too early to decide how to reduce emissions. At another meeting held in Nairobi in September 1991 to draft a treaty to prevent global warming, the United States rejected mandatory cuts in emissions of heat-trapping carbon dioxide. Meanwhile, the United Nations Intergovernmental Panel on Climate Change warned that man-made emissions could melt the polar ice-caps, cause ocean levels to rise and wreak havoc among the low-lying island nations. In November 1991 Japan agreed to comply with the UN moratorium on using driftnets in the Pacific which destroyed dolphins, whales, turtles, birds and fish. Such recurrent meetings and the pressures arising out of them did have some impact upon those nations whose levels of consumption threaten the greatest damage to the environment but, as a rule, only at the margins.

The United Nations Conference on Environment and Development (UNCED), popularly known as the Rio Earth Summit, was held on 3–14 June 1992 in Rio de Janeiro, Brazil. It was attended by over 100 Heads of State and Government and representatives of 178 countries altogether and was the largest ever world summit meeting. It was also, given the momentous world events then taking place, the first opportunity in the post-Cold War world for members of the United Nations to express their confidence in the world body and particularly for its developmental work. The conference was held at a time of growing concern about the use – and misuse – of the earth's resources and when they were being depleted at an unprecedented rate. The summit focused attention upon this escalating depletion rate of resources and upon the differences of approach to consumption and conservation by the North and the South. It was apparent from the beginning that the divide between North and South would be as acute as ever: the North wished to safeguard its right to consume, the South to exploit what resources it possesses.

The conference turned into a confrontation of opposing approaches to development. US President George Bush refused to sign the Convention on Protecting Species and Habitats (the bio-diversity convention) in order to protect US patents on products developed from materials obtained from overseas. Governor Gilberto Mestrinho, from Brazil's state of Amazonas, said (of the North): 'The developed world sold $200 billion of products based on molecules from the tropical forests last year, yet not one cent came to the Amazon region.' Prior to the conference Malaysia's prime minister, Mahathir Mohamad, had put the case of the South succinctly when he argued: 'If the rich North expects the poor to foot the bill for a cleaner environment, Rio would become an exercise in futility.' He also said: 'There will be no development if the poor countries are not allowed to extract their natural wealth ... fear by the North of environmental degradation provides the South with the leverage that did not exist before. If it is in the interest of the rich that we do not cut down our trees, then they must compensate us for the loss of income.' There was no indication in these and other similar exchanges that anyone from either North or South was concerned with resources as a common possession of mankind that required a careful husbanding for the future on behalf of the world community as a whole. Rather, they were treated solely as the focus of North–South suspicions of each other. While it was possible to sympathize with Malaysia's Mahathir Mohamad when he berated the North for expecting the poor to foot the bill for a cleaner environment, his demand that the rich should pay if they did not want Malaysia to cut down its trees missed the point of the conference: the trees, once gone, cannot be replaced. They – or some of them – are Malaysia's trees and once destroyed it is Malaysia that will be the poorer as a result.

In his opening address to the conference the UN Secretary-General, Boutros Boutros-Ghali, described the planet as being 'sick with over- and under-development' while, towards the end of the conference, Cuba's Fidel Castro said: 'We need less luxury and waste in a few countries so there can be less poverty and hunger in the greater part of the world.' In theory, few would disagree with either statement; in pactice, there were equally few signs that the rich North was prepared to alter its ways or that the poor South expected to see any changes. So what, it might be asked, was the point of the conference? Did it achieve anything?

The Conference produced two conventions and an agenda – Agenda 21. The two conventions were the Framework Convention on Climate Change (which aims to stabilize 'greenhouse' gases so as to prevent global warming) and the Convention on Biological Diversity (to curb the destruction of biological species, habitats and ecosystems). Agenda 21 outlines recommendations for action on a range of environmental problems which include climate change, depletion of the ozone layer, air and water pollution, wastes, depletion of stocks of fish and other marine resources. Just which of these decisions will be translated into firm practice remains to be seen. At least, it could be argued, the Rio Earth Summit was the first occasion when the world as a whole – both North and South – recognized in theory that problems relating to the world's resources are joint problems that must be tackled by everyone on a global basis. Just what the world intended to do in practice remained an open question.

In the four years after the Rio Earth Summit the United Nations continued to hold conferences which covered an apparently inexhaustible agenda of social and developmental problems: on human rights (Vienna 1993), on small island states (Barbados 1994), on population and development (Cairo 1994), a world summit on social development (Copenhagen 1995), a world conference on women (Beijing 1995) and human settlements (Istanbul 1996). Although such conferences clearly keep their subjects in the public (international) eye, it is debatable how much else they achieve. Cynics may argue that since the United Nations is unable to achieve much in concrete terms it can at least discuss what ought to be done. In fact, even if such an observation is partially true there is, nonetheless, more to be gained from such conferences than might appear on the surface. They establish the multiple responsibilities which have been undertaken by the United Nations and in the process have created a body of conventions and agreed principles that can be referred to at a later date. When, which seems the most likely scenario for progress, some major catastrophe forces the world to seek a new approach to a particular problem the framework for action will already exist under the auspices of the United Nations.

As the Rio Earth Summit and other conferences have repeatedly demonstrated, groups of countries pursue totally contradictory priorities. The major consumer nations, led by the United States, do not wish to have their rights to unfettered consumption and the consequent ability to raise living standards curtailed by controls on carbon emissions. The oil states do not wish to see the adoption of policies which would imply a cutback in the use of oil. The countries which possess the world's great tropical forests do not wish to see any curtailment of the immense profits to be earned from cutting down this non-renewable heritage. Whenever questions of population control are raised the views of the Vatican, if not of all Catholic countries, have to be taken into account. Reconciling these essentially self-interested and selfish views must be the primary concern of the United Nations.

When the UN Global Warming Summit opened in Berlin at the end of March 1995 it was considered as a victory that the oil producing nations had been persuaded not to block the proceedings from the outset. The object of the conference was to examine the threat of climate change and rising sea levels caused by the build-up of pollutant gases in the atmosphere. These are the result of burning coal, oil and gas and the major fossil fuel exporters, led by Saudi Arabia and Kuwait, made plain from the outset that they were determined to defend their interests (exporting oil) while some OPEC countries wanted the right to veto any resolutions which threatened their ability to do so. Over 1000 delegates representing 130 countries took part in the conference which was the first meeting of those countries which had ratified the UN climate change treaty arising out of the Rio Earth Summit. The conference president, the German environment minister, Angela Merkel, warned the conference: 'The peoples of the world expect us to take the decisions necessary to protect them from the harm that threatens.' The conference ended without any agreement to reduce the emission of 'greenhouse gases' although a mandate was given to the developed nations to prepare targets and proposals for their implementation in 1997. Angela Merkel insisted that the agreement had set 'very strong and tough guidelines'. While Greenpeace described the conference as a 'challenge to developed countries to show their good faith', the US-based Sierra Club decribed it as a 'shocking abdication of leadership'. Some advances in the theory of world behaviour (if not the actuality) were recorded. The final conference document emphasized that developed countries should 'take the lead in combating climate change ... The largest share of historical and current emissions of greenhouse gases has originated in developed countries, and the per capita emissions in developing countries are still relatively low.[4] More importantly, the agreement accepted the argument of the developing countries that their carbon dioxide emissions should be allowed to increase as their economies expand while developed countries are forced to cut back. It was also accepted that the rich North had to bear the burden of responsibility for change. The United States, as seems increasingly to be the case in relation to questions of the environment, was the most reluctant of the advanced economies to make any commitments about cutting back its emissions or otherwise agreeing to policies which, in effect, would restrict American consumption patterns.

The developed countries were set a target to produce an agreement to limit or reduce their emissions of global warming gases by 1997 over a five-, ten- or twenty-year period which should start in 2000, but the language was sufficiently vague that it could be interpreted to mean stabilization, reduction or even increases in emissions. No targets were set for the developing world.

A breakdown of participants showed them dividing into predictable groupings: the United States, Canada and Australia of the advanced economies were seen to be the most reluctant to meet any targets for cutting back emissions; in addition, they argued that the Third World should also limit its emissions if any deal is to be struck. The European Union (possibly influenced by its densely populated industrial areas) was prepared to cut emissions between the years 2000 and 2010. The Organization of Small Island States, understandably enough since some of them are threatened with total disappearance if sea levels rise, argued forlornly that the developed countries should cut their carbon dioxide emissions by 20 per cent by 2005. Third World countries, generally, wanted the rich to curb their 'greenhouse gas' emissions without, however, making any commitments about their own rapidly rising rates of pollution, while the oil-exporting countries were opposed to any measures that could threaten the export of their oil. After ten days of such discussions the chances of curbs on a scale that would have a significant impact upon climate changes seemed as remote as ever because, as usual, the wording of UN agreements is more concerned to obtain the semblance of agreed approaches, which is a possibility, than hard commitments to action, which are far rarer.

If the Global Warming Summit of 1995 did more to reveal the extent of the differences between the various interest groups than to produce solutions, the Habitat II conference, held in Istanbul during June 1996, was both more interesting and more productive. It met at a time when the majority of the world's population is about to become urban; by 2000 more people worldwide will live in towns than in the countryside while, by 2025, two-thirds of the world's population will be urban dwellers as opposed to one-third in 1975. These figures represent a revolution of huge dimensions. The Habitat II meeting hoped to produce an international strategy to deal with this change. In 1900 there were only 11 cities world-wide with a population in excess of one million; in 1996 there were 300; by 2015 there are expected to be 570. Moreover, 90 per cent of this growth will be in the Third World. Half the urban growth results from population increase, the balance from migrations as increasing numbers of people in the Third World flee rural poverty and hope to find employment in already overcrowded cities and their spreading slums. A high-level group of experts preparing for the Habitat II conference said of cities:

> Our values are made concrete in towns and cities. They are expressions of the dynamism of the human spirit, the centres of culture, creativity and the exchange of ideas. But they also concentrate the extremes of wealth and poverty and take a disproportionate toll on the life support systems

of the planet. The scale of urbanisation and growing inequality have resulted in new levels of poverty while cities already nearing breaking point will have to accommodate an unprecedented growth in numbers.[5]

Many of the problems of large cities are common to both advanced and Third World cities; they include pollution, violence, slums, drug addiction and various forms of social disintegration. For once, therefore, the problems could be presented as universal ones rather than belonging only to the Third World so that efforts to find solutions would be of equal value to both sides in the North–South divide.

As the group of experts meeting in Marmaris, Turkey, prior to the conference, also reported:

> There is no hope of addressing the crisis of towns and cities or of realising their potential to create solutions, without the full participation of their peoples. Decisions must be devolved as far as possible to the community level ... Cities are successful if they are hospitable, participatory, equitable and in balance with the natural resource base they utilise. Some towns and cities have already taken substantial steps along this path, but the journey is only beginning.[6]

Much of the message from this group was positive: that urbanization is reducing population growth; that Third World cities exploding out of control was not going to happen; that from a number of major cities such as Calcutta or Rio de Janeiro more people are moving out than coming in; and that urban farming is now carried on by some 800 million urban dwellers. In China it is estimated that 90 per cent of the vegetables consumed in the cities are also grown in them. What was new about this conference was an approach that did not simply call upon governments to act but, rather, addressed its concerns to local authorities, the private sector, citizens' groups and community organizations. The United Nations claims that this huge process of urbanization has both the potential for immense social progress and economic advance and a capacity for disaster and human degradation. Which way it develops will depend to a great extent upon decisions made at the present time. The provision of jobs in the cities will be the key to urban progress. As the ILO deputy director, Katherine Hagen, claims:

> By 2000, one half of humanity will be living and working in cities, with developing countries accounting for the major share of the world's new urban population. These people will need jobs if the new cities are to develop as centres of economic opportunity and civilisation rather than zones of inequality and misery.[7]

As the UN Population Fund argues: 'This urban future is inevitable and it should not be feared.' And as many observers of the New China have discovered, work in miserable conditions in a great city like Shanghai may still be preferable to the desperate poverty of the countryside.

Any anlysis of these UN conference activities will produce conflicting judgements. On the debit side they can be seen as huge and costly jamborees, hot-air factories which produce endless well-meaning statements and call for actions that no one will take seriously. Leaders sign 'solemn declarations' and 'plans of action' but these are no more than pious statements of suitably vague intent without any accompanying means of enforcement. They do not, as cynics argue, bear any relationship to the real world of hard-headed politics or the self-interest of nations. As one European diplomat said scathingly of the Poverty Summit held in New York at the beginning of 1995:

> We had this amazing fight over whether it [the report] should say 'eliminate poverty' or 'substantially reduce poverty'. Really, it is the worst of the UN, where everyone is vying with each other for the most extreme language. The fact that it may be totally impossible to deliver in the real world is totally irrelevant to most of them.[8]

On the credit side there is, perhaps, one major advantage in such affairs. They publicize the problems and needs and, just a little, they do succeed in eliciting commitments from participants to take small steps towards agreed solutions, even if the original agreement was more of a political gesture than an actual intent. Once governments have accepted the principles set out in a UN document they can be held to them at a future date. The United States which has always been sceptical of such UN conferences nonetheless does not like to ignore the world body entirely and most of the rich countries of the North, under pressure, can usually be persuaded to make commitments to programmes in principle which, at a later date, they are obliged to acknowledge and do something about in practice. The rich countries of the North often find these conferences extremely tiresome since the programmes they produce are almost always tilted towards the needs of the South while the North is expected to foot the subsequent bills. Yet this is the only way in which the United Nations can proceed: if there is to be eventual world government – preceded by consensus upon how problems should be tackled – there must also be a form of world taxation. The North has the wealth and should expect to meet the bills.

12 Human Rights: The Specialized Agencies

Article 1 of the United Nations Charter states that one of the principal purposes of the United Nations is to achieve international cooperation in promoting and encouraging respect for human rights and fundamental freedoms for all without distinction as to race, sex, language or religion. On 10 December 1948, the General Assembly adopted the Universal Declaration of Human Rights and proclaimed the Declaration to be 'a common standard of achievement for all peoples and all nations'. Thereafter, 10 December was to be observed annually as Human Rights Day. Articles 1 and 2 of the Declaration state that 'all human beings are born equal in dignity and rights', and that all are entitled to the rights set forth in the Declaration regardless of 'race, colour, sex, language, religion, political or other opinion, national or social origin, property, birth or other status'. Given the state of the world then and today, these rights, although universally accepted in theory, must appear near impossible to attain for a large proportion of mankind in practice.

The rights which the Declaration then enumerates are magnificent in concept but, too often, they are ignored in reality whether by governments, communities, groups, institutions or individuals. The main rights set down are as follows: the right to life, liberty and security of person; freedom from slavery and servitude; freedom from torture or cruel, inhuman or degrading treatment; the right to recognition everywhere as a person before the law; the right to effective judicial remedies, equality of treatment before the law and the right to be presumed innocent until proved guilty; the right to freedom from arbitrary interference in private life and freedom from attacks upon honour and reputation; freedom of movement, the right to asylum, the right to nationality; the right to marry, to have a family, to own property; freedom of thought, conscience and religion; freedom of opinion and expression; the right to peaceful assembly and association; the right to take part in government and to have equal access to the public service.

The Declaration also enumerates economic, social and cultural rights to which all human beings are entitled; these include the right to social security, the right to work, the right to equal pay for equal work, the right to form and join trade unions, the right to rest and leisure, the right to a standard of living adequate to health and well-being, the right to education and the right to participate in the cultural life of the community.

These rights, of course, represent a goal towards which to strive in an ideal world and for many millions they are no more than a dream. In the world's more dictatorial societies many of these rights – security of person, freedom from torture, equality before the law, freedom from arbitrary arrest, freedom of conscience or religion, or freedom of expression, or the right to peaceful assembly – are positively denied and though the United Nations, through its various mechanisms, constantly exerts pressures upon regimes which do deny such rights there is little more it is capable of doing as a general rule other than publicizing such behaviour.

Similarly, the economic rights enumerated, such as the right to work, the right to a standard of living adequate to health and well-being or the right to education, are not provided in many poor countries. This is not the result of tyranny but of poverty and, in these latter circumstances, gives point to the constant efforts of the United Nations to assist the development of the LDCs so as to bring all their populations closer to the possibility of enjoying such rights.

It is one of the paradoxes of our world that the most advanced economies often, though certainly not always, have the best human rights records. This is not because their governments or leaders are inherently better than those in poor countries but because economic well-being and wealth allow margins for the provision of rights, including the luxury of political dissent, since these governments feel able to cope with the criticisms, opposition and pressures that the full enjoyment of such rights inevitably encourages. In very poor countries many of these rights – education for example – cannot be provided adequately for all because the resources do not exist while governments whose political basis is precarious are those most likely to resort to repression such as the denial of free speech or a clamp-down on many forms of dissent.

Since 1948 the United Nations has produced a number of additional covenants covering further aspects of human rights or spelling out rights in greater detail. Its long campaigns against colonialism and against apartheid in South Africa both came under its human rights umbrella and at least in these two areas it can claim very substantial success for colonialism, at any rate in the form in which it existed after World War II, has virtually disappeared as did apartheid by 1994. The emergence of the Third World coincided with the sustained pressures of the United Nations for an end to colonialism and the new nations which achieved their independence between 1945 and 1980 owed a good deal to the efforts of the world body on their behalf.

An agreed charter of human rights is one thing; their universal observance is something quite different. Each of the human rights enumerated above is constantly violated somewhere in the world and some of them, either as a result of deliberate policy (denial of free speech or rights of political opposition) or as a result of poverty (the right to work, for example) are violated on a massive scale. In the case of the deliberate denial of political or other rights the United Nations can try, first by exposure and the use of the media, then by steady appeals, pressures and a process of education, and ultimately by action through the Security Council, to force a government to change its ways. Where economic rights are lacking as a result of poverty the United Nations must continue its campaigns to persuade the rich North to assist in programmes to achieve sustainable development in the LDCs.

In *Our Global Neighbourhood* the authors deal with human rights under a section entitled 'Neighbourhood Values', and one passage which reflects all the values so carefully enumerated in the United Nations Charter and the 1948 Universal Declaration of Human Rights is worth quoting if only to show just how difficult is the task the United Nations has set itself.

> We believe that all humanity could uphold the core values of respect for life, liberty, justice and equity, mutual respect, caring, and integrity. These provide a foundation for transforming a global neighbourhood based on economic exchange and improved communications into a universal moral community in which people are bound together by more than proximity, interest or identity. They all derive in one way or another from the principle, which is in accord with religious teachings around the world, that people should treat others as they would themselves wish to be treated. It is this imperative that was reflected in the call made in the UN Charter for recognition of 'the inherent dignity and equal and inalienable rights of all members of the human family'.[1]

Anyone who has followed the brutal denial of a whole range of human rights, the ethnic cleansing, the genocide, torture and degradation meted out to hundreds of thousands of human beings during the present decade alone in Angola, Bosnia, Burma, Burundi, Cambodia, Georgia, Iraq, Liberia, Rwanda, Sierra Leone, Tajikistan or Timor, to name only a few of the countries that more obviously made the world's headlines during the 1990s, is bound to ask whether UN human rights aspirations have any hope of full implementation unless the world body has at its disposal both the authority and the power to intervene in societies which consistently deny human rights to their populations. Yet, even if the answer to that question is no, the United Nations has an absolute duty to insist upon these human rights loudly and consistently, no matter what governments it offends and no matter how little assistance it receives from its members, especially its most powerful members, in implementing human rights policies.

The United Nations Development Programme (UNDP) has made a substantial contribution to the human rights debate through the publication of its Human Development Reports. The *Human Development Report 1992* emphasized markets as the means to achieve human development. This approach was in tune with the general political thrust of the principal powers and also coincided with the new search for market answers to problems by the members of the former USSR.

> One of the great lessons of recent decades is that competitive markets are the best guarantee for human development. They open up opportunities for creative enterprise, and they increase the access of people to a whole range of economic choices.[2]

This particular report concentrated upon the global dimensions of human development and, despite the approval of competitive markets expressed above, pointed out how unequal competition is between rich and poor countries. The report pinpoints three aspects of development that require particular attention: first, economic growth does not automatically improve people's lives whether within a nation or internationally; second, rich and poor countries compete in the global marketplace as unequal partners and if developing countries are to compete on a more equal footing they will require massive investments in human capital and technological development; third, global markets do not operate freely and this fact, together with the unequal partnership, costs developing countries an estimated US$500 billion a year or ten times what they receive in foreign assistance.[3]

The *Human Development Report 1994* was concerned with human security. In a summary of progress over the preceding 50 years it indicated the huge improvements which had taken place: most nations had won their freedom; the world had become safer from the threat of nuclear holocaust; and human advance could be measured in rising life expectations, falling infant mortality, increasing educational attainment and greatly improved nutrition. In statistical terms, the report claimed that while in 1960 70 per cent of humanity survived in abysmal conditions measured below a human development index of 0.4, only 32 per cent suffered similar conditions in 1992, while the proportion of the world population enjoying fairly satisfactory human development levels (above a human development index or HDI of 0.6) had increased from 25 per cent in 1960 to 60 per cent in 1992. These were impressive figures and both the United Nations at the political level and the various UN agencies at the more technical working levels could claim a fair proportion of the credit for such achievements.

Over the same period, the wealth of nations has multiplied with the global GDP increasing from about US$3 trillion (1 trillion=1million million) to US$22 trillion against a population increase from 2.5 billion to 5.5 billion, allowing per capita incomes to triple. Huge technological changes – telephone, television or fax – have made most parts of the world far more accessible while computers now move more than a trillion dollars between the world's financial markets every 24 hours, though whether this last development works to the advantage of the Third World is, at least at present, open to question. Between half and three-quarters of the world's people were living under democratic systems in 1992, some for the first time, and the year witnessed elections in 45 countries, in some cases again for the first time.[4]

What these improvements demonstrated was the world's capacity, selectively no doubt, to engineer changes and this touches upon what may well turn out to be an area of acute tension for the United Nations over the next decade. If the belief in market forces which became an article of faith in leading Western nations during the 1980s continues to dominate the politics of the North, then how much will the rich nations subscribe to United Nations policies which in many respects represent the antithesis of this approach? The United States, for example, has shown considerable impatience with UN concern over economic problems in the Third World. Moreover, should economic conditions generally become more difficult over the next decade the temptation for the rich to insist that all progress must depend upon market force answers may become greater as the 'market' alone is looked to for solutions when, in fact, the 'market' is being used as an excuse for no action under other headings. In all its activities in relation to the Third World – political, social, economic – the United Nations has engineered change and this, of course, is a socialist approach; had the world body left such changes to the workings of the market many would not have taken place at all. If the North is now about to enter upon a period in which it becomes increasingly fearful of the growing numbers in the South, and their more strident demands for better economic conditions, it may well draw in upon itself and set its face against greater social or economic engineering by the United Nations – and that is a consideration which must be taken into account in the immediate future.

There is a certain lack of realism about these Human Development Reports, however well-meaning they may be. The following passage is a good example:

> The new demands of global human security require a more positive relationship among all nations of the world – leading to a new era of development cooperation. In such a design, economic partnership would be based on mutual interests, not charity; cooperation, not confrontation; equitable sharing of market opportunities, not protectionism; far-sighted internationalism, not stubborn nationalism.[5]

Here the expression of hope is far greater than any likely reality. The report goes on to make the point that during the Cold War foreign assistance was given to strategic allies rather than in support of agreed policy objectives. 'Now is the time', the report says, 'for a major restructuring of existing foreign aid allocations'. The restructuring that does take place is far more likely to be in terms of reducing aid altogether than in providing equivalent amounts (to those provided through the Cold War) to meet these UN policy objectives. It is, however, a necessary UN imperative always to work upon the premise that its members wish to improve the human condition as a whole.

Much of the *Human Development Report 1996* makes gloomy reading. The report centres upon the links between economic growth and human development and comes up with two disturbing findings:

> Growth has been failing over much of the past 15 years in about 100 countries, with almost a third of the world's people. And the links between growth and human development are failing for people in the many countries with lopsided development – with either good growth but little human development or good human development but little or no growth.

The report concludes that more economic growth rather than less will be needed in the twenty-first century but that more attention should go into the structure and quality of that growth to ensure that it is 'directed to supporting human development, reducing poverty, protecting the environment and ensuring sustainability'.[6]

What this report and *The Least Developed Countries 1996 Report* of UNCTAD (see below, Chapter 16) are both examining is the growing impact of the so-called global economy. Perhaps central to this is the phenomenon, referred to above, of the movement worldwide of more than a trillion dollars a day between financial institutions. Increasingly, countries are no longer able to control their money or their business operations, both of which are becoming more international and less national in the ways in which they operate or are moved about. This is a development that is worrying major economic powers such as Britain; for small developing countries it could turn into a disaster. Over 15 years from 1980 to 1995 there occurred spectacular growth in some 15 countries with a combined population of 1.5 billion but this was paralleled by economic decline or stagnation in about 100 countries with a comparable population of 1.6 billion. The world is becoming more rather than less polarized as the gap between rich and poor continues to widen and, on present evidence, the trend is being assisted by the rapid development of the new global market. Should the major economies begin to find that their own workforces are at risk, as a result of rapid global shifts in the operations of transnational corporations, they will have little interest in assisting UN-sponsored programmes of sustainable development in the LDCs.

Emphasis upon human rights became a feature of UN activity through the 1990s: partly, this was a response to such catastrophes as Rwanda or Yugoslavia; and partly, perhaps, it reflected an ever more complicated world which had become both less predictable and less manageable as a consequence of the loosening structures which followed the end of the Cold War. The annual Human Development Reports of the UNDP were part of this process. Other aspects of it included the unanimous adoption by the General Assembly of a Convention on the Rights of the Child in November 1989 followed in 1990 by a declaration and plan of action to improve the lives of the world's poorest children. In January 1990, as a consequence of the new freedom in Eastern Europe, Czechoslovakia, East Germany, Hungary and Romania asked the UN Human Rights Centre in Geneva to assist their governments to write guarantees of individual rights into their constitutions and teach officials administering justice about obligations under the Universal Declaration of Human Rights. Here, for once, advanced nations were asking for UN assistance over human rights.

Leaders in the Horn of Africa called for a meeting with United Nations officials in Addis Ababa for early 1992 to establish the principle that governments had no right to hinder UN humanitarian relief agencies working in disaster areas or to appropriate emergency food and medical supplies as weapons in civil conflicts. Governments or factions in civil wars have been only too ready to manipulate such agencies or seize their supplies and, as the United Nations learnt in Somalia and Yugoslavia, even with armed forces at its disposal to safeguard such supplies, these often fell into the wrong hands. Such a principle, if accepted worldwide and made enforceable, could have a major impact upon civil conflicts.

Through the years 1991–6 the United Nations was obliged, again and again, to condemn human rights abuses in many parts of the world, led by Serbia for ethnic cleansing, Rwanda for genocide and so on. In March 1992 the UN Commission on Human Rights criticized 22 countries for human rights abuses, especially Iran and Cuba, and placed other countries under surveillance. On 27 May 1992, it also suggested that the United States might be violating human rights by returning Haitian refugees to Haiti before allowing them to appeal for asylum. A measure of constant pressure or a sense of embarrassment, or a combination of both, might explain the ratification by the US Senate in 1992 of the International Covenant on Civil and Political Rights which had been adopted by the United Nations in 1966 and entered into force in 1976. The United States was the 104th country to ratify the treaty. During 1993 the Security Council established a UN War Crimes Tribunal for the former Yugoslavia and the Commission on Human Rights condemned Sudan and Iraq for employing terror against their own people. In addition the Commission criticized serious human rights abuses in Afghanistan, Equatorial Guinea, Haiti, Iran, Israel, Myanmar (Burma) and Togo and expressed 'deep concern' at human rights violations in East Timor. A UN 'Commission on the Truth' investigating violations of human rights in the 12-year civil war in El Salvador held active and retired military officers responsible for killing thousands of civilians and called for the government to dismiss them or bar them from public leadership posts for a minimum of ten years. In December 1993 the General Assembly established a new office of High Commissioner on Human Rights. While many of these condemnations or expressions of deep concern may make little impact upon abuses that have taken place, they do have a growing importance in a world where the media, and especially television, has become so important. And though the use of sanctions against offending states has, so far, been a lopsided affair principally dictated by the major powers, and then only when it suits them, fear of UN sanctions is not a negligible factor in influencing government behaviour.

*   *   *

Apart from its peacekeeping bodies, the United Nations has created a wide range of agencies, 15 of which are known as specialized agencies. The work of some of these, such as the Universal Postal Union (UPU) or International Telecommunications Union (ITU), is mainly technical although they provide substantial expertise which is available to all member nations. A number have become powerful and influential bodies in their own right. The economic institutions, headed by the autonomous World Bank and including the United Nations Development Programme (UNDP) and the Food and Agricultural Organization (FAO), are mainly concerned with aid and development problems. Others deal with living standards and social conditions and include the International Labour Organization (ILO), the United Nations Educational, Scientific and Cultural Organization (UNESCO) and the World Health Organization (WHO). A majority of these organizations are, in fact, of far greater importance to the developing countries of the Third World than to the advanced economies although in theory their expertise is available to all UN members. It is not the intention to examine the work of all these bodies in detail here but aspects of the work of some of them have particular bearing upon the arguments of this book and deserve study.

Sometimes an agency becomes the centre of controversy: this may be confrontational, as between North and South, which was the case in UNESCO in the early 1980s; sometimes it is about economic control as are the periodic rows about the operations of the International Monetary Fund (IMF); and sometimes it is about corruption as in the 1995 row involving the WHO. The work of some agencies – the United Nations High Commissioner for Refugees (UNHCR) for example – simply demonstrates the sheer extent of the problems which the United Nations faces.

UNESCO was formed in 1946 with the primary aim of promoting collaboration among nations through education, science, culture and communications and it has many achievements to its credit. In the early 1980s, however, it became involved in growing controversy which led to a classic confrontation between its Third World members (supported by the USSR) and the major Western powers. Although there were a number of underlying strains, including the personality of its director and accusations of corruption, the principal cause of the row was the demand by a majority of its members for a new 'information order': that is, a news service comparable to such established services as Reuters, providing information supplied by Third World governments. This was bitterly opposed by the West which objected to any curtailment of the liberties of the press in favour of government-censored news. The row culminated in the withdrawal from UNESCO of the United States at the end of 1984 and Britain at the end of 1985. The confrontation highlighted those problems endemic to all North–South arguments. In this particular case the Western powers were heavily outvoted by the majority of UNESCO members, yet they provide the greater part of the organization's funds and in 1984, for example, the withdrawal of the United States meant UNESCO lost 25 per cent of its budget (and another 5 per cent when Britain left). As so often in UN confrontations, the argument resolved itself into one of power: the Third World countries have the votes; the rich countries of the North the power (in the form of finance).

The IMF, arguably, has become the most controversial of all UN agencies. Born out of the Bretton Woods talks of 1944 and closely allied to the World Bank, the IMF, originally, was not seen as a development agency at all but as a permanent instrument for establishing a world multilateral system of payments. It is, in theory, a form of cooperative deposit bank upon which members with balance of payments problems can draw funds. However, if members wish to draw funds over and above their full drawing rights which are determined by their deposits they are obliged to submit to stringent IMF conditions. These conditionalities go beyond normal banking requirements and have become a continuing bone of political contention between the Fund and many would-be borrowers from the South. The problem for the poor countries is that the IMF has come to be seen, with its seal of approval which Western bankers require if they are to lend, as a form of policeman for Western financial interests, prescribing policies which developing countries are then obliged to adopt whether or not these are in tune with their own political aims. Moreover, the IMF is seen to be controlled by the North (which means the rich countries of the Western world) and to be the key to multilateral economic assistance. At the end of the 1980s the IMF sought to increase its resources by 67 per cent (US$80 billion) so as the better to meet the shocks of the 1990s and allow it to expand its role into Eastern Europe. In May 1990 it did increase its resources by 50 per cent in order to provide assistance to Eastern European countries in their moves towards a market economy. The importance of the IMF in North–South deliberations was emphasized in 1990 when the United States participated in the Third World economic debate 'with a lot of scepticism' and reluctance, preferring to leave development questions to the IMF. Indeed, the rich countries have been able to shield behind the IMF when development questions involving loans or aid to the South arise, for instead of addressing these directly they can refer them to the IMF whose seal of approval must first be obtained before a loan will be considered. In January 1991, for example, the IMF made a loan of US$1.8 billion to Czechoslovakia to help it create a market economy. This was certainly not the role originally envisaged for the IMF.

According to the *Human Development Report 1992*, the IMF no longer performs the function for which it was created, which was to maintain monetary stability with the burden of adjustments shared between surplus and deficit countries; moreover, it has ceased to perform this original function because it is unable to control or exert authority over the rich industrial nations. From the 1980s onwards it became clear that the rich nations (in effect the Group of Seven), who between them control IMF voting, had come to see it as their instrument and not as their mentor and though the IMF ought to have become the guardian of the poor, in fact it became the policeman for the rich. As a result an increasing proportion of highly vulnerable Third World countries have been obliged to operate IMF-inspired structural adjustment programmes (SAPs) through which the IMF instructs governments how to run their economies in return for a measure of debt relief in the form of rescheduling.

The World Health Organization (WHO) was established in 1948 and has as its objective 'the attainment of all peoples of the highest possible level of health' and its record has been largely benign and uncontroversial. It is mainly concerned with primary health care in developing countries and reinforces national health systems by building up infrastructures and promoting research. It has promoted a series of worldwide health campaigns: the provision of safe drinking water, for example, or the provision through the 1980s of immunization to prevent the six major communicable diseases of childhood – diptheria, measles, poliomyelitis, tetanus, tuberculosis and whooping cough.

In 1995, however, the WHO was affected by a major scandal when a report by the British Auditor-General accused its African regional office in Brazzaville (the Congo) of fraud, irregular payments and accounting malpractices. Sir John Bourn, the British Auditor-General, told the United Nations that the National Audit Office was resigning its job of auditing the WHO accounts and would not reapply for the contract in 1996. The WHO declined to comment. The list of malpractices detailed by the British Auditor-General was long and extraordinary. The WHO Director-General, Dr Hiroshi Nakajima, and his staff refused to cooperate with Sir John Bourn and his staff.[7] The row illustrated many of the worst forms of corruption that bedevil the United Nations and its agencies. One reaction of such an organization when in trouble is simply to ignore awkward facts and hope that the row will die down. Another problem lies with the political ambition of the agency head: in this case Dr Nakajima was hoping for a third term of office as Director-General of the WHO and, therefore, clearly wished to avoid any public scrutiny. Part of the problem could be described as North–South confrontation since the auditors came from the North while the office under scrutiny was in a poor country in the South. As a result, what in business terms would be dealt with as a straight case of corruption, in UN terms takes on acute political dimensions. Another aspect of such a problem, which appears to be endemic to UN structures, is the perpetuation of incompetent or second-rate management. Again and again such questions return to the political dimension of who (what nationality) is in charge of an organization, so that what ought to be a simple problem of management (sacking the incompetent) becomes, instead, a question of offending a member state whose personnel are at fault. There are no easy answers to such problems unless the management structure of such organizations is changed. This could be done in two ways. First, if the Director-General is only appointed for one term and is barred from running for a second term, he would be far more likely to take tough stands on issues such as this where offence to a member nation is a possible outcome. Second, if all jobs in UN organizations are put out to tender and are never in the gift of member nations, this, in large measure, would eliminate the temptation for governments to defend their nationals when they have behaved corruptly because not to do so is to lose face.

One of the most genuinely overworked UN agencies is the UNHCR. Figures released in March 1990 showed that the numbers of refugees which it had to deal with had doubled since 1980 yet it was only to receive US$550 million of the US$700 million it required that year to meet the minimum needs of 15 million refugees. The 1990s has seen an increasing number of refugees created by civil wars rather than wars between states and this has added another dimension to UNHCR problems. Humanitarian aid always has a political impact, no matter how non-partisan it is intended to be, and for example, it is estimated that about 300 000 people in Sarajevo were saved from becoming refugees because UNHCR relief supplies reached them. Perhaps the most important question now facing the UNHCR concerns the changing nature of wars, most of which are now civil wars so that refugees are created but remain within their own national borders. In 1995, 26 million people fell into this category, and unless the situation develops into a 'Yugoslavia' where the UNHCR has a mandate to intervene, it is unable to provide assistance. Here is a new problem: should the UNHCR mandate be extended to cover refugees within a country where a civil war is taking place? Most governments are unwilling to allow interference within their national boundaries. The UNHCR has raised the consciousness of the world to the plight of refugees but finding solutions is far more difficult. Addressing this problem in 1995, the United Nations High Commissioner for Refugees, Sadako Ogata, claimed that 27 million people worldwide had fled their homes because of war and persecution. She called for new political thinking to prevent conflicts and deal with the changing character of war and displacement. As the High Commissioner pointed out,[8] figures for 1995 included the following: four countries – Germany, Pakistan, Iran and Zaire – were each hosting more than one million refugees and another 28 nations were hosting more than 100 000 each; the three countries with the most refugees were Afghanistan, Rwanda and Liberia, with 2.74 million Afghans still living as refugees 16 years after the Soviet invasion of 1979, and 2.26 million Rwandans also living in exile; there were more refugees in Africa (6.75 million) than in any other continent. While traditionally a refugee was someone who crossed an international border and sought asylum in another state, present-day civil conflicts and the break-up of states such as Yugoslavia and Somalia have created a new category of refugee who have been named 'internally displaced persons'. If such people are to be assisted the UNHCR must be given a new mandate, which may happen for, as the United Nations Secretary-General has admitted, 'the time of absolute and exclusive sovereignty has passed'.

13 Arms: Nuclear and Conventional

The paramount concern of the United Nations has always been the maintenance of peace which at the best of times is difficult; and a world awash with arms has made such a task infinitely harder. If the production and trade in arms can be drastically reduced so that potential and actual antagonists experience serious difficulty in obtaining arms this will make peacekeeping an easier proposition for the United Nations. During the 1990s, and despite attempted embargoes, few combatants ever experienced serious problems in obtaining the arms they required. The United Nations Charter is specific in the responsibilities it assigns to both the General Assembly and the Security Council in the matter of disarmament. The General Assembly has the duty to consider 'principles governing disarmament and the regulation of armaments' and can make recommendations to UN members or the Security Council. The Security Council is responsible for formulating 'plans to be submitted to the members of the United Nations for the establishment of a system for the regulation of armaments'. Over the years of the Cold War, UN efforts to limit armaments or encourage disarmament were constantly thwarted by the massive scale of military preparedness that both sides in that confrontation saw fit to maintain. Even so, various steps were taken by the United Nations during its first 40 years, though these did not bring an end to the arms race.

Between 1959 and 1985 the United Nations promoted a series of treaties designed principally to restrict the spread of nuclear weapons and to limit nuclear testing and these form the basis of an international arms control system. They include: the Antarctic Treaty of 1959 which provides for the demilitarization of Antarctica and prohibits any military activities in the region; the 1963 Partial Test-Ban Treaty which banned nuclear weapons tests in the atmosphere, outer space and under water; and a 1967 Treaty on Principles Governing the Activities of States in the Exploration and Use of Outer Space which banned the placing of nuclear or other weapons of mass destruction in orbit. Also, in 1967, the Treaty of Tlatelolco created the world's first nuclear-weapon-free zone to cover Latin America and the Caribbean. In 1968 came the Treaty on the Non-Proliferation of Nuclear Weapons which aimed to prevent the spread of nuclear weapons and to promote the peaceful uses of nuclear energy. The 1970s saw another four treaties of relative significance: the 1971 Sea-Bed Treaty which banned the

144

placement of nuclear or other weapons on the seabed; the 1972 Biological Weapons Convention which prohibited the development and production of bacteriological weapons; the 1977 Convention which prohibited the use of Environmental Modification Techniques (the ENMOD Convention); and the 1979 Agreement Governing the Activities of States on the Moon and Other Celestial Bodies which complemented the 1967 space treaty. In 1981 the Inhumane Weapons Convention prohibited the use of conventional weapons deemed to be excessively injurious or to have indiscriminate effects. In 1985 a second nuclear-free zone was created by the South Pacific Nuclear Free Zone Treaty (the Treaty of Rarotonga). None of these treaties curtailed the arms race between the United States and the USSR and their respective allies; nor did they have any impact upon the growth of the international arms trade.

The explosion of the first atomic bomb at Hiroshima on 6 August 1945 ushered in a new age in terms of destructive armaments as well as the very real fear that a nuclear holocaust could eliminate the human race, and concern with nuclear weapons became central to all efforts at arms control thereafter. Indeed, it may be argued that the growth of ordinary (non-nuclear) armaments was given a boost because of the nuclear question since almost all the international efforts to control arms were focused upon nuclear weapons so that, by the mid-1980s, the world arms trade had grown to be worth US$500000 million a year and more.

Unfortunately, after 1945 the possession of nuclear weapons came to be seen as the badge of great power status and by the 1990s, despite some genuine efforts to reduce nuclear armaments, their possession was still regarded in this light and there were no measurable indications that the nuclear big five (the United States, Russia, China, Britain and France) had any intention of renouncing their own weapons although they were ready enough to insist that no other nation should be permitted to obtain them. The argument for their possession is that they are a shield against a potentially hostile world; what the main nuclear powers have never satisfactorily explained is how, if this is the case, other states should not also have nuclear weapons for the same reason. Israel, sitting in the middle of what it sees as a highly hostile Arab world, has ignored big power pleas and created its own nuclear arsenal which is generally believed to include some 200 nuclear bombs or warheads. Israel apart, Argentina, Brazil, India, Iraq, North Korea, Pakistan and South Africa have the capability to produce nuclear weapons and in at least three of these cases have done so already while, altogether, about 40 countries are believed either to possess the capacity to make such weapons or to be well on the way to achieving the capability to do so. On the plus side, it appears that Argentina, Brazil and South Africa have halted their nuclear weapons development. The break-up of the Soviet Union meant a further dispersal of both nuclear weapons technology and material so that by the mid-1990s, despite the reduction of American and Russian nuclear stockpiles, more rather than less countries either did possess or were measurably closer to possessing nuclear weapons than at the height of the Cold War. Furthermore, other means of mass destruction such as biological or chemical weapons appear to be on the increase as the United Nations discovered to be the case in Iraq following the Gulf War of 1991.

Leaving aside questions relating specifically to nuclear arms, by the mid-1990s there were many signs that a number of medium powers were anxious to acquire the most up-to-date weaponry available while there were very few indications that many such powers, if any, wished to reduce the level of their armaments or arsenals. Between 1945 and 1990 approximately 140 wars have been fought; these all occurred in the Third World although major powers were sometimes directly involved (as in the Korean and Vietnam wars); otherwise their involvement was by proxy and, as a rule, they supplied the bulk of the weaponry. One of the greatest – and saddest – contradictions of the principles upon which the United Nations was founded lies in the behaviour of the permanent members of the Security Council in relation to the spread of arms. It is their responsibility above all others to work to maintain international peace and yet they have always been the leading suppliers of arms worldwide and derive immense profits from selling arms to the countries of the Third World or South.

Expectations that the end of the Cold War would also bring about a drastic reduction in the arms trade were not fulfilled:

> Although the demand for arms has declined as many countries face economic difficulties or feel less threatened since the end of the cold war, those that are buying find many countries eager to sell. The five permanent members of the Security Council provide 86 per cent of the arms exported to developing countries. In 1992 the United States alone accounted for 46 per cent of the deliveries of weapons to these states. For arms exporters – the United States, Russia, United Kingdom, France, and Germany are the top five – strategic considerations now matter less than protecting jobs and industrial bases. And the huge research and development costs of major weapons often mean that even the largest domestic market cannot guarantee a profit.[1]

As the world rearranges itself in the post-Cold War era, there is a danger that North–South divisions will become more marked and that large areas of the South will be affected, more or less constantly, by civil conflicts as poverty leads to the break-up of states and the emergence of power-hungry warlords. In such circumstances supplying arms may appear to be an easier and more lucrative option for the North than acting as an international policeman for, short of putting troops in place on the ground which the North appears increasingly reluctant to do, such conflicts cannot be controlled. Areas most likely to be affected in this way 'would include large areas of Africa, the Middle East, and South Asia and possibly bits of Central and South America'.[2]

The world's military expenditure peaked in 1987 (at the height of the United States' 'star wars' build-up) but then, as the Cold War came to an end, the USSR made major cuts in its military budget to change this picture with the principal Western military powers following on a more modest scale. Between 1987 and 1994 world expenditure on arms dropped steadily from a peak of US$995000 million in 1987 to US$767000 million in 1994, roughly by a fifth. A breakdown of these figures as between the industrial countries (including China) and the developing countries shows that the greater reductions came in the industrial countries whose costs for their most sophisticated weapons are, in any case, astronomical and it was among these that many cutbacks took place. In 1987 the total expenditure of US$995000 million divided as follows: industrial countries, US$850000 million; developing countries US$145000 million. Seven years later, in 1994, the breakdown was US$649000 million expenditure for industrial countries and US$118000 million for developing countries.[3] The industrial countries had reduced their military expenditure by nearly a quarter, the developing countries by just over a sixth and, in the latter case, this was more a question of economics than as a result of any ideological decision to reduce armaments. At the same time, countries such as Angola which had been in a more or less permanent state of civil war for 30 years were, in any case, awash with arms.

Hopes for a peace dividend at the end of the Cold War in the form of a real reduction in the worldwide arms trade proved illusory. While Russia reduced its arms budget drastically to allow it to cope with its immense problems of economic and social adjustment, civil wars in four of the successor states to the USSR – Armenia, Azerbaijan, Georgia and Tajikistan – added another tier of instability to the immediate north of one of the most unstable regions in the world which includes Afghanistan, Iraq and Iran. The power and influence of the world's military-industrial complexes remains pervasive in the industrial countries despite the end of the Cold War, while in developing countries the military is either in political control or very closely allied to the political leadership so that all efforts at arms reductions or limiting the arms trade meet with formidably entrenched opposition. Apart from the widely held conviction of governments that a powerful military establishment is essential to defence there is the equally widely held determination of arms-producing countries to reap the huge profits that can be earned from selling their arms while, at the same time, divorcing themselves from any responsibility for the consequences of such sales, particularly in the developing world.

Expenditure upon arms and weapons systems is reflected in world research and development figures: in 1990, of between five and seven million people engaged in research and development 1.5 million were working in the military sector.[4] Another factor of relevance in the mid-1990s emerges from the break-up of formal unions or federations: the 15 successor states of the USSR will each create and build up its own separate military establishment; and the break-up of Yugoslavia, after a brutal civil war that has left behind bitter hatreds, means that instead of one military establishment for Yugoslavia as a whole there will be five, one each for Bosnia, Croatia, Macedonia, Serbia and Slovenia. Furthermore, the change in the nature of conflicts may well signal an even greater proliferation of military establishments than ever before and a wider spread of arms, whether to newly formed states or to guerrilla or dissident groups fighting civil wars.

This new trend has been much commented upon since the end of the Cold War although it began much earlier. The great majority of conflicts are now within states rather than between states and, for example, the first Gulf War between Iraq and Iran (1980–8) or the second Gulf War consisting, first, of the Iraqi invasion of Kuwait in 1990 and, then, of the UN-sponsored US-led coalition to drive Iraqi forces out of Kuwait in 1991, were the exceptions rather than the rule. 'Of 82 armed conflicts between 1989 and 1992, only three were between states. Although often cast in ethnic divisions, many also have a political or economic character.'[5] Moreover, a majority of all conflicts now take place in developing countries and this was true throughout the years of the Cold War. Some 52 major conflicts were being fought in 42 countries during 1993 while there was substantial political violence in a further 37 countries, while more than half the conflicts in 1993 had been in progress for ten years or longer, accounting for between four and six million people. In addition, these conflicts had created millions of refugees; in 1992, for example, there were 31 countries from which more than 50 000 refugees had fled. These civil conflicts and the huge numbers of refugees they give rise to present the United Nations with two basic problems, one new and one old. The new problem, judging by events during the 1990s in the former Yugoslavia, Somalia or Rwanda, faces the United Nations with the essentially new dilemma of when it should intervene in the internal affairs of a sovereign state: when should a civil war become the concern of the world, either because it threatens to spread into neighbouring countries or because it puts at risk the human rights, at worst by genocide, of the population in a country at war with itself? The old problem, with a new dimension, is how to look after an apparently ever growing number of refugees of whom an increasing proportion are displaced persons within their own states?

Hopes that general disarmament would follow the end of the Cold War did not materialize while conflicts, if anything, have become more destructive and more widespread, especially in the Third World, and far too many of the poorest countries spend more money on their military estalishments than they do on education or health, which is nothing short of tragic in countries as poor as Angola or Pakistan. The determination of so many Third World countries to purchase as many of the most up-to-date arms as they can afford (or, rather, not afford) is fuelled by the industrial countries whose governments provide major credits to their defence industries. They do this, in part, to safeguard jobs but still more because the arms business is so profitable and though the governments of industrial countries sometimes pay lip-service to the principle of reducing the international arms trade they rarely do anything more positive.

The *Human Development Report 1994*, which devotes a considerable section to the problems of disarmament, suggests seven ways in which it could be promoted:

1. by establishing forums for disarmament;
2. by defusing tensions around the globe;
3. by phasing out military assistance;
4. by regulating the arms trade;
5. by designing a new aid policy dialogue;
6. by agreeing on criteria for UN mediation in conflicts within states; and
7. by creating more effective information systems.

Two of the above approaches to the problem, options 1 and 7, could be readily implemented. Under the first heading would come the mobilization of the various regional Third World forums such as the OAU, the OAS or ASEAN, as well as the Non-Aligned Movement, to undertake to work positively in their regions to reduce military tensions and persuade their members to work towards disarmament. There have been welcome signs that the OAU is willing to undertake an increasing role as a peacemaker in Africa as it has attempted to do, for example, in relation to the Liberian civil war during the 1990s. Under option 7 there is a wide range of activities whose adoption would make it harder for individual countries to ignore pressures to reduce their level of armaments if only by persuading them to explain why they needed so much. In 1992, for example, the United Nations established an arms register in which 80 countries were persuaded to report on their imports and exports of conventional weapons although there remained glaring omissions – but it was a start.

Defusing tensions around the globe (option 2) is obvious enough; part of the difficulty here lies in the number and nature of such tensions – Israel and Palestine and Israel's neighbours are one example, Iraq and her neighbours, another – for in some such cases the root cause of the tensions is long-standing and bitter or the participants are powerful and obdurate. Moreover, where a major power is involved on one side in such disputes, defusing tensions becomes even more difficult: US partiality for Israel in the long-standing Middle East dispute means, in terms of *realpolitik*, that it always sides with Tel Aviv when a crisis erupts, a fact which Israel depends upon and plays with great skill. The United Nations role is to defuse tensions but it can only do this effectively if it has the impartial support of the major powers, and especially the members of the Security Council, in doing so.

Phasing out military assistance (option 3) ought to be straightforward. Military assistance grew directly out of the Cold War with the major powers, and especially the United States, creating worldwide networks of bases and providing arms, free in some circumstances, paid for by loans in others, to friendly states. The disintegration of the USSR brought an end to Soviet aid in Eastern Europe and to Cuba. The West, on the other hand, has been reluctant to do very much. Some phasing-out of bases has taken place, the United States in the Philippines for example, although the closing of the Subic Bay naval facility or the Clark Air Base was involuntary. There has also been a reduction in the provision of military training to allies but the provision of arms continues (by the United States to Israel and Egypt, the two major recipients of its military assistance) while NATO has shown its determination to expand rather than contract despite the formal disbanding of the Warsaw Pact.

Regulating the arms trade (option 4) constitutes the core of the problem and here the difficulties are formidable, not simply because the arms trade is so profitable but also because its leading beneficiaries are the world's leading powers. The principal arms exporters in the years 1988–92, in order, were the United States, the USSR (Russia), France, Germany, China, Britain, Czechoslovakia, the Netherlands, Italy, Sweden and Brazil and the total value of their exports over this five-year period came to US\$151 014 million with the United States alone accounting for US\$54 968 million, or more than a third of that amount. Further, a high proportion of all their sales go to the poorest countries in the world such as India, Afghanistan or Pakistan.

Not only do arms exporting countries fight for contracts to export highly sophisticated weaponry to countries where a high proportion of the populations lack basic necessities but arms dealers show little or no concern about shipping weapons to trouble-spots that help prolong conflicts. As the *Human Development Report 1994* claims:

> The arms trade is a notoriously murky business. When weapons are being bought and sold, the purpose for which they are intended is rarely clear – whether for legitimate needs of national security, for wars of external aggression, for campaigns of internal repression, or for merely satisfying the greed of those who benefit from the transactions. There has never been any satisfactory accounting for arms sales – to the citizens of the buying and selling countries, or to the international community.[6]

Given the amoral readiness of arms supplying countries to sell to any customer who is able to pay, the major suppliers could hardly complain when, in the 1991 Gulf War against Saddam Hussein's Iraq, for example, they found their own weapons turned against them. Apart from the movement of finances around the world, the top three global trades are the arms business, the oil business and drugs and the profits in each case are so enormous that there is probably little prospect that the United Nations can do more than make a few dents in the trade, at least until it has far greater real authority and power at its command than is the case at present, more especially as the worst arms trade offenders are its own Security Council permanent members. Nonetheless, it must keep trying and minor breakthroughs – such as the United Nations Register of Conventional Armaments – represent genuine if small advances.

The design of a new aid dialogue policy (option 5) could become an effective weapon in reducing the arms trade: its central idea is simply to relate aid to the recipient country's ratio of military to social spending so that the more it spends on armaments the less aid it can expect to receive, and vice versa. The concept is simple enough; it will only work if the principal arms suppliers accept the morality of such logic and that appears doubtful.

Finally, agreeing on criteria for UN mediation in conflicts within nations (option 6), is potentially one of the most important UN developments to be expected in the near future. Given the range of conflicts that have taken place in the 1990s in which the United Nations has intervened – Angola, Bosnia, Haiti, Somalia, Iraq and the Kurds – as well as its growing role in monitoring elections after long periods of civil war or civil confrontation – as in Mozambique and South Africa – the idea has now taken hold that there are a growing range of circumstances in which the United Nations must intervene in the internal affairs of a member nation although for decades such a suggestion has been taboo. According to the *Human Development Report 1994*, four situations warrant international intervention in the affairs of a particular state. These are: mass slaughter of the population by the state (genocide as in Rwanda in 1994); decimation through starvation or the withholding of health and other services (as in Bosnia or Somalia); forced exodus (ethnic cleansing throughout much of the former Yugoslavia); and occupation and the denial of the right to self-determination.[7]

Although the United Nations and enlightened opinion may be moving towards an acceptance of those four criteria for UN interventions, their implementation faces formidable difficulties. If we take the four considerations in turn we find that in the most glaring recent example of mass slaughter, in Rwanda, the United Nations effectively did nothing because the major powers refused to become involved. Decimation through starvation or the withholding of health or other supplies saw considerably more action by the United Nations: in Bosnia because, however reluctantly, the major powers decided it was too dangerous to do nothing, although in the case of Somalia the United Nations was forced to withdraw once the United States decided intervention was too costly. Forced exodus presents some of the most difficult of all problems and in the former Yugoslavia, in fact, the United Nations has largely accepted the results of the ethnic cleansing which took place despite condemnations to the contrary (see below). The last criterion, occupation and the right to self-determination, ought to be straightforward and accords with the UN tradition of helping bring an end to colonialism; yet the 20 million Kurds in Iraq, Iran, Syria and Turkey represent the largest cohesive ethnic group in the world that does not have a state of its own and it is far from clear what the United Nations intends in relation to this problem although the major powers and the four nations in which the Kurds are now living are probably quite clear as to what they intend: to leave the Kurds as they are without a state. In the end we always come back to the interests of the great powers and the extent to which, for whatever reasons, they are prepared to support a UN policy.

At the negotiating level the 1990s saw some limited successes and some abysmal failures. At the forty-fourth meeting of the General Assembly in 1989, as the Cold War marched rapidly towards its demise, the general atmosphere, for a change, was optimistic. US President George Bush urged delegates to 'rid the earth' of chemical weapons and offered to destroy 80 per cent of the US stockpile if the USSR would match the Americans which they were willing to do. In January 1993 120 nations meeting in Paris signed a treaty to ban the production, stockpiling and use of chemical weapons and agreed that existing stocks were to be destroyed over a ten-year period. In 1995, however, an attempt to halt the spread of landmines which currently kill or maim 20000 people a year worldwide was thwarted by China, India, Iran, Pakistan and Russia which manufacture such mines and do not want restrictions upon their production and sale. On the bright side that year, a protocol prohibiting laser weapons which blind the enemy was adopted at

Vienna and in May 1995, following four weeks of debate, 170 nations agreed to extend the Nuclear Non-Proliferation Treaty for 25 years. In May 1996 humanitarian agencies described the United Nations Inhumane Weapons Convention conference, which had failed to impose a total ban on anti-personnel landmines, a 'dismal failure' and the British working group on landmines, consisting principally of NGOs, said the decisions of the conference were 'riddled with loopholes, delays and lack of enforcement. In essence this is a mine layers' charter.'[8] In August 1996 India refused to sign a global treaty to ban nuclear test explosions despite pressure from the major nuclear powers. This was in line with a new tough Indian policy aimed at securing for itself a permanent seat on the Security Council (see below, Chapter 14).

Disarmament, apart from the maintenance of peace itself, is arguably the most difficult of all the problems the United Nations has to tackle because the reduction of arms touches upon three basic aspects of national policies. First, it concerns the determination by each individual power of its own security and the level of arms it deems necessary to ensure this and very few powers, even quite small ones, will permit others to dictate what that level should be. Second, it concerns support for allies which is partly about security but still more, perhaps, about a state's notion of its own place in the world. The United States is unlikely to accept any directions about the amount or kind of weapons it supplies to its allies, whether from the United Nations or anyone else. Third, it concerns national greed or, as governments would prefer to describe it, the needs of their economies. Countries making large profits out of arms sales will not easily be persuaded to curtail the trade, especially if they believe that any markets they give up will simply be taken over by other, less scrupulous rivals. Given these obvious restraints, the United Nations nonetheless must continue to persevere with its measures to reduce the world arms business, as always, nibbling away at the edges and occasionally securing substantial advances.

14 The Future of the Security Council

Just as the Security Council represents the core of United Nations power, so, too, does its present composition also reflect the weakness and rigidity of the United Nations in the mid-1990s, for whatever the intentions in 1945, 50 years later the world order had changed so profoundly that the entrenched position of the big five permanent members with their powers of veto could no longer be justified. If the United Nations is to enter the twenty-first century as a viable, working organization there is need for fundamental reforms and these must begin with the Security Council.

The principal victorious powers in World War II – the United States, the USSR, Britain, China and France – first proclaimed the principles of universality and the equality of member states and then reserved to themselves an entrenched position as permanent members of the Security Council with a veto, on the less lofty assumption of *realpolitik* that to the victors go the spoils. 'The Security Council was the only organ of the UN with power to take decisions that bound all member-states and to authorize enforcement action under the collective security provisions of Chapter VII of the Charter.'[1] It has been argued that without the right of veto neither the USSR nor the United States would have ratified the UN Charter; if so, the other permanent members – Britain, France and China – were as anxious for the privilege as the remaining 45 founder members were opposed to it.

The United Nations represented the world's second attempt to create the structures of world government. The failure of the League of Nations, and most particularly its failure in the face of fascism during the 1930s, induced a degree of cynicism about the concept of world government and this, ironically, may have worked in favour of the United Nations: no one has expected too much of it. The ability of the big powers to obstruct the wishes of the UN majority – formally embodied in the existence of the veto – is easier to understand when it is realized that even today most of the world's really important decisions are still taken by only a handful of nations and, until 1990, these were led by the two superpowers. Ever since its inception in 1945 the major powers have rejected the idea that collective decisions of the world body as a whole should become the practice of the United Nations. On the other hand, weak nations which make up the greater part of UN membership see collective action as the best way for them to influence events and towards the end of the Cold War even the superpowers were finding it politic not entirely to ignore this majority opinion. Perhaps subconsciously, and certainly with political realism, the majority of members have worked upon the assumption that a United Nations with limited powers was better than no United Nations at all and that, bit by bit, the majority could slowly enlarge the areas over which it exercised control. It has done this through the specialized agencies, through the Economic and Social Council, in the long battles to persuade the European colonial powers to relinquish their empires and by the persistence with which, again and again, issues repugnant to the major powers have, nonetheless, been raised and in some cases the majority view has eventually prevailed over the wishes of one or more of the permanent members of the Security Council.

As long as the fixed rigidities of the Cold War lasted fundamental changes in the structure of the United Nations were not to be expected, nor did they represent practical politics. The mid to late 1990s, however, coincide with the best opportunity to effect changes that will make the United Nations more representative of the world as a whole and, therefore, better able to deal with its problems. The world is in a period of flux, major powers and regional organizations are having to rethink their purpose and leading nations such as Germany, Japan and India which were barred from any place on the Security Council in 1945 should now be considered.

Recourse to the United Nations to resolve problems increased dramatically from the end of the Cold War:

> From 1946 until the end of 1989, the cold war seriously sapped the vigour of the Council. Only rarely was its true potential used. The Council held 2903 meetings and passed 646 resolutions in that period. But from the beginning of 1990 through mid-1994, it had almost daily informal consultations and 495 formal meetings, and passed 288 resolutions – 26 on the Gulf War and 53 in relation to the situation in the Balkans. Between January 1993 and June 1994 alone, there were 134 resolutions. ...
>
> Peacekeeping has registered a similar increase. At the end of 1990, the United Nations was involved in eight operations with a total of 10000 troops. At the end of June 1994, seventeen operations were being conducted, with more than 70000 troops, costing about $3 billion on a yearly basis.[2]

Apart from anything else, the end of the Cold War has simply made it easier and more practicable for the big powers to use the mechanisms of the United Nations to tackle problems and this represents a substantial advance. The next stage, however, is crucial to the future well-being and, probably, survival of the United Nations and depends upon the goodwill of the five permanent members of the Security Council: reforms that will both enlarge the Security

Council to make it more truly representative of the world in which we now live and a gradual (but not too gradual) phasing out of the veto. Demands for reform of the United Nations as a whole grew steadily through the 1990s; in 1992 India proposed reform in the General Assembly and in December 1993 the General Assembly established a Working Group to consider reform of the Security Council. Two reforms are required, one general and positive, the other particular and 'negative'. The general reform must consist of a restructuring of the Security Council both as to its membership and as to its powers and *modus operandi*. The 'negative' reform, upon which everything else depends, is the requirement for the five permanent members of the Security Council to recognize that the conditions which prevailed in 1945 no longer exist and that, as an act of statesmanship, they should relinquish their rights of veto. Whether or not this will happen must depend upon the statesmanship of the permanent five on the one hand, and the judicious exercise of the collective will of the majority on the other. There is unlikely to be a more propitious time for such a change than during the remaining years of the twentieth century.

The United States holds the key to change. It is the world's sole remaining superpower and by far the most powerful state in the world; if it sets its face against UN reform little advance will be possible even if, in the end, Washington finds that it has isolated itself. The Americans have rarely been more than lukewarm about the United Nations and right from the beginning, when they insisted upon the veto, demonstrated their suspicions of such a body: in 1945, aware of its new-found, immense power, the United States wished to exercise it untrammelled by any likely restrictions which might come from the United Nations. In part the reason was historical. The efforts of President Woodrow Wilson after World War I which led to the creation of the League of Nations were subsequently repudiated by the US Senate, not least because it was believed in Washington that the President had been duped in the 1919 Versailles peace process by the principal European statesmen of the day – Britain's Lloyd George and France's Clemenceau. The United States then retreated into isolation. Following the outbreak of World War II and after he had become Britain's Prime Minister in 1940, Winston Churchill applied his rhetorical skills and much of his political effort to persuading President Roosevelt to support Britain against Germany; when the war came to an end it was at Churchill's suggestion that the headquarters of the United Nations were sited in New York. He hoped, or so the story goes, that the highly visible presence of the United Nations on American soil would persuade the American people to support the world body as they had not been persuaded in relation to the League of Nations. Then came the Cold War and the superpower stalemate that characterized the first 40 and more years of UN existence and while the Americans, as they saw themselves, were 'containing' the threat of communism the Third World steadily grew in numbers and in its readiness to criticize the United States and the other Western powers for their alleged shortcomings. US impatience with the inadequacies of the United Nations – real or imagined – was very apparent during the 1980s. Then came the end of the Cold War and the collapse of the Soviet Union and with it the prospect that the United Nations could be made to work effectively, provided the United States and Russia were prepared to act together. It was an alluring prospect whose brief realization came at the time of the Gulf War.

The euphoria, if such it could be called, did not last. The unsatisfactory nature of the US intervention in Somalia (under UN auspices), the careful refusal of Washington to become involved in Rwanda and the long drawn-out refusal to become involved with troops on the ground in Bosnia signalled a growing American reluctance to work under the direction of the United Nations. Under President Clinton the first US international concern was with Russia and the mutual agreements about nuclear weapons reached with President Boris Yeltsin when Clinton visited Moscow in January 1994 were seen as a triumph. The next US concern was trade and Washington's relations with Japan on the one hand and the prospects for greatly increased involvement in the new China on the other. The American intervention in Haiti, after a long period of hesitation, was dictated far more by concern at the arrival of Haitian boat people in the United States than by any sense of working through the United Nations to reverse an injustice. When finally the United States committed itself to brokering a Balkan peace – the Dayton Treaty of November 1995 – this was the superpower sorting out the mess Europe had made of the Balkan war rather than an effort to use the United Nations for the purpose.

The September 1996 US air strikes against Saddam Hussein, following his intervention with troops on the ground in support of Massoud Barzani's Kurdish Democratic Party at Arbil (in, or rather under, the Kurdish no-fly zone) was a unilateral US decision that, as much as anything, demonstrated the precarious level of unfinished business left behind by the Gulf War. Subsequently, the United States faced unease among its regional allies and, with a more conciliatory stance from Saddam Hussein, decided to hold back on further action even as it built up its forces in the Gulf. This new mini-Gulf crisis highlighted new concerns about the US role. According to the much respected US newspaper, the *Washington Post*, elements of the US armed forces were fighting one another for the right to fight Saddam Hussein in any second wave of punitive attacks. The reason for such service in-fighting, apart from normal service rivalry and pride, was the desire to try out new high-tech weapons, especially as a major Pentagon review of US military programmes was to be carried out in 1997. The various branches of the services believed their chances of keeping and developing their favourite weapons systems would be greatly helped if these had been used in Iraq.[3] Criticism of the US attacks on Iraq came from an unexpected source when President Nelson Mandela of South Africa argued that no country had the right to assume the role of 'policeman to the world'. Mandela did not condone Iraq's attacks upon the Kurds but said the United States should respect the UN Charter and seek to resolve problems by peaceful means.[4]

In this instance the United States acted as a great power in its own right and according to its own judgement of the situation rather than through the United Nations – and, very clearly, this is what Washington prefers to do. How, then, to persuade the United States that the prospects of eventual world government can only be brought closer if the United States acts through the world body rather than outside it? In 1994 the US GNP stood at over US$6.7 trillion, just under a third of the world's GNP, and given that such figures provide only a very approximate guide to a nation's standing and resources, nonetheless this represents awesome power, both absolutely and in relation to the rest of the world; for the foreseeable future, therefore, no organization or combination of other powers will be able to force the United States against its will to give greater backing to the United Nations than it wishes. Whether it chooses to be more conciliatory towards the world body and work harder to make it effective remains to be seen.

The break-up of the USSR deprived the world of its second superpower; it also gave rise to the impression that Russia, the successor to the USSR, was very much in the second rank of powers, an impression which was greatly enhanced by its immediate economic and political problems, the rapid growth of an apparently all-pervasive criminal mafia, the poor showing of the Russian military in the Chechnya crisis and its need for Western and IMF aid to assist the switch from a command to a market economy. Western triumphalism following the end of the Cold War and the determination of both the European Union and NATO to increase their membership by advancing into Eastern Europe led President Yeltsin to warn the December 1994 Conference on Security and Cooperation in Europe (CSCE) that there was a danger of the Cold War giving way to a Cold Peace. And though the USSR may have disappeared as a political entity, within the councils of the Commonwealth of Independent States (CIS) Russia has moved steadily to expand its political, economic and military influence among the former Soviets; the creation of an Interstate Economic Committee by CIS in 1994 suggested that such moves were welcome to the other CIS members. Russia has also worked hard to improve relations with China and Japan. During 1995, despite excellent personal rapport between President Clinton and President Yeltsin, Russia insisted upon supplying nuclear reactors to Iran (against US pressures), firmly opposed any NATO expansion into Eastern Europe and refused to allow its forces in Bosnia to serve under a NATO general. And though throughout the messy Bosnian crisis Russia played a subsidiary role to that of the Western powers, its presence in the background had always to be taken into account.

Russian opposition to the expansion of NATO to its borders is understandable as is its wariness about EU expansion. If the West makes the mistake of believing and behaving as though the break-up of the USSR also signalled the end of Russia as a great power the consequences will be extremely grave. Once Russia has sorted out its internal problems of transition it will reassert itself on the international stage; at that point its role as a permanent member of the Security Council will be crucial to its own *amour propre* and to the United Nations. Moscow will never contemplate any surrender of the veto unless this is also envisaged by the United States. What it may be far more willing to do is encourage a general reform and expansion of the Security Council.

China has maintained a relatively low profile in the United Nations since 1990 while concentrating upon relations with its Asian neighbours and the rapid development of its economy. Arguments with the United States about its most favoured nation (MFN) trading status and the row which erupted in 1995 with Washington for permitting the President of Taiwan, Lee Teng-hui, to visit the United States which led China to carry out missile and artillery tests just north of Taiwan emphasized two contradictory developments: on the one hand, China urgently seeks to expand its trade with the United States as it goes flat out to create a market economy; on the other, old enmities and suspicions from the Cold War era still survive and can easily be reignited.

China reinforced its big power status throughout 1995: Beijing played host to the UN Fourth World Conference on Women although it angered many participants in the concurrent non-governmental women's forum by severely limiting their contact with Chinese women. In the South China Sea it pursued its claim to the Spratly Islands where it risked antagonizing ASEAN, four of whose members – Brunei, Malaysia, the Philippines, and Vietnam – also advance claims to the islands. It defied world opinion by carrying out nuclear tests and it used the occasion of the UN fiftieth anniversary to join other victims in condemning Japan's wartime aggression. In Asia generally China's rapid economic growth and developing military power were cause for concern: if China decides upon a policy of cooperation with the world community after its long years of isolation it could make a major contribution to the United Nations, not least because it shows a real sympathy with the viewpoint of the Third World (the result of its own poverty) that is now conspicuously lacking among the other great powers.

Britain and France, the other two permanent members of the Security Council, may both be described as powers in decline: each has seen its empire disappear in the years since 1945 and in each case through the years of the Cold War they found themselves overshadowed by the superpowers although their insistence upon becoming nuclear powers gave them a pretence of superior authority which now looks hollow. Britain reinforced its declining influence by acting as the loyal lieutenant of the United States, invoking the so-called 'special relationship' in order to do so; France, over the same period, asserted its independence by removing itself from NATO and creating its own nuclear *force de frappe*. An unhappy Britain, still hankering after past glories, has found great difficulty in submerging its individual claims to world influence in the European Union with which it is fairly constantly in disagreement. France, on the other hand, operated at the centre of the European Union which, in France's case, it saw first and foremost as a means of containing the greater power of a renascent Germany. When France carried out a series of nuclear tests in the South Pacific during 1995 to cause a great international outcry the reason was as much to assert its great power status as it was necessary for the attainment of fresh nuclear knowledge. Both countries committed substantial armed forces to the UN-sponsored peacekeeping operation in the former Yugoslavia at least in part to demonstrate that they deserved their special position as permanent members of the Security Council.

Now, in power terms, while the United States, Russia and China merit a continuing permanent seat on the Security Council whatever new arrangments may be made, this cannot any longer be argued automatically on behalf of Britain and France. They are there for historic reasons. Germany, Japan and India have strong claims to a place: Germany and Japan on economic grounds, India in terms of its huge population. And though both countries have GNPs in excess of one trillion dollars, that of Germany is nearly double Britain's, while that of Japan, at nearly US\$4.7 trillion, is second only to that of the United States and equivalent to the combined GNPs of Germany, France and Britain.

A report submitted to the UN Human Rights Commission in February 1996 called on the Japanese government to set up a war crimes tribunal to prosecute former soldiers and officials responsible for the forced prostitution of thousands of women during World War II. It claimed that between 100000 and 200000 'comfort women' including Chinese, Koreans, and a handful of European internees were confined in military brothels where they were forced to serve as many as 70 men a day. War scandals, fresh claims for compensation or demands that Japan apologize for war crimes still surface periodically more than 50 years after the end of World War II to embarrass the Japanese government. In this particular case Tokyo was especially put out since the government was in the process of conducting a low-key campaign for a permanent seat on the Security Council. The UN special rapporteur on violence against women, Sri Lanka's Radhika Coomaraswamy, said: 'We sincerely hope that the Japanese government will at least compromise by meeting us half-way, and make some kind of gesture worthy of a superpower.'[5] This statement was doubly interesting in that it both fixed blame on Japan for the past sins which ensured it had no seat on the Security Council in the first place while at the same time acknowledging that Japan had become a superpower, certainly in economic terms. In 1995 Japan was the world's leading creditor nation with net overseas assets at a record US$689 000 million; it was the largest provider of foreign aid (at a level of US$13 billion a year) for the fourth successive year; while its economic power was felt increasingly in every sphere of international activity.

The German economic miracle of the 1950s and 1960s, the painstaking efforts by West Germany ever since 1949 to achieve rehabilitation among the nations after the Nazi period and, finally, the reunification of Germany in 1990 resulted in the re-emergence of Europe's strongest state. During the 1990s Germany dominated EU economic arguments (it is the world's third economic power after the United States and Japan) and embarked with increasing confidence upon an independent East European policy of its own rather than submerging its initiatives in those of the EU. In June 1995, after long and agonized debate, Germany decided to reverse the policy of 50 years and allow its armed forces to be used outside Germany in support of the UN forces in Bosnia. It was the first time since the defeat of Hitler's armies that Germans would be sent into war and it was seen as a traumatic turning point. As Germany's Foreign Minister, Klaus Kinkel, said: 'Germany has in the post-war era received protection and solidarity from its partners and friends, with no ifs and buts ... now we must show solidarity.'[6] The forces involved were moderate – Tornado combat planes but ground forces consisting only of medical and other back-up forces. Both Western leaders and the UN Secretary-General, Boutros-Ghali, had long pressed for Germany to play a more active role and welcomed the decision which marked a turning point in German foreign policy: as President Roman Herzog had outlined German foreign policy earlier in the year, on 13 March, the new and larger Germany resulting from reunification 'must be prepared to articulate its own economic and security interests, and it must also be prepared to use military power in concert with other democracies'.[7] With a population of 82 million, a GNP of just under US$2 trillion and the third largest economy in both output and sophistication in the world, Germany could advance a major claim to a permanent seat on the Security Council, and one that it has become increasingly difficult to deny.

In March 1996 Italy enraged Britain and France by suggesting that they should be prepared to surrender their permanent seats on the Security Council in favour of a single seat for the European Union. The proposal was advanced by the Italian Ambassador to the United Nations, Francesco Fulci, in the debate within the organization about an expanded Security Council. Italy is opposed to the idea, backed by the United States, Britain and France, that two new permanent seats on the Security Council should be given to Germany and Japan. Whatever the Italian motive for this suggestion – a desire to prevent Germany becoming a permanent member of the Security Council is believed to be the prime reason – the Italians opened up the debate in a doubly interesting way. First, there is a case to be made for permanent seats for organizations or unions rather than countries; second, there is an element of Western haste in the proposal to give Germany and Japan permanent seats before other claims have been fully considered. Given the possibility that the European Union will have expanded by the year 2000 to include the Czech Republic, Hungary, Poland and Slovenia – and possibly some other states such as the three small Baltic Republics as well – a single EU seat on the Security Council would make a great deal of sense. The suggestion also opened up the debate to other possibilities such as a seat for the Organization of African Unity (OAU) since, at present, the African continent has no permanent representation on the Security Council.

First, however, two other major countries – India and Brazil – deserve consideration. India has as good a claim to a permanent seat as does China and, barring the accident of history which meant it was still part of the British Empire in 1945, it would almost certainly have been considered for a seat at the time the United Nations was formed. The Indian population in 1995 stood at 935 million, approximately one-sixth of the world's total; it is the world's largest democracy and though extremely poor with an economy less advanced than that of China, has long played a leading role in Asia, in the councils of the Non-Aligned Movement and the Commonwealth and as a supporter of UN initiatives. In August 1996 India made an unequivocal bid for 'big power' status with a permanent seat on the Security Council. It did so, first, by blocking the Comprehensive Test-Ban Treaty which had been endorsed by 60 other nations at Geneva on the grounds that the five nuclear powers had taken no steps towards eliminating nuclear weapons with the result that a test-ban treaty would freeze the present nuclear club. The stand of the five nuclear powers has long been regarded as hypocrisy and not just by India. India's UN envoy in Geneva, Arundhai Ghose, claimed that the Comprehensive Test-Ban Treaty ignored India's security needs – her neighbours China and Pakistan both have nuclear weapons – and that the treaty gave an unfair edge to countries already in possession of nuclear weapons. The logic of the Indian position was unassailable and a test-ban treaty only makes sense if the existing nuclear powers proceed to eliminate all their weapons – and of that there is as yet no sign. Second, Prime Minister Deve Gowda, speaking on India's Independence Day, claimed that India deserved a permanent seat on an expanded Security Council because of its long contribution to peacekeeping efforts and other UN programmes.[8] If there is to be an expansion of the permanent seats on the Security Council it would be very difficult to do this without including India; moreover, should India be excluded while Germany and Japan were given seats this would be seen as a snub to the whole South.

The other obvious claimant to a permanent seat on the Security Council is Brazil. Latin America is not represented and Brazil, which is continental in size, is its largest country, rich in resources, with a population of 155 million in 1995 and a rapidly expanding economy with a GNP of US$471.978 million (1993). Both US President Franklin D. Roosevelt and Secretary of State Cordell Hull had promised Brazil a permanent seat on the Security Council during the war, in the preliminary discussions which led to the creation of the United Nations, although the promise was never honoured. In 1995, at the UN fiftieth anniversary celebrations, Brazil's President, Fernando Henrique Cardoso, reminded President Clinton of this fact and argued that the time had come for Brazil to obtain a permanent seat on the Council. If Security Council membership is to be widened so that it more accurately represents the world's principal powers, regions and peoples, Brazil is an obvious contender for a permanent seat.

An expansion of the Security Council could be achieved in several ways. First, the present structure could be kept but with an increase in permanent members and an increase in the number of rotating members. The obvious candidates for permanent seats are Germany, Japan, India and Brazil. Second, a new kind of member could be considered – the collective member as envisaged in the Italian suggestion of an EU seat which would then subsume Britain, France and Germany. There are substantial difficulties in such an idea though these are not insuperable. Africa has no permanent seat on the Council, as yet, nor has it any single power with sufficient claims to such a seat but it could be represented by the OAU. Similarly, Latin America and the Caribbean could be represented by a regional seat – a revamped

Organization of American States (less the dominant United States). The idea of collective seats has its attractions – after all, if the eventual aim is collective world government through the United Nations why not begin by collective seats for regions, more especially as the United Nations has been looking at ways in which regional organizations can assist it in peacekeeping operations? The difficulties, however, are of major proportions. In the case of the European Union, to take the most obvious example, given the existing suspicions of any more political power being ceded to the centre that exist most overtly in Britain but among other members as well, and given also the inability of the EU to produce a European policy over the Balkan crisis, it is unrealistic to suppose that Britain or France would be prepared to agree to such a seat whose effect would be to eliminate their own places on the Security Council.

The Commission on Global Governance examined the question of reforming the Security Council and recommended that a new class of 'standing members' should be established: two to be drawn from industrial countries and three from the larger developing countries (one each from Asia, Africa and Latin America). As the authors of *Our Global Neighbourhood* suggest, and this would seem to be a crucial condition of permanent membership of the Council:

> In many respects, the new standing members suggest themselves; but we recommend that the General Assembly propose them, and in doing so be guided by the consideration that standing members of the Security Council should be able to contribute in more than a token way to the maintenance of international peace and security and to the other purposes of the United Nations.[9]

On the veto the same authors suggest, first, that new permanent members should not be given a veto; second, that the existing five veto holders should agree not to use their vetoes except in 'circumstances they consider to be exceptional and overriding in the context of their national security'; and third, that by 2005, perhaps, they should be prepared to surrender their vetoes entirely. Assuming that some such scenario could be achieved, the new Security Council would have something of the following composition and powers: nine permanent members – the present five plus Germany, Japan, India and Brazil; 15 rotating members; and a provision that in peacekeeping operations which required UN intervention, a two-thirds majority of the Security Council would have to be obtained for such action, the two-thirds majority automatically including two-thirds of the nine permanent members.

The sooner proposals along these or similar lines can be tabled and considered by both the General Assembly and the present Security Council, the sooner there will be a real prospect of reform. Immediately, perhaps, it is important to familiarize members with concrete suggestions for reform; thereafter, the five permanent members must be persuaded, gently but firmly if that is possible, that their powers of veto are no longer compatible with the kind of democratic world the United Nations is trying to build.

15 United Nations Reform

The question of reforming the United Nations moved close to the top of the UN agenda during the 1990s and the reforms discussed and required fall into two broad categories: the first category concerns the role of the United Nations as such, and what its members expect of it, and these reforms have been touched upon, at least in part, by considerations relating to the Security Council (see above, Chapter 14); the second category concerns the mechanics of running the United Nations and includes such subjects as the position of the Secretary-General, the finances, the recruitment of personnel and ways of dealing with the pervasive corruption which seems to become a part of any international organization.

Corruption takes many forms: in the United Nations system its effects can be seen in relation to power, to money, to job security and to national pride. Four of the five permanent members of the Security Council (the United States, Britain, France and post-Cold War Russia) are political democracies but though the three Western powers have been quick enough to extol the superior merits of democracy, especially when dealing with Third World countries seeking their aid, they are not democratic at all in relation to the world body and clearly (as of the mid-1990s) had no intention of surrendering their vetoes in order to abide by the democratic majority decisions of the United Nations.

There is a good deal of venal corruption in the United Nations, principally in the form of fiddling the books in, for example, regional offices or fiddling expense accounts and this can be done in two ways. The first is by making up expenses that were not in fact incurred, and a number of senior ranking UN personnel have been found guilty of this practice. The second is by deliberately incurring expenses, for example, by unnecessary travel in order to earn per diem allowances. What are needed in relation to these practices are much firmer guidelines and some form of watchdog to ensure that the guidelines are kept with far tougher sanctions including dismissal for those who are discovered corruptly to enhance their incomes.

Another corrupt practice which is difficult, if not impossible, to pin down, and really depends upon the calibre of person recruited, is that of 'playing safe': the official who never takes any decision that risks upsetting his or her superiors, whose only concern is to hold on to a safe job indefinitely rather than take on responsibility for difficult decisions. Such people are to be found in all organizations; the surest way to root them out is to have regular career performance checks and not allow indefinite security of tenure.

Perhaps most pervasive of all throughout the United Nations is the quota system which allows countries to nominate a prescribed number of their nationals to jobs at different levels – the principle of 'buggins' turn'. There are several different problems involved here. First, the nominating country may send indifferent personnel to the United Nations – because the government wants to keep its best people at home, or because it wishes to send abroad political troublemakers whose only claim to a job is some connection with a powerful (and corrupt) minister, or simply in order to take up its quota to have as full a representation as possible for nationalist reasons. There is a further complication, and this concerns the pride of governments which are at least as likely to defend one of their nationals who is accused of corruption than agree to his being disciplined or sacked, since this is thought to reflect as much upon the country as upon the individual.

Such malpractices are to be found worldwide and it is easy to dismiss them along familiar lines – that human nature being what it is they are to be expected and too much should not be made of them. The United Nations, however, is the world's political 'shopfront' and as such should insist upon the highest possible standards at all times and from all its members. It is clear that it has not done this for many years.

The heads of the specialized agencies have near autocratic authority over very extensive fiefdoms and in recent years corruption charges of one kind or another have been levelled at a High Commissioner for Refugees, a Director-General of the World Health Organization, and the Kenya UNICEF office. Why, it should be asked, are international institutions so prone to such scandals? In case after case corruption is passed over, inefficiency is ignored or, indeed, accepted as the norm while UN jobs are seen as vehicles for personal aggrandisement that has very little to do with the task in hand. In part the problem results from a selection process that has nothing to do with merit or skills and everything to do with political bargaining between member nations. Members squabble as to which nominee should be given a post and, too often, it goes to a particular candidate because it is his or her country's turn or because another plum job has just been awarded to a rival country. There is, moreover, no system whereby talent can be found and nurtured for top UN posts; instead, with luck, some good people will be discovered amongst those that countries post to the United Nations, often with a view to getting them away from their home political scenes – a form of 'kicking upstairs'. A further great weakness, and one that is not easy to remedy, is the lack of any organized global public opinion. At least in countries like Britain or the United States, a poor performer, in the end, can be forced from office because of adverse public opinion and criticism. There is no such equivalent at work in the United Nations or its agencies. Further, both the

United Nations heaquarters in New York and its many ancillary bodies resist any scrutiny from outside. In the end, therefore, the only way to force a change is for a major power (and, as a result, a major financial contributor to an agency) to threaten to withhold funds unless change is forthcoming. This at once creates another political problem since the major funding members are all from the North and if they use this weapon (as did the United States and Britain in relation to UNESCO in 1984 and 1985) they are liable to create a North–South conflict with the usual accusations that the rich North is using its wealth and the size of its financial contributions to dominate the United Nations unfairly at the expense of the South. Despite considerations such as this, Article 100 of the United Nations Charter laid down clearly what was required:

> In the performance of their duties, the Secretary-General and the staff shall not seek or receive instructions from any government or from any authority external to the Organization. They shall refrain from any action which might reflect on their position as international officials accountable only to the Organization.

It is wrong in both principle and practice that the only effective means of forcing reform are the threat of withdrawal or the threat of reducing funding. The United Nations must devise an internal system that forces reform before any such threats need to be made.

One set of precise proposals to prevent corruption in international agencies is as follows:

1. Impose a limit of one term on chief executives of all international agencies;
2. Give auditors powers to requisition any information they believe they need;
3. Require the public registration of all the private interests of international diplomats, UN agency chief executives and senior managers;
4. Hand over the appointment of agency chief executives to an independent multinational commission of Supreme Court judges from leading nations;
5. Introduce automatic budget cuts for agencies in which corruption is discovered;
6. Require all agencies to publish breakdowns of their expenditure in several different ways at once – showing not just budget line items but attaching expenditures across all departments to particular outcomes, and showing all spending made under each of their constitutional powers to act;
7. Make agency chief executives personally liable for overspending that is poorly accounted for.[1]

Perhaps the most effective reform of all would be to abolish any quota system and insist that all UN officials, apart from national delegations, must be recruited by competitive tender worldwide, preferably by an independent agency created specifically for this purpose; that contracts for the top appointments are never for more than one term; and that the same appointing agency should be responsible for checking the performance of UN personnel and recommending disciplinary procedures where these are applicable. This, at least, would remove the political pressures which currently operate to keep second-rate, incompetent or corrupt personnel in office once their inadequacies have been uncovered.

The position and capacity of the Secretary-General are clearly crucial to the success of the United Nations; yet the election of the Secretary-General is anything except democratic and results from what has been described as a Byzantine process of political horse-trading at the highest levels of world diplomacy. According to Article 97 of the UN Charter, the General Assembly will approve the appointment of a Secretary-General for a renewable five-year term; a single candidate must be recommended to the General Assembly beforehand by the Security Council. Permanent members of the Security Council may exercise their veto over the choice, an action which, clearly, would kill it.

The authors of *Our Global Neighbourhood*[2] suggest the following reforms should be applied to the choosing of a Secretary-General:

1. The veto should not apply to the nomination of the Secretary-General, but candidates from the five permanent members could be considered (to date, they have been excluded);
2. Individuals should not campaign for the office;
3. The appointment should be for a single term of seven years;
4. Governments should consider seriously the qualifications required of the Secretary-General;
5. The Security Council should organize a world-wide search for the best-qualified candidates;
6. The qualifications and suitability of candidates should be systematically checked.

(The same report suggests that similar conditions should apply to the selection of heads of UN programmes and specialized agencies.)

The single-term condition for a Secretary-General is especially important as it would eliminate the need for a first-term occupant of the office to campaign for reappointment. Speaking in London in December 1995, Australia's Foreign Minister, Gareth Evans, said: 'It's debilitating in any international organisation when towards the end of the first term the person has to turn his sights towards what's necessary to getting another one. A single seven-year term is the best way to address that.'[3] Early in 1996, as though to make the Australian Foreign Minister's point, it was reported that a high-level deal was underway at the United Nations to guarantee the re-election of the Secretary-General, Boutros-Ghali, on condition he then stepped down after two years in office. His unpopularity was with both the leading Western powers – to whom he has refused to kow-tow – but also with some members of the General Assembly whom he has succeeded in upsetting. By the beginning of 1996 the United States had become bitterly opposed to his continuation in office, partly for his failure to initiate wholesale reforms of the UN structure, and partly because of sharp conflicts between the United States and the Secretary-General over the peacekeeping operations in Somalia and Bosnia where the US role had been open to substantial criticisms while Washington tended to blame the United Nations when the operations went wrong.

American anger at Boutros-Ghali appeared to surface at the time of US deaths in Somalia and continued with consistent attacks upon the UN peacekeeping operations although the United States had often refused to give these adequate support. It also appears that the American public often entertains unrealistic expectations of what the United Nations can achieve, partly because UN aims have not been sufficiently well presented. At the same time the United States is the most persistent offender in the matter of not paying its dues on time: as of May 1996, for example, its arrears stood at US$1.5 billion or 55 per cent of total UN arrears.

Boutros-Ghali has been reviled, in undiplomatic terms, by the US delegate to the United Nations, Madeleine Albright, as well as being attacked by the Republican leader Bob Dole and the Republican Right. Ironically, Boutros-Ghali was elected in the first place because the African candidates for the post (it was Africa's 'turn' to provide the Secretary-General) were not acceptable to the main Western powers which then asserted (a form of reverse racialism) that Boutros-Ghali (an Egyptian) was an African; this was technically correct but hardly what black Africa had in mind. Boutros-Ghali subsequently won the support of the non-aligned nations by his readiness to attack the United States.[4] Rumours about plots to oust Boutros-Ghali persisted through 1996 with the names of potential successors including the Irish President, Mary Robinson, the Prime Minister of Norway, Gro Harlem Brundtland, and the Ghanaian UN official, Kofi Annan, being suggested for the job.

This was not a healthy way to deal with the question of the Secretary-General, with the United States expressing its 'irrevocable' determination to stop Boutros-Ghali being re-elected, if necessary by using its veto. After

Boutros-Ghali had announced his intention of seeking another term, in June 1996, a White House spokesman said: 'We must turn our attention to identifying another candidate. Our minds will not be changed.' Never before in the history of the United Nations had a major power reacted in such a way to the incumbent Secretary-General. However, the American stand seemed certain to stir up bitter resentment among the majority of developing nations which make little secret of their anger at the US role in the United Nations, especially as it adopts its hectoring attitudes while refusing to pay its arrears of dues.

In an interview with the London *Independent* during September 1996 the Secretary-General, Boutros-Ghali, lamented the 'neo-provincialism' which, he said, gripped many world governments, and he made plain his determination to defy American efforts to prevent him serving a second term. He cited his successes as Secretary-General ranging from peace in El Salvador and Mozambique to the adoption of a zero-growth UN budget as well as a series of world conferences on such issues as poverty and the environment. He claimed that aborted missions such as Somalia and Bosnia were ultimately the responsibility of member governments. He said, of the suggestion that he should depart in December 1996 without seeking a second term, that he believed 'my departure would create more problems for this institution. Because you need the continuity at this particular period. We have begun a series of reforms; it is important if not to achieve them completely – it is a continuous process – then to achieve at least a certain amount of them.' He argued that there was a new provincialism, a new neo-isolationism and that the majority of UN members were not interested in international affairs which, he said, was the real problem faced by the United Nations. At the same time, member nations constantly made the United Nations a scapegoat when international peace efforts went wrong. Explaining the UN failure in Bosnia, Boutros-Ghali said it had been impossible to defend safe-havens without the 34000-strong force he had requested for this task: 'The mistake was not only the number was not corresponding to the number we demanded, but that it took two years to get up to this number, and the soldiers came with very light armaments. It was a mistake ... of the international community.'[5]

Two days after he gave this interview to the *Independent*, the US envoy to the United Nations, Madeleine Albright, insisted that Washington would not go back on its threat to veto his reappointment and said: 'We would hope very much that Mr Boutros-Ghali understands this. We would hope that we would not have to use our veto.' The confrontation between the Secretary-General and the United States was becoming one of the most unpleasant in the history of the United Nations. The Secretary-General's case – that he was carrying through reforms – was weakened at this point when it appeared that he had backed down from plans to make 37 members of the UN staff redundant; these lay-offs would have been the first involuntary ones in UN history but had provoked furious opposition from certain developing countries. Madeleine Albright seized upon the fact that the sackings were not going to be implemented and said: 'It is essential for the UN to have a Secretary-General whose main priority, top priority, every-day focus of his job is to reform the UN.' Despite having cut down staff by nearly 10 per cent, this had been by wastage and voluntary departure. The Secretary-General was now up against what has become the jobs-for-life culture of the United Nations in which the idea of sacking an official, regardless of his performance, has been unthinkable and he found himself opposed in his attempts to alter this tradition by many of the developing countries.[6] His enemies, however, no doubt detected a desire not to upset such governments just as his re-election approached, which was another reason for changing the system and adopting a one-term only approach to the top UN job.

The crisis surrounding the Secretary-General was resolved at the end of 1996 when Boutros Boutros-Ghali was replaced by the Ghanaian Kofi Annan, a long-serving, highly respected UN civil servant who had been responsible for peacekeeping operations. The crisis, however, was resolved to the satisfaction of the United States after the world's only superpower had forced an unwilling United Nations to accept its absolute determination not to allow Boutros-Ghali a second term. Kofi Annan may or may not prove an effective Secretary-General but the manner in which US power rather than any more democratic process forced his predecessor to stand down was an ill-omen for the United Nations. The suspicion remained that the final reason dictating this US action was anger in Washington that Boutros-Ghali had insisted upon publishing the UN report on the Qana massacre of 18 April 1996 despite US objections.

The fact that the United Nations constantly faces financial problems has less to do with any deficiencies of the organization itself than with the willingness of its members to pay the very modest contributions which are required for its maintenance. Countries should be penalized for falling into arrears of payments; at the same time, those (rich) countries assessed at the highest rates should not have any special privileges for in fact, on a pro rata basis, they pay less than the poorest members. The rule that each member state must pay at least 0.01 per cent of the regular budget while no member should pay more than 25 per cent (as does the United States) in fact casts a heavier burden upon poor members than it does upon rich ones. Just to take four examples: Sao Tome and Principe (one of the world's poorest counries) pays 0.01 per cent of the UN regular budget and this represents 0.2511 per cent of its national income; the Maldives also pays 0.01 per cent of the UN regular budget and in this case it represents 0.1626 per cent of its national income; at the other end of the scale, the Netherlands pays 1.5 per cent of the UN budget which represents only 0.0104 per cent of its national income, while the United States pays 25 per cent of the UN budget although this only represents 0.0076 per cent of its national income. The United Nations originally imposed a limit of 25 per cent on the payment that any country makes to the budget.[7] On the other hand, the finances to pay for peacekeeping operations are not included in the regular budget and are raised from member states according to a different formula which places more of the burden upon the rich members. As early as August 1993 in his term of office, Boutros-Ghali was obliged to write to the permanent members of the Security Council to warn that the United Nations was then facing the gravest financial crisis of its history because member nations would not pay their assessments on time. Whatever his failings, no other Secretary-General has faced the financial problems that have bedevilled the United Nations through the 1990s.

The United Nations has individual budgets for peacekeeping operations and members are assessed separately for them. By the early 1990s, the overall peacekeeping budget had outgrown the UN regular budget, but, 'although all the main powers have fully endorsed the UN's enhanced peacekeeping role, particularly its costly operations in Bosnia, Croatia, Somalia and Cambodia, many have failed to contribute to this budget'.[8] Members are assessed for peacekeeping on a modified version of the formula used for the regular budget with countries divided into four categories: the A group comprises the permanent members of the Security Council and they are expected to pay more pro rata than the rest; the B group contributes on the same scale as their regular budget assessment; the C group pays only 20 per cent of their regular rate; and the D group pays only 10 per cent of their regular assessment. If members fall behind in these payments they jeopardize the operations which they have authorized.

In a speech to the UN General Assembly of September 1995, the British Foreign Secretary, Malcolm Rifkind, challenged the United States and other member nations to pay their dues in full so as to stave off the collapse of the world body and called for tighter penalties for UN members who do not pay. At the time of his speech the United Nations was owed more than US$3.7 billion in unpaid contributions from 39 countries and US$1.6 billion of this sum was owed by the United States. In world terms this represented a minute sum of money as it also did for the major powers. As Malcolm Rifkind added, clearly aiming his remarks at the US Congress: 'The bill for all UN peacekeeping, all aid and development work last year, was slightly over 3.5 per cent of the US defence budget. One day of Operation Desert Storm cost as much as all that year's peacekeeping.' Moreover, he added, 'Even in the

United States, polls are clear: people support the UN; they support international peacekeeping. We have a duty to our electorates to continue the UN's work.'[9] The US Secretary of State, Warren Christopher, told the General Assembly that his government was committed to meeting its financial obligations but called for wide-ranging reform to help convince the US Congress that the organization deserved American funds. There is an article in the UN Charter that stipulates that any country which falls two years in arrears should lose its assembly voting rights, although the provision has long been ignored. By this time in the debt crisis, the United States had become extremely unpopular in the United Nations generally and with its usual allies in Europe, in particular for its persistent refusal to pay its dues. The problem of debts is not really about money at all; it is about the readiness of the major powers to make the United Nations work effectively and in this respect it concerns the United States most of all.

There are many ways in which the United Nations needs to be reformed, some of which have been discussed here. The three most important reforms concern power, the Secretary-General and patronage. As far as power is concerned, what is needed is a fundamental reorganization of the Security Council to include the abolition of the veto, the expansion of its permanent members to make it more representative of world power structures as a whole and a re-examination of its powers, especially as relating to interventions in countries where either civil wars or massive denials of human rights threaten the lives of large numbers of their populations. As far as the Secretary-General is concerned (and this can also be applied to the heads of specialized agencies) he should be appointed for a single seven-year term so that he is not obliged to modify his actions in order to obtain country support for re-election. As far as patronage is concerned, the most effective way to reform the United Nations would be to abolish any form of quota system whereby countries have the right to nominate staff and put all jobs out to competitive tender with clear limits upon the length of employment available. Few if any of these reforms will mean very much, however, unless the world at large and most especially its leading powers want to make the United Nations effective and are prepared to work through it and not against it.

16   Reflections

Any international organization – the United Nations, NATO, the European Union, the Commonwealth – takes on a character and personality of its own, yet ultimately it is the creation as well as the prisoner of its members and if they become disenchanted with it the organization will either die or, at the very least, become moribund and ineffective. The United Nations which was established in the immediate aftermath of the greatest, most destructive war in history was intended to keep the peace in a world weary of war but soon found itself sidelined by the superpower confrontation of the Cold War in which its effectiveness, at most, was limited and heavily circumscribed. Many people thought that in these circumstances merely to have survived for 50 years was an achievement. The end of the Cold War in 1990 and the opening up of international politics to a new set of power variables faced the United Nations with both a new opportunity and new dangers: the new opportunity was to move centre-stage again and, at last, be used as originally intended to keep the peace and the 1990s presented all too many occasions for it to attempt to fulfil this role; the dangers arose out of the sense of release that came with the collapse of Cold War tensions and the consequent temptation of the great powers, and most especially of the United States, to revert to a form of international behaviour that placed individual power above collective action while using the United Nations as a convenient scapegoat whenever things go wrong. Perhaps the most encouraging sign during the 1990s has been the readiness of the world community to call upon the United Nations, despite its obvious limitations, to solve problems because using the United Nations is seen as less of a risk than dependence upon the unilateral intervention of the major powers who have done little enough to earn the trust of the world's weaker nations.

The world appears to have entered a phase in which wars between states are comparatively rare while civil wars and the breakdown of states have become all too common. The question that such a situation poses for the United Nations, therefore, is whether and when it should intervene in civil wars or at what point should it become involved after a major breakdown of law and order has occurred in a particular state? The principle that the United Nations should not intervene in the internal affairs of member states has, increasingly, been put aside during the 1990s. The United Nations intervened in Yugoslavia as that federal state fell apart; it intervened in Somalia, originally to ensure that humanitarian aid was delivered to those in need. In Angola it attempted to keep a precariously achieved peace between the two sides after more than

15 years of civil war but the effort was thwarted when UNITA went back to the bush to continue the fight. It intervened far more successfully in Mozambique as a peacekeeping force between two sides which had exhausted themselves after 15 years of civil war. Beginning in 1991 with the imposition of a 'no-fly' zone in northern Iraq (to safeguard the Kurds from attack by Saddam Hussein in the aftermath of the Gulf War) the United Nations has shown an increasing readiness to intervene in states once a certain level of violence has been reached, although it is, as yet, far from clear in either theory or practice exactly when it should intervene, why it should do so and who expects it to do so.

An intervention in a civil war whose effect is to freeze the fighting is necessarily partial since, without the intervention, one side might well go on to win the conflict and change the existing political situation. A primary question for the United Nations must be whether the suffering inflicted in a civil war should be a world concern or whether it only becomes a world concern when a certain level of suffering is reached? Most civil wars achieve a degree of savagery that is appalling to outsiders yet either side will resent any intervention that is not obviously going to work to its advantage. Should the United Nations intervene if, for example, a people rise in revolt against a government that denies human rights or treats a large segment of its population as second-class citizens? During the 1990s the United Nations believed it should intervene to prevent ethnic cleansing in Yugoslavia (without success); it saw the need to safeguard the delivery of humanitarian aid as a justification for interventions in Bosnia and Somalia; and it wanted to intervene in Rwanda and Burundi to prevent genocide, although in these cases the major powers (the members of the Security Council) were not prepared to provide the means for such intervention. On the other hand, in Indonesia where, since 1975, the government has conducted a brutal war of oppression against the people of Timor who have been fighting for their independence, the United Nations has done no more than protest. And in the case of Chechnya seeking its independence from Russia the United Nations has been silent. Despite this apparently haphazard pattern, certain ground rules do seem to be emerging although the UN capacity to intervene must necessarily be tempered by the willingness of its members to support its actions. Broadly, the world community appears ready in principle if not always in practice to support intervention in order to prevent genocide, to prevent or at least lessen the effects of ethnic cleansing and to ensure that humanitarian aid can be delivered to those in need when a large proportion of a population is clearly at risk as a result of a civil conflict. It is a murky area for decision makers and, as an anonymous diplomat asked in August 1996 when Burundi appeared to be descending into a new phase of genocidal killings: 'Nobody in Burundi wants outside intervention, so do you impose yourself?' As the century comes to an end the phenomenon of the failed state appears to be on the increase: should it be the business of the United Nations to undertake responsibility for such states and, if so, what, short of imposing its own form of law and order upon them, can it do?

The duty of humanitarian intervention and the need to safeguard the oppressed are replacing the concept of the sanctity of states with a new concept of the sanctity of people's rights. Such rights, of course, are set out in the United Nations Charter but in general during its first 50 years of existence the United Nations only saw it as its duty to protest at the violation of such rights, especially if the violation occurred within a major member state, rather than actively to intervene to see that they were enforced. Increasingly during the 1990s, however, it has moved away from the acceptance of the sacrosanct nature of states and shown a greater readiness to intervene in support of certain rights which it sees as absolute. So far, however, such interventions have only been contemplated with regard to 'failed' states or states in violent conflict with the world body as in the case of Iraq and the Kurds.

A number of new ideas about peacekeeping are beginning to emerge from the experiences of the 1990s – in relation to events in Angola, Burundi, Iraq, Rwanda, Somalia and Yugoslavia (especially Bosnia). One such idea is that member states should earmark a sector of their armed forces for peacekeeping operations. A second idea, and one that may well become vital to future UN operations, is that of the regional peacekeeping force or authority. When the United Nations relinquished its authority in Bosnia to NATO it was actively endorsing this concept. There are a number of regional organizations which ought to be seen as the frontline agents for peacekeeping in their regions. In the civil war in Liberia the members of the Economic Community of West African States (ECOWAS) through their military arm, ECOMOG, intervened, with the endorsement of the OAU, to bring an end to the hostilities. In this case, while supporting these efforts, the United Nations stayed in the background. Here is a potential pattern for the future: the immediate neighbourhood organization – in this case ECOWAS – acting as the actual arm of intervention; this (ECOWAS), in its turn, being supported by the OAU and the whole operation being backed and if necessary reinforced by the United Nations. Such a pattern makes obvious sense in a world where the range of civil wars is likely to be far greater than the ability of the United Nations alone to deal with them. There exists a wide range of regional organizations that should consider peacekeeping as a necessary part of their activities: in the Americas the OAS and, under its umbrella, a number of mainly economic groupings which, nonetheless, might act as did ECOWAS in Liberia – the Andean Group, the Caribbean Community and Common

Market (CARICOM) or the Central American Common Market (CACM). In Europe both NATO and the CSCE; in Africa, under the umbrella of the OAU, such regional organizations as ECOWAS and SADC. In Asia the obvious regional group to turn to is ASEAN except that so far it has ruled out any military role for itself. There is also the Commonwealth and the Commonwealth of Independent States (CIS). Certain major powers, and most notably France in Africa, are prepared to intervene under treaty obligations in countries with which they have close ties. As the United Nations learned in respect to both Rwanda and then Burundi, the major powers of the Security Council preferred not to become involved. Had the United Nations at once encouraged the OAU and the regional neighbours of those two countries to act and at the same time undertaken the task of persuading the Security Council to bankroll the operation such a pragmatic compromise approach may well have worked – at least it could hardly have been worse than what happened in fact – and since both the neighbours of Rwanda and Burundi as well as the OAU had immediate reasons of self-interest to prevent these genocidal conflagrations they could have been persuaded to act where non-African powers held back.

Interventions can rarely be simple and quite often they will produce unlooked-for side effects. The delivery of humanitarian aid – food, clothing and medicine for example – to those who have been put at risk in a civil conflict exercises a powerful appeal upon the public imagination, and in relation to both Somalia and Bosnia, non-government organizations (NGOs) were, at times, to take the lead in demanding action where governments preferred to hold back. Yet the delivery of humanitarian aid may help to prolong rather than shorten a conflict. If the international community insists upon delivering humanitarian aid and then calls upon the United Nations to safeguard such delivery this may assist one or both sides in a conflict since it takes from them both the responsibility and obligation to look after the people on either side who have been rendered homeless and starving by the conflict. Moreover, as happened in both Somalia and Bosnia, at least a proportion of the humanitarian supplies fall into the hands of the combatants and so assist them directly. Second, precisely because of its appeal to an international public, the delivery of humanitarian aid may first be used as an excuse for holding back on other forms of intervention on the grounds that these might endanger the delivery of aid and then be used to rationalize the absence of more urgent political and military action designed to stop the conflict.

The Nuremberg trials after World War II familiarized the world with the idea of bringing war criminals to trial and justice; the practice was revived in relation to the former Yugoslavia when the United Nations War Crimes

Tribunal was established to deal especially with those guilty of ethnic cleansing excesses. In September 1996 the Chief Prosecutor, Judge Richard Goldstone, complained bitterly at NATO's deliberate failure to arrest the indicted Serb war criminals Radovan Karadzic and Ratko Mladic who had been blamed for the mass murder of up to 8000 Bosnian Muslim civilians in the UN 'safe haven' of Srebenica in July of 1995. This failure, he said, 'could prove a fatal blow to this tribunal and to the future of international justice'.[1] As the judge explained, Western leaders had made plain that they were not prepared to put their soldiers at risk and NATO forces in Bosnia had been ordered to arrest wanted war criminals only if they saw them but were not to seek them out. Unfortunately, such political pusillanimity characterizes many of the actions of the big powers in relation to the United Nations tasks which they undertake to support. In the former Yugoslavia the Western powers simply did not want or intend to put their soldiers unnecessarily at risk and, as a result, have to explain too many 'body bags' to their political supporters at home. Here the power of the media clearly plays an important role which reinforces another lesson that the wars of the 1990s have taught the United Nations: the major powers will only take the risk of substantial casualties in engagements where their own interests are at stake (such as the Gulf War with Iraq) while the more remote a conflict in terms of their interests, the less the likelihood of any commitment to action on the ground. Such attitudes are reinforced by the promise – often unfulfilled – that is held out by 'high-tech' weaponry which can be employed from the air, as opposed to the use of infantry on the ground.

There is not a great deal the United Nations can do if the major powers refuse to become involved in a problem as was the case in Burundi. It has learnt, for example, that effective military intervention requires the support of at least one of the major Western powers (the United States, Britain or France) and though other smaller powers and a number of Third World countries are prepared to provide military forces, they lack both the logistical capacity to transport their troops to the operation zone and the finances to pay for the operation. Africa, as the conflicts of the 1990s have demonstrated, comes low on the list of big power priorities. Failure to support UN operations, despite initial approval of action through Security Council resolutions, poses the question: does the United Nations attempt to do too much? In purely pragmatic terms the simple answer is clearly 'Yes'. In any long-term assessment of United Nations aims, however, the answer must be 'No'. In the first place, the United Nations cannot refuse to look at one problem as opposed to another simply on the grounds that the major powers are not interested or not prepared to intervene or it would lose all credibility. The United Nations must become involved and then hope that by persuasion and a constant representation of the problem and what is required to bring about a solution it may eventually obtain the support it requires for its policy.

Throughout the years of the Cold War the United Nations acted both as the forum for and the champion of the least developed and weakest countries of the Third World or South. In the post-Cold War world their need for a champion will be even greater for they no longer attract big power interest as possible Cold War allies and with fading donor interest in aid their economic plight may well become intolerable. Indeed, the marginalization of the poorest economies has aleady become a theme of international economic discussions and was brought out clearly in *The Least Developed Countries 1996 Report* of UNCTAD which was published in April 1996.[2] In any case, the Group of Seven which to all intents still monopolizes economic decision making rarely gives much attention to development issues. And though United Nations special programmes such as its Development Decades or years set aside for concentration upon particular problems are designed to highlight the needs of the least developed countries, they may in fact do more to emphasize differences than to bridge gaps.

The effective resolution of international problems as well as the future of the United Nations can only be determined by the major powers, beginning with the five permanent members of the Security Council. In the mid-1990s the leading Western powers, and most especially the United States, demanded reforms (and there are many reforms which, by any standards, are urgently needed), yet can the Security Council justifiably instruct the Secretary-General to reform the United Nations as a whole if they are not prepared to give a lead and reform themselves? If the five permanent members of the Security Council are not prepared to contemplate fundamental reforms which would include the rapid phasing-out of their veto and the creation of a more equitable distribution of decision making powers within the system, how can they instruct the world body as a whole to reform?

The big powers have shown themselves ready enough to use the United Nations when it suits them; most notably, for example, in calls for UN embargoes upon states that have incurred their displeasure as in the case of the United States, Britain and France in relation to Libya, or the United States in relation to Sudan. In other cases, however, they either ignore the United Nations, bypass it or use their vetoes as the United States has done most particularly in relation to Israel. Over the issue of the arms trade the big five of the Security Council, followed by other major industrial countries, are the world's worst offenders in spreading arms worldwide for their own profit. And though they have worked hard to control nuclear weapons this has been to prevent their spread to other nations rather than to eliminate their own weapons.

In the end these issues resolve themselves, as always, into questions of power. If the major nations, and most especially the United States, are willing to work through the United Nations and are prepared to ensure that its decisions are carried out then it has a significant future before it. If, on the other hand, they treat it with cynical disregard, invoke its support as an umbrella of legality when it suits them (as in the Gulf War of 1991) or make a scapegoat of it as in Bosnia because they had failed to provide it with the military forces it required for the task they had assigned it in the first place, then its future will indeed be at risk. The reluctance of the world's leading powers to subordinate their interests to wider considerations of world justice lies at the centre of all the problems of the United Nations. Such attitudes cannot easily be changed and those who would reform the United Nations understand this perfectly well. Changes will have to be introduced gradually. Yet, so great are the problems now piling up for the world – the spread of chaos in failed states, the proliferation of arms, the constant escalation of pressures upon resources as populations both increase and demand higher living standards, the increasing likelihood of wars in the next century over the control of dwindling world supplies of fresh water – that it will become increasingly difficult to resolve these and other problems unless there is some form of world government in operation. It is as much in the interests of the big powers as it is in those of the weakest states to make the United Nations effective, and now, in the latter years of the twentieth century as the world reappraises its future in the aftermath of the Cold War, is the best time to provide the United Nations with the authority and finances it requires but, so far, has always been denied. This means, above all, that the leading nations first insist upon wide-ranging reforms; then provide the United Nations with adequate funds; and finally insist that it is given the authority it requires to carry out the mandates which the world is ready enough to thrust upon it.

References

CHAPTER 1

1. *Observer* 25/06/1995.
2. Ibid.
3. Ibid.
4. *Independent* 30/09/1995.
5. *Independent* 24/10/1995.
6. *Annual Register 1995* (A Record of World Events), Cartermill Publishing, 1996 p. 373.
7. *Annual Register 1993* (A Record of World Events) Longman Current Affairs, 1994 p. 388.
8. *Our Global Neighbourhood* (The Report of the Commission on Global Governance) Oxford University Press 1995, p. 2.
9. Ibid p. 6.

CHAPTER 2

1. *Basic facts about the United Nations* United Nations 1992, Department of Public Information, New York p. 30.
2. Ibid p. 30.
3. *Our Global Neighbourhood* (The Report of the Commission on Global Governance), Oxford University Press, 1995 p. 84.
4. Ibid p. 102.
5. Ibid p. 106.
6. Ibid p. 340.
7. Flora Lewis, *Legacy of 1991: Phoenix or Empty Ashes, Britannica Book of the Year 1992* p. 4.
8. *Annual Register 1994* (A Record of World Events), Cartermill Publishing, 1995 pp. 109–10.
9. Interview in *Independent* 27/10/1994.
10. *Independent* 29/05/1995.
11. *Standard* 1/05/1995.
12. *Independent* 10/05/1995.
13. Anthony Parsons, *From Cold War to Hot Peace* (UN Interventions 1947–1994), Michael Joseph, 1995.
14. *Independent* 27/09/1995.
15. Christopher Bellamy, *Knights in White Armour – the New Art of War and Peace*, Hutchinson, 1996.
16. Quoted in *Independent* 23/07/1996.
17. Ibid.

CHAPTER 3

1. For a fuller account of the Kurdish problem see Guy Arnold, *Wars in the Third World since 1945* (2nd edn), Cassell, 1995 pp. 75–84.
2. *Annual Register 1993*, Longman Current Affairs, 1994 p. 396.
3. *Annual Register 1994* (A Record of World Events), Cartermill Publishing, 1995 p. 415.
4. *Independent* 18/01/1995.
5. *Annual Register 1995* (A Record of World Events), Cartermill Publishing, 1996 p. 37.
6. *Independent* 19/01/1996.
7. *Independent* 21/05/1996.

CHAPTER 4

1. *Independent* 19/08/1992.
2. Anthony Parsons, *From Hot War to Cold Peace*, Michael Joseph, 1995 p. 234.
3. Ibid p. 238.
4. Richard N. Swift, *The United Nations, Britannica Book of the Year 1995* p. 354.
5. Ibid.
6. Ibid.
7. *Independent* 10/05/1995.
8. Ibid.
9. *Observer* 23/07/1995.
10. *Independent* 16/05/1995.
11. *Independent* 17/05/1995.
12. *Independent* 23/07/1995.
13. *Observer* 25/05/1995.
14. *Observer* 30/07/1995.
15. *Independent* 16/06/1995.
16. *Independent* 30/09/1995.
17. Jonathan Eyal, Director of Studies Royal United Services Institute, *Independent* 21/07/1996.

CHAPTER 5

1. Guy Arnold, 'Burundi: Civil War by Massacre', *Wars in the Third World since 1945* (2nd edn), Cassell, 1995 pp. 383–9.
2. *Annual Register 1994* (A Record of World Events), Cartermill Publishing, 1995 p. 294.
3. *Annual Register 1995* (A Record of World Events), Cartermill Publishing, 1996 p. 267.
4. Anthony Parsons, *From Cold War to Hot Peace*, Michael Joseph, 1995 pp. 212–13.
5. *Observer* 21/01/1996.
6. *Independent* 25/07/1996.

7. *Independent* 26/07/1996.
8. Ibid.
9. Anthony Parsons, op cit. p. 184.
10. Guy Arnold, op cit., 'Rwanda: The Peasants' Revolt' p. 426.
11. *Annual Register 1995* (A Record of World Events), Cartermill Publishing, 1996 p. 376.
12. *Independent* 7/01/1995.
13. Christopher Bellamy, *Knights in White Armour,* Hutchinson, 1996 p. 106.
14. Guy Arnold, op cit., 'Somalia: Civil War – North versus South' pp. 427–34.
15. *Britannica Year Book 1995* p. 353.
16. *Annual Register 1993* (A Record of World Events), Longman Current Affairs, 1994 p. 391.
17. Anthony Parsons, op cit. p. 216.
18. Ibid pp. 218–19.

CHAPTER 6

1. Anthony Parsons, *From Cold War to Hot Peace*, Michael Joseph, 1995 p. 142.
2. Ibid p. 144.
3. *Annual Register 1995* (A Record of World Events), Cartermill Publishing, 1996 p. 375.
4. *Observer* 09/06/1996.
5. Anthony Parsons, op cit. p. 146.
6. Guy Arnold, 'Namibia: the Independence Struggle' *Wars in the Third World since 1945* (2nd edn), Cassell, 1995 pp. 46–53.
7. Anthony Parsons, op cit. p. 114.
8. Anthony Parsons, op cit. p. 104.

CHAPTER 7

1. Guy Arnold, 'Kampuchea/Cambodia: Border War, Civil War, Vietnam invasion' *Wars in the Third World since 1945* (2nd edn), Cassell, 1995 pp. 284–97.
2. Anthony Parsons, *From Cold War to Hot Peace*, Michael Joseph, 1995 p. 165.
3. *Annual Register 1993* (A Record of World Events), Longman Current Affairs, 1994 p. 393.
4. Anthony Parsons, op cit. p. 166.
5. Guy Arnold, op cit., 'Haiti: Ripe for Revolution' pp. 606–7.
6. *Independent* 26/02/1996.

CHAPTER 8

1. Guy Arnold, 'Western Sahara: Desert War' *Wars in the Third World since 1945* (2nd edn), Cassell, 1995 pp. 56–63.
2. *Annual Register 1994* (A Record of World Events), Cartermill Publishing, 1995 p. 258.

3. *Independent* 29/11/1991.
4. *Annual Register 1994* (A Record of World Events), Cartermill Publishing, 1995 p. 410.

CHAPTER 9

1. Trevor Burridge, *Clement Attlee*, Jonathan Cape, 1985 p. 248.
2. Anthony Parsons, *From Cold War to Hot Peace*, Michael Joseph, 1995 p. 26.
3. Ibid p. 24.
4. *Annual Register 1993* (A Record of World Events), Longman Current Affairs, 1994 p. 397.
5. *Keesings* Record of World Events, April 1996.

CHAPTER 10

1. United Nations Economic and Social Commission for Asia and the Pacific (ESCAP), New York 1991.
2. World Bank, *World Development Report 1991*, Oxford University Press, 1991.
3. United Nations Development Programme (UNDP), *Human Development Report 1992*, Oxford University Press, 1992.
4. A World Bank Policy Research Report, *Adjustment in Africa*, Oxford University Press, 1994 pp. 3–4.
5. Ibid p. 4.
6. The World Bank, *Accelerated Development in Sub-Saharan Africa – An Agenda for Action*, Washington DC, 1981 p. v.
7. Ismael Serageldin, The World Bank, *Poverty, Adjustment, and Growth in Africa* 1981.
8. The World Bank, *Annual Report 1995*, Washington DC, p. 10.
9. The Report of the Commission on Global Governance, *Our Global Neighbourhood*, Oxford University Press, 1995 p. 21.
10. Ibid p. 139.
11. Ibid pp. 147–8.
12. Ibid p. 162.
13. United Nations Development Programme (UNDP), *Human Development Report 1994*, New York, 1994 p. 3.
14. *Independent* 11/03/1996.

CHAPTER 11

1. See *Basic Facts about the United Nations*, Department of Public Information, United Nations, New York, 1992.
2. The Report of the Commission on Global Governance, *Our Global Neighbourhood*, Oxford University Press, 1995 p. 27.
3. Ibid p. 30.
4. *Independent* 08/04/1996.

5. *Independent* 22/05/1996.
6. Ibid.
7. *Independent* 30/05/1996.
8. *Independent* 30/01/1995.

CHAPTER 12

1. The Report of the Commission on Global Governance, *Our Global Neighbourhood*, Oxford University Press, 1995 p. 49.
2. *Human Development Report 1992*, United Nations Development Programme (UNDP), Oxford University Press, 1992 p. iii (Foreword).
3. Ibid pp. 3–5.
4. *Human Development Report 1994*, United Nations Development Programme (UNDP), Oxford University Press, 1994 pp. 1–2.
5. Ibid p. 4.
6. *Human Development Report 1996*, United Nations Development Programme (UNDP), Oxford University Press, 1996 p. 1.
7. *Independent* 06/05/1995.
8. *Independent* 16/11/1995.

CHAPTER 13

1. The Report of the Commission on Global Governance, *Our Global Neighbourhood*, Oxford University Press, 1995 p. 15.
2. Ibid p. 17.
3. Ibid p. 124.
4. *Human Development Report 1994*, United Nations Development Programme (UNDP), Oxford University Press, 1994 p. 47.
5. Ibid p. 47.
6. Ibid p. 55.
7. Ibid p. 57.
8. *Independent* 04/05/1996.

CHAPTER 14

1. The Report of the Commission on Global Governance, *Our Global Neighbourhood*, Oxford University Press, 1995 p. 234.
2. Ibid pp. 236–7.
3. *Independent* 14/09/1996.
4. Ibid.
5. *Independent* 07/02/1996.
6. *Independent* 01/07/1995.
7. *Britannica Book of the Year 1995*, Robert Sigel p. 410.
8. *Observer* 18/08/1996.

9. The Report of the Commission on Global Governance, *Our Global Neighbourhood*, Oxford University Press, 1995 p. 240.

CHAPTER 15

1. *Independent* 11/05/1995.
2. The Report of the Commission on Global Governance, *Our Global Neighbourhood*, Oxford University Press, 1995 p. 293.
3. *Independent* 22/12/1995.
4. *Observer* 19/05/1996.
5. *Independent* 17/09/1996.
6. *Independent* 19/09/1996.
7. *Our Global Neighbourhood* op cit., see table, p. 247.
8. *Guardian* 04/08/1993.
9. *The Times* 27/09/1995.

CHAPTER 16

1. *Independent* 17/09/1996.
2. *The Least Developed Countries 1996 Report*, United Nations Conference on Trade and Development (UNCTAD), New York, 1996.

Appendix   Charter of the United Nations and Statute of the International Court of Justice

INTRODUCTORY NOTE

The Charter of the United Nations was signed on 26 June 1945, in San Francisco, at the conclusion of the United Nations Conference on International Organization, and came into force on 24 October 1945. The Statute of the International Court of Justice is an integral part of the Charter.

Amendments to Articles 23, 27 and 61 of the Charter were adopted by the General Assembly on 17 December 1963 and came into force on 31 August 1965. A further amendment to Article 61 was adopted by the General Assembly on 20 December 1971, and came into force on 24 September 1973. An amendment to Article 109, adopted by the General Assembly on 20 December 1965 came into force on 12 June 1968.

The amendment to Article 23 enlarges the membership of the Security Council from eleven to fifteen. The amended Article 27 provides that decisions of the Security Council on procedural matters shall be made by an affirmative vote of nine members (formerly seven) and on all other matters by an affirmative vote of nine members (formerly seven), including the concurring votes of the five permanent members of the Security Council.

The amendment to Article 61, which entered into force on 31 August 1965, enlarged the membership of the Economic and Social Council from eighteen to twenty-seven. The subsequent amendment to that Article, which entered into force on 24 September 1973, further increased the membership of the Council from twenty-seven to fifty-four.

The amendment to Article 109, which relates to the first paragraph of that Article, provides that a General Conference of Member States for the purpose of reviewing the Charter may be held at a date and place to be fixed by a two-thirds vote of the members of the General Assembly and by a vote of any nine members (formerly seven) of the Security Council. Paragraph 3 of Article 109, which deals with the consideration of a possible review conference during the tenth regular session of the General Assembly, has been retained in its original form in its reference to a "vote, of any seven members of the Security Council", the paragraph having been acted upon in 1955 by the General Assembly, at its tenth regular session, and by the Security Council.

CHARTER OF THE UNITED NATIONS

WE THE PEOPLES
OF THE UNITED NATIONS
DETERMINED

to save succeeding generations from the scourge of war, which twice in our lifetime has brought untold sorrow to mankind, and

to reaffirm faith in fundamental human rights, in the dignity and worth of the human person, in the equal rights of men and women and of nations large and small, and

to establish conditions under which justice and respect for the obligations arising from treaties and other sources of international law can be maintained, and

to promote social progress and better standards of life in larger freedom,

AND FOR THESE ENDS

to practice tolerance and live together in peace with one another as good neighbours, and

to unite our strength to maintain international peace and security, and

to ensure, by the acceptance of principles and the institution of methods, that armed force shall not be used, save in the common interest, and

to employ international machinery for the promotion of the economic and social advancement of all peoples,

HAVE RESOLVED TO COMBINE OUR EFFORTS TO ACCOMPLISH, THESE AIMS

Accordingly, our respective Governments, through representatives assembled in the city of San Francisco, who have exhibited their full powers found to be in good and due form, have agreed to the present Charter of the United Nations and do hereby establish an international organization to he known as the United Nations.

CHAPTER I
PURPOSES AND PRINCIPLES

Article 1

The Purposes of the United Nations are:

1. To maintain international peace and security, and to that end: to take effective collective measures for the prevention and removal of threats to the peace, and for the suppression of acts of aggression or other breaches of the peace, and to bring about by peaceful means, and in conformity with the principles of justice and international law, adjustment or settlement of international disputes or situations which might lead to a breach of the peace;

2. To develop friendly relations among nations based on respect for the principle of equal rights and self-determination of peoples, and to take other appropriate measures to strengthen universal peace;

3. To achieve international co-operation in solving international problems of an economic, social, cultural, or humanitarian character, and in promoting and encouraging respect for human rights and for fundamental freedoms for all without distinction as to race, sex, language, or religion; and

4. To be a centre for harmonizing the actions of nations in the attainment of these common ends.

Article 2

The Organization and its Members, in pursuit of the Purposes stated in Article 1, shall act in accordance with the following Principles.

1. The Organization is based on the principle of the sovereign equality of all its Members.

2. All Members, in order to ensure to all of them the rights and benefits resulting from membership, shall fulfil in good faith the obligations assumed by them in accordance with the present Charter.

3. All Members shall settle their international disputes by peaceful means in such a manner that international peace and security, and justice, are not endangered

4. All Members shall refrain in their international relations from the threat or use of force against the territorial integrity or political independence of any state, or in any other manner inconsistent with the Purposes of the United Nations.

5. All Members shall give the United Nations every assistance in any action it takes in accordance with the present Charter, and shall refrain from giving assistance to any state against which the United Nations is taking preventative or enforcement action.

6. The Organization shall ensure that states which are not Members of the United Nations act in accordance with these Principles so far as may be necessary for the maintenance of international peace and security.

7. Nothing contained in the present Charter shall authorize the United Nations to intervene in matters which are essentially within the domestic jurisdiction of any state or shall require the Members to submit such matters to settlement under the present Charter; but this principle shall not prejudice the application of enforcement measures under Chapter VII.

Chapter II
MEMBERSHIP

Article 3

The original Members of the United Nations shall be the states which, having participated in the United Nations Conference on International Organization at San Francisco, or having previously signed the Declaration by United Nations of 1 January 1942, sign the present Charter and ratify it in accordance with Article 110.

Article 4

1. Membership in the United Nations is open to all other peace-loving states which accept the obligations contained in the present Charter and, in the judgment of the Organization, are able and willing to carry out these obligations.

2. The admission of any such state to membership in the United Nations will be effected by a decision of the General Assembly upon the recommendation of the Security Council.

Article 5

A Member of the United Nations against which preventive or enforcement action has been taken by the Security Council may be suspended from the exercise of the rights and privileges of membership by the General Assembly upon the recommendation of the Security Council. The exercise of these rights and privileges may be restored by the Security Council.

Article 6

A Member of the United Nations which has persistently violated the Principles contained in the present Charter may be expelled from the Organization by the General Assembly upon the recommendation of the Security Council.

CHAPTER III
ORGANS

Article 7

1. There are established as the principal organs of the United Nations: a General Assembly, a Security Council, an Economic and Social Council, a Trusteeship Council, an International Court of Justice, and a Secretariat.

2. Such subsidiary organs as may be found necessary may be established in accordance with the present Charter.

Article 8

The United Nations shall place no restrictions on the eligibility of men and women to participate in any capacity and under conditions of equality in its principal and subsidiary organs.

CHAPTER IV
THE GENERAL ASSEMBLY

Composition

Article 9

1. The General Assembly shall consist of all the Members of the United Nations.

2. Each Member shall have not more than five representatives in the General Assembly.

Functions and Powers

Article 10

The General Assembly may discuss any questions or any matters within the scope of the present Charter or relating to the powers and functions of any organs provided for in the present Charter, and, except as provided in Article 12, may make recommendations to the Members of the United Nations or to the Security Council or to both on any such questions or matters.

Article 11

1. The General Assembly may consider the general principles of co-operation in the maintenance of international peace and security, including the principles governing

disarmament and the regulation of armaments, and may make recommendations with regard to such principles to the Members or to the Security Council or to both.

2. The General Assembly may discuss any questions relating to the maintenance of international peace and security brought before it by any Member of the United Nations, or by the Security Council, or by a state which is not a Member of the United Nations in accordance with Article 35, paragraph 2, and, except as provided in Article 12, may make recommendations with regard to any such questions to the state or states concerned or to the Security Council or to both. Any such question on which action is necessary shall be referred to the Security Council by the General Assembly either before or after discussion.

3. The General Assembly may call the attention of the Security Council to situations which are likely to endanger international peace and security.

4. The powers of the General Assembly set forth in this Article shall not limit the general scope of Article 10.

Article 12

1. While the Security Council is exercising in respect of any dispute or situation the functions assigned to it in the present Charter, the General Assembly shall not make any recommendation with regard to that dispute or situation unless the Security Council so requests.

2. The Secretary-General, with the consent of the Security Council, shall notify the General Assembly at each session of any matters relative to the maintenance of international peace and security which are being dealt with by the Security Council and shall similarly notify the General Assembly, or the Members of the United Nations if the General Assembly is not in session, immediately the Security Council ceases to deal with such matters.

Article 13

1. The General Assembly shall initiate studies and make recommendations for the purpose of:

a. promoting international co-operation in the political field and encouraging the progressive development of international law and its codification;

b. promoting international co-operation in the economic, social, cultural, educational, and health fields, and assisting in the realization of human rights and fundamental freedoms for all without distinction as to race, sex, language, or religion.

2. The further responsibilities functions and powers of the General Assembly with respect to matters mentioned in paragraph l(b) above are set forth in Chapters IX and X.

Article 14

Subject to the provisions of Article 12, the General Assembly may recommend measures for the peaceful adjustment of any situation regardless of origin, which it deems likely to impair the general welfare or friendly relations among nations, including situations resulting from a violation of the provisions of the present Charter setting forth the Purposes and Principles of the United Nations.

Article 15

1. The General Assembly shall receive and consider annual and special reports from the Security Council; these reports shall include an account of the measures

that the Security Council has decided upon or taken to maintain international peace and security.

2. The General Assembly shall receive and consider reports from the other organs of the United Nations.

Article 16

The General Assembly shall perform such functions with respect to the international trusteeship system as are assigned to it under Chapters XII and XIII, including the approval of the trusteeship agreements for areas not designated as strategic.

Article 17

1. The General Assembly shall consider and approve the budget of the Organization.

2. The expenses of the Organization shall be borne by the Members as apportioned by the General Assembly.

3. The General Assembly shall consider and approve any financial and budgetary arrangements specialised agencies referred to in Article 57 and shall examine the administrative budgets of such specialised agencies with a view to making recommendations to the agencies concerned.

Voting

Article 18

1. Each member of the General Assembly shall have one vote.

2. Decisions of the General Assembly on important questions shall be made by a two-thirds majority of the members present and voting. These questions shall include: recommendations with respect to the maintenance of international peace and security, the election of the non-permanent members of the Security Council, the election of the members of the Economic and Social Council, the election of members of the Trusteeship Council in accordance with paragraph 1(c) of Article 86, the admission of new Members to the United Nations, the suspension of the rights and privileges of membership, the expulsion of Members, questions relating to the operation of the trusteeship system, and budgetary questions.

3. Decisions on other questions, including the determination of additional categories of questions to be decided by a two-thirds majority, shall be made by a majority of the members present and voting.

Article 19

A Member of the United Nations which is in arrears in the payment of its financial contributions to the Organization shall have no vote in the General Assembly if the amount of its arrears equals or exceeds the amount of the contributions due from it for the preceding two full years. The General Assembly may, nevertheless, permit such a Member to vote if it is satisfied that the failure to pay is due to conditions beyond the control of the Member.

Procedure

Article 20

The General Assembly shall meet in regular annual sessions and in such special sessions as occasion may require. Special sessions shall be convoked by the Secretary-

General at the request of the Security Council or of a majority of the Members of the United Nations.

Article 21

The General Assembly shall adopt its own rules of procedure. It shall elect its President for each session.

Article 22

The General Assembly may establish such subsidiary organs as it deems necessary for the performance of its functions.

CHAPTER V
THE SECURITY COUNCIL

Composition

Article 23

1. The Security Council shall consist of fifteen Members of the United Nations. The Republic of China, France, the Union of Soviet Socialist Republics, the United Kingdom of Great Britain and Northern Ireland, and the United States of America shall be permanent members of the Security Council. The General Assembly shall elect ten other Members of the United Nations to be non-permanent members of the Security Council, due regard being specially paid, in the first instance to the contribution of Members of the United Nations to the maintenance of international peace and security and to the other purposes of the Organization, and also to equitable geographical distribution.

2. The non-permanent members of the Security Council shall be elected for a term of two years. In the first election of the non-permanent members after the increase of the membership of the Security Council from eleven to fifteen, two of the four additional members shall be chosen for a term of one year. A retiring member shall not be eligible for immediate re-election.

3. Each member of the Security Council shall have one representative.

Functions and Powers

Article 24

1. In order to ensure prompt and effective action by the United Nations, its Members confer on the Security Council primary responsibility for the maintenance of international peace and security, and agree that in carrying out its duties under this responsibility the Security Council acts on their behalf.

2. In discharging these duties the Security Council shall act in accordance with the Purposes and Principles of the United Nations. The specific powers granted to the Security Council for the discharge of these duties are laid down in Chapters VI, VII, VIII, and XII.

3. The Security Council shall submit annual and, when necessary, special reports to the General Assembly for its consideration.

Article 25

The Members of the United Nations agree to accept and carry out the decisions of the Security Council in accordance with the present Charter.

Article 26

In order to promote the establishment and maintenance of international peace and security with the least diversion for armaments of the world's human and economic resources, the Security Council shall be responsible for formulating, with the assistance of the Military Staff Committee referred to in Article 47, plans to be submitted to the Members of the United Nations for the establishment of a system for the regulation of armaments.

Voting

Article 27

1. Each member of the Security Council shall have one vote.
2. Decisions of the Security Council on procedural matters shall be made by an affirmative vote of nine members.
3. Decisions of the Security Council on all other matters shall be made by an affirmative vote of nine members including the concurring votes of the permanent members, provided that, in decisions under Chapter VI, and under paragraph 3 of Article 52, a party to a dispute shall abstain from voting.

Procedure

Article 28

1. The Security Council shall be so organized as to be able to function continuously. Each member of the Security Council shall for this purpose be represented at all times at the seat of the Organization.
2. The Security Council shall hold periodic meetings at which each of its members may, if it so desires, be represented by a member of the government or by some other specially designated representative.
3. The Security Council may hold meetings at such places other than the seat of the Organization as in its judgment will best facilitate its work.

Article 29

The Security Council may establish such subsidiary organs as it deems necessary for the performance of its functions.

Article 30

The Security Council shall adopt its own rules of procedure, including the method of selecting its President.

Article 31

Any Member of the United Nations which is not a member of the Security Council may participate, without vote, in the discussion of any question brought before the Security Council whenever the latter considers that the interests of that Member are specially affected.

Article 32

Any Member of the United Nations which is not a member of the Security Council or any state which is not a Member of the United Nations, if it is a party to a dispute under consideration by the Security Council, shall be invited to participate, without vote, in the discussion relating to the dispute. The Security Council shall lay down such conditions as it deems just for the participation of a state which is not a Member of the United Nations.

CHAPTER VI

PACIFIC SETTLEMENT OF DISPUTES

Article 33

1. The parties to any dispute, the continuance of which is likely to endanger the maintenance of international peace and security, shall, first of all, seek a solution by negotiation, enquiry, mediation, conciliation, arbitration, judicial settlement, resort to regional agencies or arrangements, or other peaceful means of their own choice.

2. The Security Council shall, when it deems necessary, call upon the parties to settle their dispute by such means.

Article 34

The Security Council may investigate any dispute, or any situation which might lead to international friction or give rise to a dispute, in order to determine whether the continuance of the dispute or situation is likely to endanger the maintenance of international peace and security.

Article 35

1. Any Member of the United Nations may bring any dispute, or any situation of the nature referred to in Article 34, to the attention of the Security Council or of the General Assembly.

2. A state which is not a Member of the United Nations may bring to the attention of the Security Council or of the General Assembly any dispute to which it is a party if it accepts in advance, for the purposes of the dispute, the obligations of pacific settlement provided in the present Charter.

3. The proceedings of the General Assembly in respect of matters brought to its attention under this Article will be subject to the provisions of Articles 11 and 12.

Article 36

1. The Security Council may, at any stage of a dispute of the nature referred to in Article 33 or of a situation of like nature, recommend appropriate procedures or methods of adjustment.

2. The Security Council should take into consideration any procedures for the settlement of the dispute which have already been adopted by the parties.

3. In making recommendations under this Article the Security Council should also take into consideration that legal disputes should as a general rule be referred by the parties to the International Court of Justice in accordance with the provisions of the Statute of the Court.

Article 37

1. Should the parties to a dispute of the nature referred to in Article 33 fail to settle it by the means indicated in that Article, they shall refer it to the Security Council.

2. If the Security Council deems that the continuance of the dispute is in fact likely to endanger the maintenance of international peace and security, it shall decide whether to take action under Article 36 or to recommend such terms of settlement as it may consider appropriate.

Article 38

Without prejudice to the provisions of Articles 33 to 37, the Security Council may, if all the parties to any dispute so request, make recommendations to the parties with a view to a pacific settlement of the dispute.

CHAPTER VII
ACTION WITH RESPECT TO THREATS TO THE PEACE, BREACHES OF THE PEACE, AND ACTS OF AGGRESSION

Article 39

The Security Council shall determine the existence of any threat to the peace, breach of the peace, or act of aggression and shall make recommendations, or decide what measures shall be taken in accordance with Articles 41 and 42, to maintain or restore international peace and security.

Article 40

In order to prevent an aggravation of the situation, the Security Council may, before making the recommendations or deciding upon the measures provided for in Article 39, call upon the parties concerned to comply with such provisional measures as it deems necessary or desirable. Such provisional measures shall be without prejudice to the rights, claims, or position of the parties concerned. The Security Council shall duly take account of failure to comply with such provisional measures.

Article 41

The Security Council may decide what measures not involving the use of armed force are to be employed to give effect to its decisions, and it may call upon the Members of the United Nations to apply such measures. These may include complete or partial interruption of economic relations and of rail sea, air, postal, telegraphic, radio, and other means of communication, and the severance of diplomatic relations.

Article 42

Should the Security Council consider that measures provided for in Article 41 would be inadequate or have proved to be inadequate, it may take such action by air, sea, or land forces as may be necessary to maintain or restore international peace and security. Such action may include demonstrations, blockade, and other operations by air, sea, or land forces of Members of the United Nations.

Article 43

1. All Members of the United Nations, in order to contribute to the maintenance of international peace and security, undertake to make available to the Security Council, on its call and in accordance with a special agreement or agreements, armed forces, assistance, and facilities, including rights of passage, necessary for the purpose of maintaining international peace and security.

2. Such agreement or agreements shall govern the numbers and types of forces, their degree of readiness and general location, and the nature of the facilities and assistance to be provided.

3. The agreement or agreements shall be negotiated as soon as possible on the initiative of the Security Council. They shall be concluded between the Security Council and Members or between the Security Council and groups of Members and shall be subject to ratification by the signatory states in accordance with their respective constitutional processes.

Article 44

When the Security Council has decided to use force it shall, before calling upon a Member not represented on it to provide armed forces in fulfilment of the obligations assumed under Article 43, invite that Member, if the Member so desires, to participate in the decisions of the Security Council concerning the employment of contingents of that Member's armed forces.

Article 45

In order to enable the United Nations to take urgent military measures, Members shall hold immediately available national air-force contingents for combined international enforcement action. The strength and degree of readiness of these contingents and plans for their combined action shall be determined, within the limits laid down in the special agreement or agreements referred to in Article 43, by the Security Council with the assistance of the Military Staff Committee.

Article 46

Plans for the application of armed force shall be made by the Security Council with the assistance of the Military Staff Committee.

Article 47

1. There shall be established a Military Staff Committee to advise and assist the Security Council on all questions relating to the Security Council's military requirements for the maintenance of international peace and security, the employment and command of forces placed at its disposal, the regulation of armaments, and possible disarmament.

2. The Military Staff Committee shall consist of the Chiefs of Staff of the permanent members of the Security Council or their representatives. Any Member of the United Nations not permanently represented on the Committee shall be invited by the Committee to be associated with it when the efficient discharge of the Committee's responsibilities requires the participation of that Member in its work.

3. The Military Staff Committee shall be responsible under the Security Council for the strategic direction of any armed forces placed at the disposal of the Security Council. Questions relating to the command of such forces shall be worked out subsequently

4. The Military Staff Committee, with the authorization of the Security Council and after consultation with appropriate regional agencies, may establish regional sub-committees.

Article 48

1. The action required to carry out the decisions of the Security Council for the maintenance of international peace and security shall be taken by all the Members of the United Nations or by some of them, as the Security Council may determine.

2. Such decisions shall be carried out by the Members of the United Nations directly and through their action in the appropriate international agencies of which they are members.

Article 49

The Members of the United Nations shall join in affording mutual assistance in carrying out the measures decided upon by the Security Council.

Article 50

If preventive or enforcement measures against any state are taken by the Security Council, any other state, whether a Member of the United Nations or not, which finds itself confronted with special economic problems arising from the carrying out of those measures shall have the right to consult the Security Council with regard to a solution of those problems.

Article 51

Nothing in the present Charter shall impair the inherent right of individual or collective self-defence if an armed attack occurs against a Member of the United Nations, until the Security Council has taken measures necessary to maintain international peace and security. Measures taken by Members in the exercise of this right of self-defence shall be immediately reported to the Security Council and shall not in any way affect the authority and responsibility of the Security Council under the present Charter to take at any time such action as it deems necessary in order to maintain or restore international peace and security.

CHAPTER VIII
REGIONAL ARRANGEMENTS

Article 52

1. Nothing in the present Charter precludes the existence of regional arrangements or agencies for dealing with such matters relating to the maintenance of international peace and security as are appropriate for regional action, provided that such arrangements or agencies and their activities are consistent with the Purposes and Principles of the United Nations.

2. The Members of the United Nations entering into such arrangements or constituting such agencies shall make every effort to achieve pacific settlement of local disputes through such regional arrangements or by such regional agencies before referring them to the Security Council.

3. The Security Council shall encourage the development of pacific settlement of local disputes through such regional arrangements or by such regional agencies either on the initiative of the states concerned or by reference from the Security Council.

4. This Article in no way impairs the application of Articles 34 and 35.

Article 53

1. The Security Council shall, where appropriate, utilize such regional arrangements or agencies for enforcement action under its authority. But no enforcement action shall be taken under regional arrangements or by regional agencies without the authorization of the Security Council, with the exception of measures against any enemy state, as defined in paragraph 2 of this Article, provided for pursuant to Article 107 or in regional arrangements directed against renewal of aggressive policy on the part of any such state, until such time as the Organization may, on request of the Governments concerned, be charged with the responsibility for preventing further aggression by such a state.

2. The term enemy state as used in paragraph 1 of this Article applies to any state which during the Second World War has been an enemy of any signatory of the present Charter.

Article 54

The Security Council shall at all times be kept fully informed of activities undertaken or in contemplation under regional arrangements or by regional agencies for the maintenance of international peace and security.

Chapter IX
INTERNATIONAL ECONOMIC AND SOCIAL CO-OPERATION

Article 55

With a view to the creation of conditions of stability and well-being which are necessary for peaceful and friendly relations among nations based on respect for the principle of equal rights and self-determination of peoples, the United Nations shall promote:

a. higher standards of living, full employment, and conditions of economic and social progress and development;

b. solutions of international economic, social, health, and related problems; and international cultural and educational co-operation; and

c. universal respect for, and observance of, human rights and fundamental freedoms for all without distinction as to race, sex, language, or religion.

Article 56

All Members pledge themselves to take joint and separate action in co-operation with the Organization for the achievement of the purposes set forth in Article 55.

Article 57

1. The various specialized agencies, established by intergovernmental agreement and having wide international responsibilities, as defined in their basic instruments in economic, social, cultural, educational, health and related fields, shall be brought into relationship with the United Nations in accordance with the provisions of Article 63.

2. Such agencies thus brought into relationship with the United Nations are hereinafter referred to as specialized agencies.

Article 58

The Organization shall make recommendations for the co-ordination of the policies and activities of the specialized agencies.

Article 59

The Organization shall, where appropriate, initiate negotiations among the states concerned for the creation of any new specialized agencies required for the accomplishment of the purposes set forth in Article 55.

Article 60

Responsibility for the discharge of the functions of the Organization set forth in this Chapter shall be vested in the General Assembly and, under the authority of the General Assembly, in the Economic and Social Council, which shall have for this purpose the powers set forth in Chapter X.

CHAPTER X
THE ECONOMIC AND SOCIAL COUNCIL

Composition

Article 61

1. The Economic and Social Council shall consist of fifty-four Members of the United Nations elected by the General Assembly.

2. Subject to the provisions of paragraph 3, eighteen members of the Economic and Social Council shall be elected each year for a term of three years. A retiring member shall be eligible for immediate re-election.

3. At the first election after the increase in the membership of the Economic and Social Council from twenty-seven to fifty-four members, in addition to the members elected in place of the nine members whose term of office expires at the end of that year, twenty-seven additional members shall be elected. Of these twenty-seven additional members, the term of office of nine members so elected shall expire at the end of one year, and of nine other members at the end of two years, in accordance with arrangements made by the General Assembly.

4. Each member of the Economic and Social Council shall have one representative.

Functions and Powers

Article 62

1. The Economic and Social Council may make or initiate studies and reports with respect to international economic, social, cultural, educational, health, and related matters and may make recommendations with respect to any such matters to the General Assembly, to the Members of the United Nations, and to the specialized agencies concerned.

2. It may make recommendations for the purpose of promoting respect for, and observance of, human rights and fundamental freedoms for all.

3. It may prepare draft conventions for submission to the General Assembly, with respect to matters falling within its competence.

4. It may call, in accordance with the rules prescribed by the United Nations, international conferences on matters falling within its competence.

Article 63

1. The Economic and Social Council may enter into agreements with any of the agencies referred to in Article 57, defining the terms on which the agency concerned shall be brought into relationship with the United Nations. Such agreements shall be subject to approval by the General Assembly.

2. It may co-ordinate the activities of the specialized agencies through consultation with and recommendations to such agencies and through recommendations to the General Assembly and to the Members of the United Nations.

Article 64

1. The Economic and Social Council may take appropriate steps to obtain regular reports from the specialized agencies. It may make arrangements with the Members of the United Nations and with the specialized agencies to obtain reports on the steps taken to give effect to its own recommendations and to recommendations on matters falling within its competence made by the General Assembly.

2. It may communicate its observations on these reports to the General Assembly.

Article 65

The Economic and Social Council may furnish information to the Security Council and shall assist the Security Council upon its request.

Article 66

1. The Economic and Social Council shall perform such functions as fall within its competence in connexion with the carrying out of the recommendations of the General Assembly.

2. It may, with the approval of the General Assembly, perform services at the request of Members of the United Nations and at the request of specialized agencies.

3. It shall perform such other functions as are specified elsewhere in the present Charter or as may be assigned to it by the General Assembly.

Voting

Article 67

1. Each member of the Economic and Social Council shall have one vote.

2. Decisions of the Economic and Social Council shall be made by a majority of the members present and voting.

Procedure

Article 68

The Economic and Social Council shall set up commissions in economic and social fields and for the promotion of human rights, and such other commissions as may be required for the performance of its functions.

Article 69

The Economic and Social Council shall invite any Member of the United Nations to participate, without vote, in its deliberations on any matter of particular concern to that Member.

Article 70

The Economic and Social Council may make arrangements for representatives of the specialized agencies to participate, without vote, in its deliberations and in those of the commissions established by it, and for its representatives to participate in the deliberations of the specialized agencies.

Article 71

The Economic and Social Council may make suitable arrangements for consultation with non-governmental organizations which are concerned with matters within its competence. Such arrangements may be made with international organizations and, where appropriate, with national organizations after consultation with the Member of the United Nations concerned.

Article 72

1. The Economic and Social Council shall adopt its own rules of procedure, including the method of selecting its President.
2. The Economic and Social Council shall meet as required in accordance with its rules which shall include provision for the convening of meetings on the request of a majority of its members.

CHAPTER XI
DECLARATION REGARDING NON-SELF-GOVERNING TERRITORIES

Article 73

Members of the United Nations which have or assume responsibilities for the administration of territories whose peoples have not yet attained a full measure of self- government recognize the principle that the interests of the inhabitants of these territories are paramount, and accept as a sacred trust the obligation to promote to the utmost, within the system of international peace and security established by the present Charter, the well-being of the inhabitants of these territories, and, to this end:

a. to ensure, with due respect for the culture of the peoples concerned, their political, economic, social, and educational advancement, their just treatment, and their protection against abuses;

b. to develop self-government, to take due account of the political aspirations of the peoples, and to assist them in the progressive development of their free political institutions, according to the particular circumstances of each territory and its peoples and their varying stages of advancement;

c. to further international peace and security;

d. to promote constructive measures of development, to encourage research, and to co-operate with one another and, when and where appropriate, with specialized international bodies with a view to the practical achievement of the social, economic, and scientific purposes set forth in this Article; and

e. to transmit regularly to the Secretary-General for information purposes, subject to such limitation as security and constitutional considerations may require, statistical and other information of a technical nature relating to economic, social, and educational conditions in the territories for which they are respectively responsible other than those territories to which Chapters XII and XIII apply.

Article 74

Members of the United Nations also agree that their policy in respect of the territories to which this Chapter applies, no less than in respect of their metropolitan areas, must be based on the general principle of good-neighbourliness, due account being taken of the interests and well-being of the rest of the world, in social, economic, and commercial matters.

CHAPTER XII
INTERNATIONAL. TRUSTEESHIP SYSTEM

Article 75

The United Nations shall establish under its authority an international trusteeship system for the administration and supervision of such territories as may be placed there under by subsequent individual agreements. These territories are hereinafter referred to as trust territories.

Article 76

The basic objectives of the trusteeship system, in accordance with the Purposes of the United Nations laid down in Article 1 of the present Charter, shall be:

a. to further international peace and security;

b. to promote the political, economic, social, and educational advancement of the inhabitants of the trust territories, and their progressive development towards self-government or independence as may be appropriate to the particular circumstances of each territory and its peoples and the freely expressed wishes of the peoples concerned, and as may be provided by the terms of each trusteeship agreement;

c. to encourage respect for human rights and for fundamental freedoms for all without distinction as to race, sex, language, or religion, and to encourage recognition of the interdependence of the peoples of the world; and

d. to ensure equal treatment in social, economic, and commercial matters for all Members of the United Nations and their nationals, and also equal treatment for the latter in the administration of justice, without prejudice to the attainment of the foregoing objectives and subject to the provisions of Article 80.

Article 77

1. The trusteeship system shall apply to such territories in the following categories as may be placed thereunder by means of trusteeship agreements:

a. territories now held under mandate;

b. territories which may be detached from enemy states as a result of the Second World War; and

c. territories voluntarily placed under the system by states responsible for their administration.

2. It will be a matter for subsequent agreement as to which territories in the foregoing categories will be brought under the trusteeship system and upon what terms.

Article 78

The trusteeship system shall not apply to territories which have become Members of the United Nations, relationship among which shall be based on respect for the principle of sovereign equality.

Article 79

The terms of trusteeship for each territory to be placed under the trusteeship system, including any alteration or amendment, shall be agreed upon by the states directly concerned, including the mandatory power in the case of territories held under mandate by a Member of the United Nations, and shall be approved as provided for in Articles 83 and 85.

Article 80

1. Except as may be agreed upon in individual trusteeship agreements, made under Articles 77, 79, and 81, placing each territory under the trusteeship system, and until such agreements have been concluded, nothing in this Chapter shall be construed in or of itself to alter in any manner the rights whatsoever of any states or any peoples or the terms of existing international instruments to which Members of the United Nations may respectively be parties.

2. Paragraph 1 of this Article shall not be interpreted as giving grounds for delay or postponement of the negotiation and conclusion of agreements for placing mandated and other territories under the trusteeship system as provided for in Article 77.

Article 81

The trusteeship agreement shall in each case include the terms under which the trust territory will be administered and designate the authority which will exercise the administration of the trust territory. Such authority, hereinafter called the administering authority, may be one or more states or the Organization itself.

Article 82

There may be designated, in any trusteeship agreement, a strategic area or areas which may include part or all of the trust territory to which the agreement applies, without prejudice to any special agreement or agreements made under Article 43.

Article 83

1. All functions of the United Nations relating to strategic areas, including the approval of the terms of the trusteeship agreements and of their alteration or amendment, shall be exercised by the Security Council.

2. The basic objectives set forth in Article 76 shall be applicable to the people of each strategic area.

3. The Security Council shall, subject to the provisions of the trusteeship agreements and without prejudice to security considerations, avail itself of the assistance of the Trusteeship Council to perform those functions of the United Nations under the trusteeship system relating to political, economic, social, and educational matters in the strategic areas.

Article 84

It shall be the duty of the administering authority to ensure that the trust territory shall play its part in the maintenance of international peace and security. To this end the administering authority may make use of volunteer forces, facilities, and assistance from the trust territory in carrying out the obligations towards the Security Council undertaken in this regard by the administering authority, as well as for local defence and the maintenance of law and order within the trust territory.

Article 85

1. The functions of the United Nations with regard to trusteeship agreements for all areas not designated as strategic, including the approval of the terms of the trusteeship agreements and of their alteration or amendment, shall be exercised by the General Assembly.

2. The Trusteeship Council, operating under the authority of the General Assembly shall assist the General Assembly in carrying out these functions.

CHAPTER XIII
THE TRUSTEESHIP COUNCIL

Composition

Article 86

1. The Trusteeship Council shall consist of the following Members of the United Nations:

a. those Members administering trust territories;

b. such of those Members mentioned by name in Article 23 as are not administering trust territories; and

c. as many other Members elected for three-year terms by the General Assembly as may be necessary to ensure that the total number of members of the Trusteeship Council is equally divided between those Members of the United Nations which administer trust territories and those which do not.

2. Each member of the Trusteeship Council shall designate one specially qualified person to represent it therein.

Functions and Powers

Article 87

The General Assembly and, under its authority, the Trusteeship Council, in carrying out their functions, may:

a. consider reports submitted by the administering authority;

b. accept petitions and examine them in consultation with the administering authority;

c. provide for periodic visits to the respective trust territories at times agreed upon with the administering authority; and

d. take these and other actions in conformity with the terms of the trusteeship agreements.

Article 88

The Trusteeship Council shall formulate a questionnaire on the political, economic, social, and educational advancement of the inhabitants of each trust territory, and the administering authority for each trust territory within the competence of the General Assembly shall make an annual report to the General Assembly upon the basis of such questionnaire.

Voting

Article 89

1. Each member of the Trusteeship Council shall have one vote.
2. Decisions of the Trusteeship Council shall be made by a majority of the members present and voting.

Procedure

Article 90

1. The Trusteeship Council shall adopt its own rules of procedure, including the method of selecting its President.
2. The Trusteeship Council shall meet as required in accordance with its rules, which shall include provision for the convening of meetings on the request of a majority of its members.

Article 91

The Trusteeship Council shall, when appropriate, avail itself of the assistance of the Economic and Social Council and of the specialized agencies in regard to matters with which they are respectively concerned.

CHAPTER XIV
THE INTERNATIONAL COURT OF JUSTICE

Article 92

The International Court of Justice shall be the principal judicial organ of the United Nations. It shall function in accordance with the annexed Statute, which is based upon the Statute of the Permanent Court of International Justice and forms an integral part of the present Charter.

Article 93

1. All Members of the United Nations are *ipso facto* parties to the Statute of the International Court of Justice.
2. A state which is not a Member of the United Nations may become a party to the Statute of the International Court of Justice on conditions to be determined in each case by the General Assembly upon the recommendation of the Security Council.

Article 94

1. Each Member of the United Nations undertakes to comply with the decision of the International Court of Justice in any case to which it is a party.

2. If any party to a case fails to perform the obligations incumbent upon it under a judgment rendered by the Court, the other party may have recourse to the Security Council, which may, if it deems necessary, make recommendations or decide upon measures to be taken to give effect to the judgment.

Article 95

Nothing in the present Charter shall prevent Members of the United Nations from entrusting the solution of their differences to other tribunals by virtue of agreements already in existence or which may be concluded in the future.

Article 96

1. The General Assembly or the Security Council may request the International Court of Justice to give an advisory opinion on any legal question.

2. Other organs of the United Nations and specialized agencies, which may at any time be so authorized by the General Assembly, may also request advisory opinions of the Court on legal questions arising within the scope of their activities.

CHAPTER XV
THE SECRETARIAT

Article 97

The Secretariat shall comprise a Secretary-General and such staff as the Organization may require. The Secretary-General shall be appointed by the General Assembly upon the recommendation of the Security Council. He shall be the chief administrative officer of the Organization.

Article 98

The Secretary-General shall act in that capacity in all meetings of the General Assembly, of the Security Council, of the Economic and Social Council, and of the Trusteeship Council, and shall perform such other functions as are entrusted to him by these organs. The Secretary-General shall make an annual report to the General Assembly on the work of the Organization.

Article 99

The Secretary-General may bring to the attention of the Security Council any matter which in his opinion may threaten the maintenance of international peace and security.

Article 100

1. In the performance of their duties the Secretary-General and the staff shall not seek or receive instructions from any government or from any other authority external to the Organization. They shall refrain from any action which might reflect on their position as international officials responsible only to the Organization.

2. Each Member of the United Nations undertakes to respect the exclusively international character of the responsibilities of the Secretary-General and the staff and not to seek to influence them in the discharge of their responsibilities.

Article 101

1. The staff shall be appointed by the Secretary-General under regulations established by the General Assembly.

2. Appropriate staffs shall be permanently assigned to the Economic and Social Council, the Trusteeship Council, and, as required to other organs of the United Nations. These staffs shall form a part of the Secretariat.

3. The paramount consideration in the employment of the staff and in the determination of the conditions of service shall be the necessity of securing the highest standards of efficiency, competence, and integrity. Due regard shall be paid to the importance of recruiting the staff on as wide a geographical basis as possible.

CHAPTER XVI
MISCELLANEOUS PROVISIONS

Article 102

1. Every treaty and every international agreement entered into by any Member of the United Nations after the present Charter comes into force shall as soon as possible be registered with the Secretariat and published by it.

2. No party to any such treaty or international agreement which has not been registered in accordance with the provisions of paragraph 1 of this Article may invoke that treaty or agreement before any organ of the United Nations.

Article 103

In the event of a conflict between the obligations of the Members of the United Nations under the present Charter and their obligations under any other international agreement, their obligations under the present Charter shall prevail.

Article 104

The Organization shall enjoy in the territory of each of its Members such legal capacity as may be necessary for the exercise of its functions and the fulfilment of its purposes.

Article 105

1. The Organization shall enjoy in the territory of each of its Members such privileges and immunities as are necessary for the fulfilment of its purposes.

2. Representatives of the Members of the United Nations and officials of the Organization shall similarly enjoy such privileges and immunities as are necessary for the independent exercise of their functions in connexion with the Organization.

3. The General Assembly may make recommendations with a view to determining the details of the application of paragraphs 1 and 2 of this Article or may propose conventions to the Members of the United Nations for this purpose.

CHAPTER XVII
TRANSITIONAL SECURITY ARRANGEMENTS

Article 106

Pending the coming into force of such special agreements referred to in Article 43 as in the opinion of the Security Council enable it to begin the exercise of its responsibilities under Article 42, the parties to the Four-Nation Declaration, signed at Moscow, 30 October 1943, and France, shall, in accordance with the provisions of paragraph 5 of that Declaration, consult with one another and as occasion requires with other Members of the United Nations with a view to such joint action on behalf of the Organization as may be necessary for the purpose of maintaining international peace and security.

Article 107

Nothing in the present Charter shall invalidate or preclude action, in relation to any state which during the Second World War has been an enemy of any signatory to the present Charter, taken or authorized as a result of that war by the Governments having responsibility for such action.

CHAPTER XVIII
AMENDMENTS

Article 108

Amendments to the present Charter shall come into force for all Members of the United Nations when they have been adopted by a vote of two thirds of the members of the General Assembly and ratified in accordance with their respective constitutional processes by two thirds of the Members of the United Nations, including all the permanent members of the Security Council.

Article 109

1. A General Conference of the Members of the United Nations for the purpose of reviewing the present Charter may be held at a date and place to be fixed by a two-thirds vote of the members of the General Assembly and by a vote of any nine members of the Security Council. Each Member of the United Nations shall have one vote in the conference.

2. Any alteration of the present Charter recommended by a two-thirds vote of the conference shall take effect when ratified in accordance with their respective constitutional processes by two thirds of the Members of the United Nations including all the permanent members of the Security Council.

3. If such a conference has not been held before the tenth annual session of the General Assembly following the coming into force of the present Charter, the proposal to call such a conference shall be placed on the agenda of that session of the General Assembly, and the conference shall be held if so decided by a majority vote of the members of the General Assembly and by a vote of any seven members of the Security Council.

CHAPTER XIX
RATIFICATION AND SIGNATURE

Article 110

1. The present Charter shall be ratified by the signatory states in accordance with their respective constitutional processes.

2. The ratifications shall be deposited with the Government of the United States of America, which shall notify all the signatory states of each deposit as well as the Secretary-General of the Organization when he has been appointed.

3. The present Charter shall come into force upon the deposit of ratifications by the Republic of China, France, the Union of Soviet Socialist Republics, the United Kingdom of Great Britain and Northern Ireland, and the United States of America, and by a majority of the other signatory states. A protocol of the ratifications deposited

shall thereupon be drawn up by the Government of the United States of America which shall communicate copies thereof to all the signatory states.

4. The states signatory to the present Charter which ratify it after it has come into force will become original Members of the United Nations on the date of the deposit of their respective ratifications.

Article 111

The present Charter, of which the Chinese, French, Russian, English, and Spanish texts are equally authentic, shall remain deposited in the archives of the Government of the United States of America. Duly certified copies thereof shall be transmitted by that Government to the Governments of the other signatory states.

IN FAITH WHEREOF the representatives of the Governments of the United Nations have signed the present Charter.

DONE at the city of San Francisco the twenty-sixth day of June, one thousand nine hundred and forty-five.

STATUTE OF THE INTERNATIONAL COURT OF JUSTICE

Article 1

The International Court of Justice established by the Charter of the United Nations as the principal judicial organ of the United Nations shall be constituted and shall function in accordance with the provisions of the present Statute.

CHAPTER I
ORGANIZATION OF THE COURT

Article 2

The Court shall be composed of a body of independent judges, elected regardless of their nationality from among persons of high moral character, who possess the qualifications required in their respective countries for appointment to the highest judicial offices, or are jurisconsults of recognized competence in international law.

Article 3

1. The Court shall consist of fifteen members, no two of whom may be nationals of the same state.

2. A person who for the purposes of membership in the Court could be regarded as a national of more than one state shall be deemed to be a national of the one in which he ordinarily exercises civil and political rights.

Article 4

1. The members of the Court shall be elected by the General Assembly and by the Security Council from a list of persons nominated by the national groups in the Permanent Court of Arbitration, in accordance with the following provisions.

2. In the case of Members of the United Nations not represented in the Permanent Court of Arbitration, candidates shall be nominated by national groups appointed for this purpose by their governments under the same conditions as those prescribed for

members of the Permanent Court of Arbitration by Article 44 of the Convention of The Hague of 1907 for the pacific settlement of international disputes.

3. The conditions under which a state which is a party to the present Statute but is not a Member of the United Nations may participate in electing the members of the Court shall, in the absence of a special agreement, be laid down by the General Assembly upon recommendation of the Security Council.

Article 5

1. At least three months before the date of the election, the Secretary-General of the United Nations shall address a written request to the members of the Permanent Court of Arbitration belonging to the states which are parties to the present Statute, and to the members of the national groups appointed under Article 4, paragraph 2, inviting them to undertake, within a given time, by national groups, the nomination of persons in a position to accept the duties of a member of the Court.

2. No group may nominate more than four persons, not more than two of whom shall be of their own nationality. In no case may the number of candidates nominated by a group be more than double the number of seats to be filled.

Article 6

Before making these nominations, each national group is recommended to consult its highest court of justice, its legal faculties and schools of law, and its national academies and national sections of international academies devoted to the study of law.

Article 7

1. The Secretary-General shall prepare a list in alphabetical order of all the persons thus nominated. Save as provided in Article 12, paragraph 2, these shall be the only persons eligible.

2. The Secretary-General shall submit this list to the General Assembly and to the Security Council.

Article 8

The General Assembly and the Security Council shall proceed independently of one another to elect the members of the Court.

Article 9

At every election, the electors shall bear in mind not only that the persons to be elected should individually possess the qualifications required, but also that in the body as a whole the representation of the main forms of civilisation and of the principal legal systems of the world should be assured.

Article 10

1. Those candidates who obtain an absolute majority of votes in the General Assembly and in the Security Council shall be considered as elected.

2. Any vote of the Security Council, whether for the election of judges or for the appointment of members of the conference envisaged in Article 12, shall be taken without any distinction between permanent and non-permanent members of the Security Council.

3. In the event of more than one national of the same state obtaining an absolute majority of the votes both of the General Assembly and of the Security Council, the eldest of these only shall be considered as elected.

Article 11

If, after the first meeting held for the purpose of the election, one or more seats remain to be filled, a second and, if necessary, a third meeting shall take place.

Article 12

1. If, after the third meeting, one or more seats still remain unfilled, a joint conference consisting of six members, three appointed by the General Assembly and three by the Security Council, may be formed at any time at the request of either the General Assembly or the Security Council, for the purpose of choosing by the vote of an absolute majority one name for each seat still vacant, to submit to the General Assembly and the Security Council for their respective acceptance.

2. If the joint conference is unanimously agreed upon any person who fulfils the required conditions, he may be included in its list, even though he was not included in the list of nominations referred to in Article 7.

3. If the joint conference is satisfied that it will not be successful in procuring an election those members of the Court who have already been elected shall, within a period to be fixed by the Security Council, proceed to fill the vacant seats by selection from among those candidates who have obtained votes either in the General Assembly Or in the Security Council.

4. In the event of an equality of votes among the judges, the eldest judge shall have a casting vote.

Article 13

1. The members of the Court shall be elected for nine years and may be re-elected; provided, however, that of the judges elected at the first election, the terms of five judges shall expire at the end of three years and the terms of five more judges shall expire at the end of six years.

2. The judges whose terms are to expire at the end of the above-mentioned initial periods of three and six years shall be chosen by lot to be drawn by the Secretary-General immediately after the first election has been completed.

3. The members of the Court shall continue to discharge their duties until their places have been filled. Though replaced, they shall finish any cases which they may have begun.

4. In the case of the resignation of a member of the Court, the resignation shall be addressed to the President of the Court for transmission to the Secretary-General. This last notification makes the place vacant.

Article 14

Vacancies shall be filled by the same method as that laid down for the first election, subject to the following provision: the Secretary-General shall, within one month of the occurrence of the vacancy, proceed to issue the invitations provided for in Article 5, and the date of the election shall be fixed by the Security Council.

Article 15

A member of the Court elected to replace a member whose term of office has not expired shall hold office for the remainder of his predecessor's term.

Article 16

1. No member of the Court may exercise any political or administrative function, or engage in any other occupation of a professional nature.

2. Any doubt on this point shall be settled by the decision of the Court.

Article 17

1. No member of the Court may act as agent, counsel, or advocate in any case.

2. No member may participate in the decision of any case in which he has previously taken part as agent, counsel, or advocate for one of the parties, or as a member of a national or international court, or of a commission of enquiry, or in any other capacity.

3. Any doubt on this point shall be settled by the decision of the Court.

Article 18

1. No member of the Court can be dismissed unless, in the unanimous opinion of the other members, he has ceased to fulfil the required conditions.

2. Formal notification thereof shall be made to the Secretary-General by the Registrar.

3. This notification makes the place vacant.

Article 19

The members of the Court, when engaged on the business of the Court, shall enjoy diplomatic privileges and immunities.

Article 20

Every member of the Court shall, before taking up his duties, make a solemn declaration in open court that he will exercise his powers impartially and conscientiously.

Article 21

1. The Court shall elect its President and Vice-President for three years; they may be re-elected.

2. The Court shall appoint its Registrar and may provide for the appointment of such other officers as may be necessary.

Article 22

1. The seat of the Court shall be established at The Hague. This, however, shall not prevent the Court from sitting and exercising its functions elsewhere whenever the Court considers it desirable.

2. The President and the Registrar shall reside at the seat of the Court.

Article 23

1. The Court shall remain permanently in session, except during the judicial vacations, the dates and duration of which shall be fixed by the Court.

2. Members of the Court are entitled to periodic leave, the dates and duration of which shall be fixed by the Court, having in mind the distance between The Hague and the home of each judge.

3. Members of the Court shall be bound, unless they are on leave or prevented from attending by illness or other serious reasons duly explained to the President, to hold themselves permanently at the disposal of the Court.

Article 24

1. If, for some special reason, a member of the Court considers that he should not take part in the decision of a particular case, he shall so inform the President.

2. If the President considers that for some special reason one of the members of the Court should not sit in a particular case, he shall give him notice accordingly.

3. If in any such case the member of the Court and the President disagree, the matter shall be settled by the decision of the Court.

Article 25

1. The full Court shall sit except when it is expressly provided otherwise in the present Statute.

2. Subject to the condition that the number of judges available to constitute the Court is not thereby reduced below eleven, the Rules of the Court may provide for allowing one or more judges, according to circumstances and in rotation, to be dispensed from sitting.

3. A quorum of nine judges shall suffice to constitute the Court.

Article 26

1. The Court may from time to time form one or more chambers, composed of three or more judges as the Court may determine, for dealing with particular categories of cases; for example, labour cases and cases relating to transit and communications.

2. The Court may at any time form a chamber for dealing with a particular case. The number of judges to constitute such a chamber shall be determined by the Court with the approval of the parties.

3. Cases shall be heard and determined by the chambers provided for in this article if the parties so request.

Article 27

A judgment given by any of the chambers provided for in Articles 26 and 29 shall be considered as rendered by the Court.

Article 28

The chambers provided for in Articles 26 and 29 may, with the consent of the parties sit and exercise their functions elsewhere than at The Hague.

Article 29

With a view to the speedy dispatch of business, the Court shall form annually a chamber composed of five judges which, at the request of the parties, may hear and determine cases by summary procedure. In addition, two judges shall be selected for the purpose of replacing judges who find it impossible to sit.

Article 30

1. The Court shall frame rules for carrying out its functions. In particular, it shall lay down rules of procedure.

2. The Rules of the Court may provide for assessors to sit with the Court or with any of its chambers, without the right to vote.

Article 31

1. Judges of the nationality of each of the parties shall retain their right to sit in the case before the Court.

2. If the Court includes upon the Bench a judge of the nationality of one of the parties, any other party may choose a person to sit as judge. Such person shall be chosen preferably from among those persons who have been nominated as candidates as provided in Articles 4 and 5.

3. If the Court includes upon the Bench no judge of the nationality of the parties, each of these parties may proceed to choose a judge as provided in paragraph 2 of this Article.

4. The provisions of this Article shall apply to the case of Articles 26 and 29. In such cases, the President shall request one or, if necessary, two of the members of the Court forming the chamber to give place to the members of the Court of the nationality of the parties concerned, and, failing such, or if they are unable to be present, to the judges specially chosen by the parties.

5. Should there be several parties in the same interest, they shall, for the purpose of the preceding provisions, be reckoned as one party only. Any doubt upon this point shall be settled by the decision of the Court.

6. Judges chosen as laid down in paragraphs 2, 3, and 4 of this Article shall fulfil the conditions required by Articles 2, 17 (paragraph 2), 20, and 24 of the present Statute. They shall take part in the decision on terms of complete equality with their colleagues.

Article 32

1. Each member of the Court shall receive an annual salary.

2. The President shall receive a special annual allowance.

3. The Vice-President shall receive a special allowance for every day on which he acts as President.

4. The judges chosen under Article 31 other than members of the Court, shall receive compensation for each day on which they exercise their functions.

5. These salaries, allowances, and compensation shall be fixed by the General Assembly. They may not be decreased during the term of office.

6. The salary of the Registrar shall be fixed by the General Assembly on the proposal of the Court.

7. Regulations made by the General Assembly shall fix the conditions under which retirement pensions may be given to members of the Court and to the Registrar, and the conditions under which members of the Court and the Registrar shall have their travelling expenses refunded.

8. The above salaries, allowances, and compensation shall be free of all taxation.

Article 33

The expenses of the Court shall be borne by the United Nations in such a manner as shall be decided by the General Assembly.

Chapter II

COMPETENCE OF THE COURT

Article 34

1. Only states may be parties in cases before the Court.

2. The Court, subject to and in conformity with its Rules, may request of public international organizations information relevant to cases before it, and shall receive such in formation presented by such organizations on their own initiative.

3. Whenever the construction of the constituent instrument of a public international organization or of an international convention adopted thereunder is in question in a case before the Court, the Registrar shall so notify the public international organization concerned and shall communicate to it copies of all the written proceedings.

Article 35

1. The Court shall be open to the states parties to the present Statute.

2. The conditions under which the Court shall be open to other states shall, subject to the special provisions contained in treaties in force, be laid down by the Security Council but in no case shall such conditions place the parties in a position of inequality before the Court.

3. When a state which is not a Member of the United Nations is a party to a case, the Court shall fix the amount which that party is to contribute towards the expenses of the Court. This provision shall not apply if such state is bearing a share of the expenses of the Court.

Article 36

1. The jurisdiction of the Court comprises all cases which the parties refer to it and all matters specially provided for in the Charter of the United Nations or in treaties and conventions in force.

2. The states parties to the present Statute may at any time declare that they recognize as compulsory *ipso facto* and without special agreement, in relation to any other state accepting the same obligation, the jurisdiction of the Court in all legal disputes concerning:

    a. the interpretation of a treaty;

    b. any question of international law;

    c. the existence of any fact which, if established, would constitute a breach of an international obligation;

    d. the nature or extent of the reparation to be made for the breach of an international obligation.

3. The declarations referred to above may be made unconditionally or on condition of reciprocity on the part of several or certain states, or for a certain time.

4. Such declarations shall be deposited with the Secretary-General of the United Nations, who shall transmit copies thereof to the parties to the Statute and to the Registrar of the Court.

5. Declarations made under Article 36 of the Statute of the Permanent Court of International Justice and which are still in force shall be deemed, as between the parties to the present Statute, to be acceptances of the compulsory jurisdiction of the International Court of Justice for the period which they still have to run and in accordance with their terms.

6. In the event of a dispute as to whether the Court has jurisdiction, the matter shall be settled by the decision of the Court.

Article 37

Whenever a treaty or convention in force provides for reference of a matter to a tribunal to have been instituted by the League of Nations, or to the Permanent Court of International Justice, the matter shall, as between the parties to the present Statute, be referred to the International Court of Justice.

Article 38

1. The Court, whose function is to decide in accordance with international law such disputes as are submitted to it, shall apply:

    a. international conventions, whether general or particular, establishing rules expressly recognized by the contesting states;

    b. international custom, as evidence of a general practice accepted as law;

    c. the general principles of law recognized by civilized nations;

    d. subject to the provisions of Article 59, judicial decisions and the teachings of the most highly qualified publicists of the various nations, as subsidiary means for the determination of rules of law.

2. This provision shall not prejudice the power of the Court to decide a case *ex aequo et bono,* if the parties agree thereto.

CHAPTER III
PROCEDURE

Article 39

1. The official languages of the Court shall be French and English. If the parties agree that the case shall be conducted in French, the judgment shall be delivered in French. If the parties agree that the case shall be conducted in English, the judgment shall be delivered in English.

2. In the absence of an agreement as to which language shall be employed, each party may, in the pleadings, use the language which it prefers; the decision of the Court shall be given in French and English. In this case the Court shall at the same time determine which of the two texts shall be considered as authoritative.

3. The Court shall, at the request of any party, authorize a language other than French or English to be used by that party.

Article 40

1. Cases are brought before the Court, as the case may be, either by the notification of the special agreement or by a written application addressed to the Registrar. In either case the subject of the dispute and the parties shall be indicated.

2. The Registrar shall forthwith communicate the application to all concerned.

3. He shall also notify the Members of the United Nations through the Secretary-General, and also any other states entitled to appear before the Court.

Article 41

1. The Court shall have the power to indicate, if it considers that circumstances so require, any provisional measures which ought to be taken to preserve the respective rights of either party.

2. Pending the final decision, notice of the measures suggested shall forthwith be given to the parties and to the Security Council.

Article 42

1. The parties shall be represented by agents.

2. They may have the assistance of counsel or advocates before the Court.

3. The agents, counsel, and advocates of parties before the Court shall enjoy the privileges and immunities necessary to the independent exercise of their duties.

Article 43

1. The procedure shall consist of two parts: written and oral.

2. The written proceedings shall consist of the communication to the Court and to the parties of memorials, counter memorials and, if necessary, replies; also all papers and documents in support.

3. These communications shall be made through the Registrar, in the order and within the time fixed by the Court.

4. A certified copy of every document produced by one party shall be communicated to the other party.

5. The oral proceedings shall consist of the hearing by the Court of witnesses, experts, agents, counsel, and advocates.

Article 44

1. For the service of all notices upon persons other than the agents, counsel, and advocates, the Court shall apply direct to the government of the state upon whose territory the notice has to be served.

2. The same provision shall apply whenever steps are to be taken to procure evidence on the spot.

Article 45

The hearing shall be under the control of the President or, if he is unable to preside, of the Vice-President if neither is able to preside, the senior judge present shall preside.

Article 46

The hearing in Court shall be public, unless the Court shall decide otherwise, or unless the parties demand that the public be not admitted.

Article 47

1. Minutes shall be made at each hearing and signed by the Registrar and the President.

2. These minutes alone shall be authentic.

Article 48

The Court shall make orders for the conduct of the case, shall decide the form and time in which each party must conclude its arguments, and make all arrangements connected with the taking of evidence.

Article 49

The Court may, even before the hearing begins, call upon the agents to produce any document or to supply any explanations. Formal note shall be taken of any refusal.

Article 50

The Court may, at any time, entrust any individual, body, bureau, commission, or other organization that it may select, with the task of carrying out an enquiry or giving an expert opinion.

Article 51

During the hearing any relevant questions are to be put to the witnesses and experts under the conditions laid down by the Court in the rules of procedure referred to in Article 30.

Article 52

After the Court has received the proofs and evidence within the time specified for the purpose, it may refuse to accept any further oral or written evidence that one party may desire to present unless the other side consents.

Article 53

1. Whenever one of the parties does not appear before the Court, or fails to defend its case, the other party may call upon the Court to decide in favour of its claim.

2. The Court must, before doing so, satisfy itself, not only that it has jurisdiction in accordance with Articles 36 and 37, but also that the claim is well founded in fact and law.

Article 54

1. When, subject to the control of the Court, the agents, counsel, and advocates have completed their presentation of the case, the President shall declare the hearing closed.

2. The Court shall withdraw to consider the judgment.

3. The deliberations of the Court shall take place in private and remain secret.

Article 55

1. All questions shall be decided by a majority of the judges present.

2. In the event of an equality of votes, the President or the judge who acts in his place shall have a casting vote.

Article 56

1. The judgment shall state the reasons on which it is based.

2. It shall contain the names of the judges who have taken part in the decision.

Article 57

If the judgment does not represent in whole or in part the unanimous opinion of the judges, any judge shall be entitled to deliver a separate opinion.

Article 58

The judgment shall be signed by the President and by the Registrar. It shall be read in open court, due notice having been given to the agents.

Article 59

The decision of the Court has no binding force except between the parties and in respect of that particular case.

Article 60

The judgment is final and without appeal. In the event of dispute as to the meaning or scope of the judgment, the Court shall construe it upon the request of any party.

Article 61

1. An application for revision of a judgment may be made only when it is based upon the discovery of some fact of such a nature as to be a decisive factor, which fact was, when the judgment was given, unknown to the Court and also to the party claiming revision, always provided that such ignorance was not due to negligence.

2. The proceedings for revision shall be opened by a judgment of the Court expressly recording the existence of the new fact, recognizing that it has such a character as to lay the case open to revision, and declaring the application admissible on this ground.

3. The Court may require previous compliance with the terms of the judgment before it admits proceedings in revision.

4. The application for revision must be made at latest within six months of the discovery of the new fact.

5. No application for revision may be made after the lapse of ten years from the date of the judgment.

Article 62

1. Should a state consider that it has an interest of a legal nature which may be affected by the decision in the case, it may submit a request to the Court to be permitted to intervene.

2. It shall be for the Court to decide upon this request.

Article 63

1. Whenever the construction of a convention to which states other than those concerned in the case are parties is in question, the Registrar shall notify all such states forthwith.

2. Every state so notified has the right to intervene in the proceedings; but if it uses this right, the construction given by the judgment will be equally binding upon it.

Article 64

Unless otherwise decided by the Court, each party shall bear its own costs.

Chapter IV
ADVISORY OPINIONS

Article 65

1. The Court may give an advisory opinion on any legal question at the request of whatever body may be authorized by or in accordance with the Charter of the United Nations to make such a request.

2. Questions upon which the advisory opinion of the Court is asked shall be laid before the Court by means of a written request containing an exact statement of the question upon which an opinion is required and accompanied by all documents likely to throw light upon the question.

Article 66

1. The Registrar shall forthwith give notice of the request for an advisory opinion to all states entitled to appear before the Court.

2. The Registrar shall also, by means of a special and direct communication, notify any state entitled to appear before the Court or international organization considered by the Court, or, should it not be sitting, by the President, as likely to be able to furnish information on the question, that the Court will be prepared to receive, within a time limit to be fixed by the President, written statements, or to hear, at a public sitting to be held for the purpose, oral statements relating to the question.

3. Should any such state entitled to appear before the Court have failed to receive the special communication referred to in paragraph 2 of this Article, such state may express a desire to submit a written statement or to be heard; and the Court will decide.

4. States and organizations having presented written or oral statements or both shall be permitted to comment on the statements made by other states or organizations in the form, to the extent, and within the time limits which the Court, or, should it not be sitting, the President, shall decide in each particular case. Accordingly, the Registrar shall in due time communicate any such written statements to states and organizations having submitted similar statements.

Article 67

The Court shall deliver its advisory opinions in open court, notice having been given to the Secretary-General and to the representatives of Members of the United Nations, of other states and of international organizations immediately concerned.

Article 68

In the exercise of its advisory functions the Court shall further be guided by the provisions of the present Statute which apply in contentious cases to the extent to which it recognizes them to be applicable.

Chapter V
AMENDMENT

Article 69

Amendments to the present Statute shall be effected by the same procedure as is provided by the Charter of the United Nations for amendments to that Charter, subject however to any provisions which the General Assembly upon recommendation of the Security Council may adopt concerning the participation of states which are parties to the present Statute but are not Members of the United Nations.

Article 70

The Court shall have power to propose such amendments to the present Statute as it may deem necessary, through written communications to the Secretary-General, for consideration in conformity with the provisions of Article 69.

Index